TEACHING POST-COLONIALISM
AND POST-COLONIAL LITERATURES

THE DOLPHIN

General Editor: Tim Caudery

27

TEACHING POST-COLONIALISM
AND POST-COLONIAL LITERATURES

Edited by Anne Collett,
Lars Jensen and Anna Rutherford

AARHUS UNIVERSITY PRESS

Copyright: Aarhus University Press, 1997
Printed by The Alden Press, Oxford
ISBN 87 7288 378 2
ISSN 0106 4487

AARHUS UNIVERSITY PRESS
Building 170
University of Aarhus
DK-8000 Aarhus C, Denmark
Fax (+45) 8619 8433

73 Lime Walk
Headington
Oxford OX3 7AD
Fax (+44) 1865 750 079

Box 511
Oakville, Conn. 06779
Fax (+1) 860 945 9468

Editorial address:
The Dolphin
Department of English
University of Aarhus
8000 Aarhus C, Denmark
Fax (+45) 8942 2099
E-mail engtc@hum.aau.dk

Published with financial support from the Aarhus University Research Foundation.

The cover shows a map of Africa from Martin Vahl and Gudmund Hatt, *Jorden og Menneskelivet. Geografisk Haandbog*, vol. 3 (Copenhagen: Schultz 1925). The Danish text is a key to the map, and can be translated as follows:

Areas suitable for European colonisation; Areas where the climate is reasonably healthy for Europeans, but which are less suited to European colonization because of aridity, density of the native population or other causes; Areas which are unhealthy for Europeans, but where the natural riches can nevertheless be exploited by European planters and merchants with the help of native labour; Areas which are particularly unhealthy for Europeans.

Contents

Reading Lists, Course Descriptions, etc.

While all the texts in this book discuss the teaching of post-colonialism in various forms, the following page references may be particularly helpful for those wanting concrete suggestions for the teaching of particular subjects.

Preface

This book might aptly have been called 'Moving mountains, shifting borders, altering perspectives, moving more mountains'. The fight to teach and the teaching of post-colonial literatures is hard work, work that requires an enormous amount of faith, vitality and persistence – something to which all of the essays in this book attest. As Alamgir Hashmi declares, 'we have the responsibility – to reorganise and start off again, and again'. This Dolphin issue grew out of a sense that all the work that has been done in gaining recognition for post-colonial studies should somehow be accounted for, assessed, shared and ultimately celebrated. The book has slowly taken shape over the last four years – a period during which a conceptual base has remained relatively intact, but the materials out of which that concept was to be realized or articulated have altered with the different perspectives of those involved at various stages of the creative process (a series editor, three book editors and twenty other contributors is some mind to mess with). There are still gaps, the most conspicuous being coverage of Africa by an African outside South Africa. Nevertheless, what we hope and believe we have accomplished is the bringing together of the retrospective and the prospective – a book of ideas – not only a 'theory of' or a 'history of' book, but a how-to-do-it, where-to-get-it book – a self-help guide to teaching post-colonialism and post-colonial literatures.

Originally we had thought of the book as divided into two sections, the first being a historical survey of the pedagogy of post-colonial literatures at the various sites of origin, so to speak. The second part was to be a more practical guide to teaching those literatures within 'real' contexts – 'real' classrooms with 'real' texts (i.e. those texts that at any one time might be in print, widely available, and reasonably priced!). Of course no definitive borders (or unrealistic expectations) were maintainable. The essays we received eluded our attempts to determine in any real way what was written, how it was written or even why it was written. The various writings escaped categorization, refused selection by any kind of suggested criteria, and ultimately overlapped one another in exciting energies of flow and jostle. This left us with the problem of how to place them in relation to one another to achieve some sense of coherent whole.

It seemed fitting to begin and end in Aarhus, so the book begins with Anne Collett's first lecture on post-colonial literature to Danish students at the University of Aarhus and ends with an ex-student's reflections and observations on post-colonial studies as a salutary learning process that challenges notions of self and other. Within the osmotic borders of a university community the real world jostles with the fictional, theory contends with practice, and language struggles to create and communicate our meanings. Inevitably we rely upon the facility of language to mark out our sense of personal and communal living space and to re-adjust and re-define the parameters of that space as our sense of community grows with our sense of personal relatedness. Many of the essays, although remarking the importance of valuing local culture and textual relatedness to that culture, also remark the difficulties and even dangers of a decolonization process that can sometimes result in the reconstruction of new, but equally rigid definition. Lars Jensen's essay on Pacific literatures explores the possibilities of moving beyond the limitation of nationalistic agendas; S.A. Dseagu in his 'definition of African literatures' also insists that 'the question of who is or who is not a national' be left to politicians; Coral Ann Howells advocates the advantages of a wide selection of texts, observing that, 'the wider the selection of texts the more patterns of interrelatedness students manage to construct, tracing their own maps through a new literary territory so that it becomes familiar to them'.

When Anna Rutherford is asked how she gained access to foreign cultures to which she had no inherent right, she replies that 'I guess you could say I'm a gregarious person – and I listen – and I'm colour blind'. She travelled widely, read widely and talked with anyone and everyone – and still does. Language is power, and while there is dialogue there is hope – the hope of understanding and tolerance – the respect of difference, the satisfaction of discovering compatibility. Only in silence are we defeated. Russell McDougall begins his essay with the word *dialogue*: 'Dialogue: that is what we always tell students we want: discussion. And if they sit quietly in tutorials or seminars, expecting repeat performances of our lectures, we feel vaguely, or specifically, miffed. I begin with "us" and "them" because, despite our saying we want dialogue, we so rarely act out that desire, or demonstrate it, let alone structure our courses around its possibilities ...'. The courses outlined in these essays are evidence of the desire to make real those possibilities. Kathy Trees asks that responsibility be assumed by writers, teachers and students to value and promote interrogative learning, and Susan Gingell differentiates between education for conformity and education as 'the practice of freedom'. It is this 'practice of freedom' that is so dear to the hearts of all those who teach post-colonial literatures. Most of the essays in this book attest to the rewards of teaching post-colonialism and post-colonial literatures, and all declare their intent to 'fight another day'. Margaret Daymond writes, 'Few students find it comfortable to have life's questions written back to them, but it is through these texts that I believe I can further the "working intellectually towards genuine social change" that is the declared objective of post-colonial criticism'. May our words 'refashion futures/like a healer's hand' (Edward Kamau Brathwaite, 'Negus').

And although the stories all had different voices, and came from different times and places and understandings, though some were shown, enacted or written rather than told, each one was like a puzzle piece which tongued or grooved neatly to another. And this train of stories defined our lives, curving out from points on the spiral in ever-widening circles from which neither beginnings nor endings could be defined. (Patricia Grace, *Potiki* (Auckland: Penguin), 1986).

Anne Collett
Lars Jensen
Anna Rutherford

Perspectives on Home Ground, Foreign Territory[1]

Anne Collett

This paper is comprised in the main of the first lecture I gave on 'Post-Colonial Literatures' to a group of second-year Danish students at the University of Aarhus in September 1995. I had selected a diverse and wide range of texts from across the English speaking/writing world that had worked well in a tertiary institution in London, England – colonial home ground – but this was Denmark – this was foreign territory (although coincidentally also home ground, Sorensen being my mother's name). The first problem that necessarily faced me as a teacher of post-colonial literatures was how to approach or even begin to discuss these literatures within the context of a homogeneous community and a culture that I assumed was not only unconversant, but innocent of involvement in the history of colonization. Of course, this only attests to my ignorance, which familiarity with Ngugi's essay, 'Literature and Society'[2] should have alerted me to. An African response to Isak Dinesen's literary colonization, *Out of Africa*, was the obvious place to start. In conjunction with Achebe's impassioned reaction[3] to Conrad's *Heart of Darkness*, this writing from the heart of colonial darkness, a writing that pretended to no aesthetic distance but risked all in an intimate and deadly battle with the monster – gave students who might otherwise have maintained a safe and armoured distance (it's not about us it's about them) a sense of personal imperative – theirs and ours. It was also fortuitous that Peter Hoeg's novel, *Miss Smilla's Feeling For Snow*,[4] had achieved international renown – a Danish novel whose story follows a tortuous course through the labyrinth of Danish colonization of Greenland. The story starts at the heart of a darkness that mourns not only the loss of a child, but a loss of language:

> It is freezing, an extraordinary -18°, and it is snowing, and in the language which is no longer mine, the snow is 'qanik' –
> ...
> December darkness rises up from the grave, seemingly as limitless as the sky above us. In this darkness our faces are merely pale, shining discs, but even so I can sense the disapproval of the pastor and the verger ....
> ...

The women surrounding Juliane and the pastor and the verger all are Greenlanders, and when we sing 'Guutiga, Illimi', 'Thou, My Lord', and as Juliane's legs buckle under her and she begins weeping, the volume slowly increasing, and when the pastor speaks in West Greenlandic, taking his point of departure in the Moravians' favourite passage from St Paul about redemption through the blood, then with only a tiny lapse of concentration one might feel oneself transported to Upernavik or Holsteinsborg or Qaanaaq.

But out in the darkness, like the bow of a ship, loom the walls of Vestre Prison; we are in Copenhagen.

The Greenlanders' cemetery is part of Vestre Cemetery.

These are the opening lines of the text – a text in which Greenlander, criminal and prisoner are as one – colonized and marginalized in death even as in life. I could not have asked for a more personal, more culturally relevant text. In the teaching of any literature, but particularly in the teaching of a body of literature that, within a European context, is positioned as 'other' at outset and that is all too easily generalized and abstracted by the sometimes impenetrable linguistics of its critical discourse, it is imperative to situate that foreign body of text within home ground by beginning with the personal and the particular, thereby often bringing about the realization that what was thought to be home ground is found to be a foreign territory in which delineating boundaries of self and community are explored and renegotiated. With this belief in the pedagogical and conceptual strength of a base that is personal, particular and even anecdotal, I began the lecture series with an explanation of my inherited place within the colonialized world and the process by which I achieved some kind of consciousness of that place and an articulation of personal political position.

Like all Australian school-children, I learnt that in 1788 Captain Phillip sailed into Botany Bay, 'New South Wales', to found the first European settlement on Australian soil. What I, and many other Australians, didn't learn either in or out of school until very recently is that he planted his British Union Jack upon a land that had been declared 'terra nullius' – devoid of human inhabitants – despite the obvious and unavoidable presence of hundreds of thousands of indigenous peoples that are now believed to have inhabited the land for something more than the conservative figure of 40,000 years (their own sense of habitation does not accord to linear time-line). 'Australia' began as a penal colony – a dumping ground for 'criminals' who for the main part were comprised of the British poor – the socially unacceptable – and a fair few Irish rebels – the politically unacceptable, who were in fact representative of attempted de-colonization of Ireland. The previous year, when I was teaching a Year 8 class of London school children about Australian ballads (descendants of the Irish treason songs) and asked if anyone knew what a convict was, a teacher who had come into the room piped up with the reply 'Australians, Miss!' – very funny, but not so funny – still a convict, still a colonized subject – unacceptable and marginalized.

14

So what does it mean to be a colonial? To be a colonial means to lead a kind of double life, a kind of schizophrenic existence, and like a schizophrenic, to be largely unaware of this divided self. The most enlightening definitions of abstractions are usually based upon concrete images drawn from personal experience, so I will tell you a little about myself in order to clarify what it means to be colonial. I was born in Canberra, at that time, a small town in New South Wales – purpose-built as the capital city of Australia. Although I grew up in what was supposed to be a city it was primarily the country that impinged upon my imagination. My sense of home, if I still could be said to have one, is that of very high bright blue skies, low rolling hills more brown than green and the smell of eucalypts (gum trees). It is of white sands and blue/green surf on the south coast of New South Wales where I spent my weekends and summer holidays. I grew up with the poetry of Judith Wright, the ballads of Banjo Paterson, Blinky Bill and Nutsy (koala bears) and Norman Lindsay's magic pudding, with vegemite sandwiches and days, weeks, months of sunshine – the ground baked hard and cracked where the rain only lifted the dust.... I was a fourth generation Australian of white, middle class, Protestant school-teacher parents, with a family working history of windmill erectors, Broken Hill miners, Jackaroos or boundary riders, metal workers and the occasional missionary and teacher thrown in. But Australia was only skin deep....

My great-great-grandfather on my mother's side was a Dane (a Sørensen) who came out to Australia in the gold-rush period of the late 1840s, and it was of this Danish ancestry that my mother was very proud – the source not only of her red hair but of the tendency to poetry writing that ran in the family. This Danish blood carried the exotica, the old-world inheritance of the Viking sagas ... My father, on the other hand, was sure that we were somehow related to the Royal Stuarts ...

Although I was Australian, I was Scottish, I was Danish, I was something else because somehow it wasn't enough to be just Australian. To be wholly and entirely only Australian was to be disconnected from the world that counted – the world where real history was made. This is what it is to be colonial – not merely to be displaced, disconnected, but to believe that things of importance happen not only somewhere else in the so-called Mother Country, but also tend to have happened in the past. There is a tendency to believe that a colonial's world is mapped out and controlled by someone else – by a history that has happened somewhere else (which of course was true, but it should not continue to be true). So that although Australians are proud of their democratic supposedly classless society, proud of their toughness, their pioneering, go-it-alone, do-anything spirit, they still, at least until very recently, have a tendency to allow the rules to be made, and believe the rules should be made, by someone else.

Although Canberra, the town where I was born, has an aboriginal-sounding name (I'm not sure from what aboriginal language it originates, or if it merely sounds aboriginal), as the seat of Commonwealth government, it attempts to

15

emulate an oasis of Englishness in the heart of 'the sunburnt country', and there were certainly no aboriginal people to be seen on its streets when I was a child. Canberra is a planned city of tree-lined avenues, shopping malls, manicured gardens, an artificial lake and a predominance of diplomatic residences. Here there are no wooden houses with tin roofs and shady verandahs, but brick-box houses surrounded by daffodils, lilacs, roses and lush green lawns that must be watered incessantly if they are to survive the summer drought. Here the straggly, ragged, evergreen gums have been replaced by deciduous trees that emulate the English seasons of spring blossom, summer fruit, autumn colour and winter bareness. Canberra is a typical colonial anomaly.

As a child it did not seem peculiar to send and receive Christmas cards featuring snow-covered landscapes, deer and robins, although Christmas in Australia was a blaze of heat and the landscape invariably scorched by perennial bushfires. Year after year, in 30 degree plus heat we sat down to a 'traditional' Christmas meal in the middle of the day, a meal over which my mother and grandmother would have sweated in front of a hot stove from 5 a.m., and which featured roast chicken, baked potatoes, pumpkin, boiled Christmas pudding and rich fruit cake. We sang Christmas carols that featured the sombre English winter landscape, like Christina Rossetti's 'In The Bleak Mid Winter' and felt no sense of disparity. This was how it should be, although I do remember a carol my mother produced one year and every year subsequently that featured 'Three Drovers' rather than three shepherds.

My grandfather was a senior civil servant who always wore woollen trousers, a white shirt with starched collar and cuffs, braces, a woollen coat, tie and hat, no matter what the heat – as did my father for that matter, minus the hat, braces and starch. My grandfather was also renowned for his antipathy toward Catholics, Americans and 'Wogs' (i.e. non-British European immigrants). The real Australian was not black, or Italian or Greek or Lebanese or Asian, and it is probably only in the last twenty years that a multi-cultural Australia has had any credence or any voice. Although we bought the occasional mullet or flathead from an aboriginal fisherman and spent many summer holidays exploring an aboriginal midden (or ancient kitchen), I had no understanding of the indigenous people's place in my world. They were represented by a Europeanized painting of a piccaninny (aboriginal child) on my wall. The European and Asian population that made up a large percentage of Australia's labour force were represented by the Lithuanian lady who gave me boiled sweets and to whom my father gave English lessons, and chop suey from the local Chinese restaurant.

It was not until I went to live in Canada that I questioned or even had any awareness of my imagined or actual identity as 'an Australian' and as a 'colonial'. National identity is not something you think about particularly or question until you are confronted with an image created by others that does not fit, or with which you are unhappy.

16

When I was twelve years old I went to live in a small town in the middle of northern British Columbia, Canada. It felt as though I had been transplanted into an equal and opposite environment – south by north, heat by cold, black (of bushfire) by white (of snow) – and here, suddenly, I became 'an Australian'. I was no longer 'Anne Ridden' but 'that Australian girl who wears mini-skirts', and was nick-named 'Skippy' (the Bush Kangaroo, from a T.V. series set in the Australian bush about a boy and his pet kangaroo). Here it was assumed that I lived in terror of sharks, poisonous spiders and deadly snakes, that kangaroos and koalas frequented the streets (although I had seen many kangaroos in the bush I had only seen a koala in a zoo), and that I spoke that little known and obscure language 'Australian' – which indeed I did .... I was asked with some admiration how I had managed to learn to speak English so quickly. In fact although I did indeed speak English, it was an Australian-English, quite different to the English which the Canadians spoke. Not only was my accent different but many of the words I used were different and I was constantly asked to repeat this or that phrase – I – my language and my culture that until then had been unexamined by me – an assumed part of what I was – became the centre of attention, of remark and of appraisal.

There are a number of comments I would make about this: the first is that I discovered that my world was not the centre of the world, nor was it the only world – it was not necessarily the norm. What I considered to be normal was here considered to be exotic. The second thing I discovered was a national identity – one conceived by others, one that I found myself having to create in order to adjust the evident misconceptions held by my peers, and another that I created in my own mind to categorize what it was to be 'Canadian'. The third thing I was forced to realize was that 'the' English language came in many forms, and those various forms were often assigned a value in an hierarchical scale (something I was to be made much more aware of when I came to live in Britain – the choral director of my choir constantly cast degrading aspersions not only upon my Australian accent but also upon the ability of any Australian to partake in or be productive of 'high culture'). The last thing I would say is that Canada, sharing a history of colonization with Australia, suffered, like Australia, from the same love/hate relationship with England – the same duality of aspect or outlook – and the same marginalization and contempt for its indigenous peoples. Here I discovered small-town wilderness – the rejection and fear of difference, the desperate defence of civilized community borders from incursion and intrusion by wilderness and all that does not conform to expectation and assumption of us and ours, the complete lack of understanding or compassion for Indian or Inuit dispossession. Here the Indians comprised an under-class of drunken squalor and poverty. Here, outside home ground on foreign territory, I saw and, as an outsider, lived through to some small degree, the effects of colonization of which I had been largely unaware – home ground became foreign territory – to be explored, scrutinized, politicized and ultimately, reinvented.

After completing my secondary school education in Canada, an education in which the subject 'humanities' comprised no element of Canadian literature – I 'did' Hamlet and Chaucer – I returned to Australia where I completed a first degree in Arts, discovered Commonwealth writing, and a passion for Caribbean poetry. I did the colonial thing and spent some time in the Mother Country – discovering the colonial commonplace that what was supposed to be 'home ground' was in fact foreign territory. I also discovered the nature of colonization within a Britain that I had imagined as something meaningfully whole and that I had, like many other colonials, mistakenly equated with England. Living in Scotland, on the Scottish/English border, quickly righted this misconception, as did my acquaintance with Irish, Welsh and even Cornish people for whom loss and degradation of language was the focus of colonial discontent and site of de-colonization and reconstruction. Even London itself did not equate with my imagined London – it was not a literary London – it was not Shakespeare or Chaucer – it was not old, it was not a museum piece in itself – of course it wasn't .... There were red double-decker buses and black cabs but .... My England was an England of the imagination that did not exist except in my mind and the mind of many other colonials. During my seven years there I could not claim to have met anyone who epitomized my original conception of 'Englishness'. I lived in a community of Jews, Indians, West Indians, Iranians, ... If you asked me to image London now I would see the attempt to be cellular and insular on the packed peak-hour tube – people hidden behind newspapers or books, where the disturbance of children squabbling, babies crying, the babble of incomprehensible languages, the mix of smells, colours, sounds, the Irish mother with her deathly pale child begging for change, the young man sitting at the bottom of the tube stairs with his cardboard sign indicating his state of homelessness, the young people on the street corners selling the Big Issue of unemployment, homelessness and destitution ... are staunchly ignored – if I don't look, if I don't see, if my eyes do not meet yours, then it does not exist – none of this ugliness, none of this unhappiness, none of the consequences of greed – (call it imperialism, capitalism, whatever) will be admitted. This is not just London of course, it is any city in the world – but part of the misery of this London is the result of a general colonial imagination that believed and was in fact educated and encouraged to believe England to be a home ground only to discover it to be foreign territory. The return to imagined homeland was a disappointment and a disaster for the many who found and still find themselves 'strangers in a strange land'.

So what does all this have to do with post-colonial literature? The personal history of a colonial/post-colonial gives you a geography of mind, a psychological and social orientation – a preoccupation – that I would suggest the peoples and the writers of the colonized world share. You will come across many personal histories that parallel mine in the course of your reading, not only from Australia, but from Canada, the Caribbean, South Africa .... If I was asked what the writings of Margaret Atwood and Okot p'Bitek have in common, I would reply that firstly they both write in English. This may seem a rather obtuse answer, but because they write in English they share, at certain points, a history of language, and because they are both colonials, or colonials involved in the process of de-colonization, or post-colonials, they share the struggle to define and articulate their own distinctive social and cultural identities in a language that is both their own and not their own. Colonial English-language writing could be said to be the language of 'mimic men' (a term used by Caribbean writers George Lamming and V.S. Naipaul). This is the writing that seeks to emulate the English model, to fit the social and physiological context to the language rather than the other way round, in much the same way as early 19th-century artists drew kangaroos that looked rather like gigantic English rabbits with long tails. So some early colonial would-be-Wordsworths applied the images and verse forms of England to Australian, Canadian or Caribbean contexts with very peculiar results. A language that has not grown from the native soil is neither an adequate nor an effective tool of description because it carries built-in assumptions and perceptions – a bit like the inhabitants of the Land of Oz who see their world as green, not because it is green, but because they are looking through emerald-tinted spectacles. So if this is colonialism, what is post-colonialism? Dorothy, in the Wizard of Oz, could be said to be the post-colonial who dares to remove the spectacles, discovers and declares the world to be 'ungreen' – in fact, multi-coloured. The declaration of this discovery might inspire mockery, disbelief and anger, but it also inspires some to take off their glasses and see the particularity of their world.

Post-colonialism is about becoming self-determining. In terms of both community and self, post-colonialism is about choosing, selecting – deliberately, consciously examining the past, the present and deciding a course for the future. In terms of community, it is about economic, governmental and ideological independence – of the people by the people for the people. In terms of self, it is a process of becoming consciously aware of history – what has made me what I am, and how can I become actively participatory in that creative process? In terms of literature and the creators of that literature it is primarily about taking possession (or re-possession) of the language(s) of discourse, and it is also about encouraging community participation in that creative energy. In terms of literary criticism, post-colonial theory moves out of a process of de-construction to one of re-construction. Post-colonialism is about creating and asserting identity at the same time that it seeks to undermine the generality of stereotype – most often the stereotype nurtured by colonialism.

Many of the post-colonial writers that were studied during my first term at the University of Aarhus were, both in terms of author and audience, a rite of passage. The experience of colonialism has often been a painful and destructive one in which the sense of self, of belonging and community has been lost. The African slaves transported to the Caribbean suffered a vital disconnection from language and a devaluation of culture and of person. In her poetic journey entitled 'i is a long-memoried woman', Grace Nichols charts the pain and the fulfilment of a spiritual return to Africa, a back to roots if you like, and concludes with these words:

Unforgiving as the course of justice
Inerasable as my scars and fate
I am here
a woman ..... with all my lives
strung out like beads

It isn't privilege or pity
that I seek
It isn't reverence or safety
quick happiness or purity

the power to be what I am/ a woman
charting my own futures/ a woman
holding my beads in my hand

Epilogue

I have crossed an ocean
I have lost my tongue
from the root of the old
one
a new one has sprung[5]

I too have crossed and re-crossed oceans. I have not suffered disinheritance or the dislocation of Afro-Caribbean woman, or indeed, of Koori woman (the aboriginal people of my area of New South Wales), but in the course of my journeying I have discovered an understanding of the paradox and the complexity of creating, asserting and justifying difference, and I would say that demarcation of boundary – the delineation of self from other – is valuable only when those borders are transient and fluid – when they represent temporary structures of understanding. To return to the earlier image of Canberra, that colonial anomaly – that national disaster: the hard edges of English-green squares battle against the unrelenting encroachment of parched, cracked earth whose dust and grass seed blow across artificial borders, threatening to undermine the colonial veneer of European civilization. Outer suburbs merge into grey gum and brown hills. Unlike the artificial Lake Burley Griffin, whose borders are concrete edged, Lake George – a lake that lies just outside the precincts of the city – expands and diminishes in size with a marked lack of respect for definition or boundary demarcation of farmers' fences. Watered by a mysterious source that scientists have been unable to discover, its edges are indeterminate. It is whole – it is entity enough to be labelled 'Lake George' – but the borders of that mysterious body of water tantalize and evade the cartographer's desire for definition. If we map out our edges in the indelible and inerasable 'india ink' of my childhood geography lessons, we may find commitment to that definition as damaging and restricting as the pink bits on the map of empire. Language defines our difference but it also creates a space within which we are constantly able to redefine and remap our relationship to others – an area in which foreign territory becomes home ground. This would sound like another form of colonization if it were not for intent. I am not seeking to possess, I am seeking to understand – and they are not the same thing.

Notes

1. Margaret Atwood, *Surfacing* (London: Virago, 1979), 5: 'Now we're on my home ground, foreign territory'.
2. Ngugi, 'Literature and Society' (paper read at Nairobi School, 1973), in *Writers in Politics: Essays* (London: Heinemann), 1981.
3. Chinua Achebe, 'An Image of Africa', *Research in African Literatures*, IX/1 (1978), 1-15.
4. Peter Hoeg, *Miss Smilla's Feeling For Snow* (London: Flamingo, 1994), published Denmark 1992, English translation 1993.
5. Grace Nichols, *i is a long-memoried woman* (London: Caribbean Cultural International, 1983), 79-80.

An Interview
with Anna Rutherford

Anne Collett

AC: *As you were one of the pioneers of teaching and publishing commonwealth/post-colonial literatures, I would ask first what it was that sparked your interest and generated the energy to found both* Kunapipi *and* Dangaroo Press, *and to move what had been peripheral into the mainstream consciousness of European teaching and scholarship? Why did you become interested not only in reading and teaching post-colonial literatures, but also promoting and fostering post-colonial writers? What aspect or experience in your life do you think propelled you in that direction? And perhaps additional and anecdotal to this first question, is the one that asks how and why you – a working-class girl from Newcastle, Australia – ended up teaching, publishing and creating access to and understanding of this literature in Denmark of all places – worlds away from you own source and the source of those (at the time) little known and little valued writers and writings?*

AR: In a way it's not hard to say what led me into the field of colonialism/post-colonialism. That can be traced back to my birthplace, Newcastle, the town where I was born, grew up and return to as much as possible. Newcastle is a town which, I believe, fits perfectly into the colonial, post-colonial syndrome. It is approximately 150 km from Sydney and is built, like Sydney, on the edge of the Pacific Ocean. The city lies at the mouth of the Hunter River and was founded as a penal settlement in 1797. The convicts were transported to Newcastle to mine the coal that was found there, and along with Norfolk Island it came to be one of the most brutal penal settlements in the colony. For some years coal was to remain its main industry, with free immigrants coming essentially from the coal-mining towns of England and Wales. They were soon to learn that whatever help they needed they must provide themselves – what interested management was profit, not people. In 1912 the Government sold Crown land which, ironically enough, they had set aside in 1869 for a botanical reserve to the Broken Hill Propriety Limited to build a steelworks. Other heavy industry followed, and Newcastle became an industrial city. Growing up in Newcastle we were taught to be proud of the fact that we lived in 'the largest industrial city in the Southern Hemisphere'. We were unaware at the time that the rest of Australia regarded it as a dirty, ugly industrial city inhabited by a lot of 'bolshis' who'd go on strike at the drop of a hat. In one respect they were right. The pollution was horrendous but it was a pollution which at that time was accepted as necessary – coal trucks trundling by and black smoke belching forth over the city meant employment. Management was not concerned with the social or human cost for, like the absentee landlords in the Caribbean in the earlier centuries, they didn't live there. Today, in the name of economic rationalism, BHP has just announced its withdrawal from Newcastle, which will in turn mean the loss of 10,000 jobs. But management's continued lack of concern is reflected in the fact that on the day of the announcement of the sackings the company held a farewell party for the manager. It would seem that Nero still fiddles whilst Rome burns!

The history of Newcastle is a history of exploitation. It has from the beginning been a working-class city and it remains so. Its workers have contributed greatly to the economic wealth of Australia but little of this wealth has been returned to the city. As J.C. Docherty remarked in his book on Newcastle, 'Outsiders, both public and private have treated Newcastle like a colonial possession'. Yet, I had never thought of myself as a colonial and so it was with great surprise when I turned up at a London school for my first day at work and after announcing I was the new 'supply' the head said, 'Oh, you're a colonial'. 'No', I replied, 'I'm an Australian'. At morning tea time I was dispatched to collect a bottle of milk from the supply left over by the children who didn't drink milk. The headmistress caught me and said, 'Oh, we don't STEAL from children in this country!' Apart from Moll Flanders I thought of the British Museum, which must be the greatest monument to robbery the world has ever known.

It is little wonder then that I turned to research on the convicts, and it is even less wonder that I jumped at the chance to work for Grethe Hjort,[1] who was a remarkable woman and Professor at Aarhus University. She was a gold medalist from Copenhagen and Cambridge and had been the first head of Melbourne University Women's College. She spent many years in Australia and loved it – we always said that when she died she didn't want to go to Heaven but to Australia. She was once interviewed in *Alt for Damerne* [A Danish women's magazine], which is a bit like me being interviewed in *Vogue*, and she was asked the question 'What were Australians like?' 'Wonderful people', she replied, 'who'll do anything for you – but if you try to force them or order them to do something you'll get nowhere'. (There are of course good reasons why Australians, particularly Irish-Australians, are anti-authoritarian.) What a wise woman she was! She was both brilliant and eccentric, things that often go together, but one would have to be eccentric to have the vision to set up Commonwealth Studies in a Scandinavian country in the fifties. She concentrated on Australia, New Zealand and India and had already set up a good library. I pay this tribute to her because in many ways she fitted the image of 'Old Botany Bay': 'The nation was – / Because of me!' (Mary Gilmore). We all owe her a great deal.

In 1967 Grethe Hjort died suddenly and it was left to me to take over the Commonwealth section. My first thought was why not introduce African, West Indian, Canadian and all those other parts of the world once coloured red but on which the sun, in spite of Britain's proud boast, had now sunk. Not that I knew much of them at that stage.

AC: You successfully established Commonwealth Literature as part of the core curriculum in the English Department at the University of Aarhus, Denmark. Could you tell us a little about the battle, the blood and the glory?

AR: The times were with me. 1968 was of course the time of the student revolts all over Europe and I was more than sympathetic to their course. They in turn were curious, as students should be, and supported my proposals and courses. The major aim was to get Commonwealth Literature on an equal par with English and American Literatures. It was no easy task and required the approval of the external examiners as well as the teachers and students. Once again luck was on my side because the head of the external examiners had just read Peter Cowan's short story 'The Tractor', and he said that any literature that was as good as that was worth its place alongside British and American. As I said, my knowledge of all those other countries didn't at that stage extend far beyond the 'map of the world' pool in Newcastle, but I started making it my business to learn about them, their history, their culture and their literature. I travelled widely, went to as many conferences as possible, swapped ideas.

In 1964 Derry Jeffares decided to form the Association of the Commonwealth Literature and Language Studies and we held the first conference in Brisbane in 1968. We determined that ACLALS should comply with Joseph Furphy's 'temper democratic' – that there would no hierarchy. We never used titles – it was more like a family ... Three years later, the next conference was held in the Caribbean – the one at which Naipaul was booed off the stage. It had been an interesting but perhaps not very successful conference and when I came back to Aarhus I decided that I could do better. The first Commonwealth Conference took place at the University of Aarhus three months later and that was the beginning. We cancelled all classes for the week, and all 200 students went. There were many writers – Randolf Stow, Les Murray, Wilson Harris – it was something I wanted to continue beyond the conference, and so EACLALS (the European Association for Commonwealth Language and Literature Studies) was formed and a *Commonwealth Newsletter* was produced to maintain the links we had created. This was the first step towards *Kunapipi*, which began in 1979. I would like to pay tribute here to Signe Frits, who was with us from the beginning when we started *Kunapipi*

– without her we could never have continued – she was a perfectionist and had an eye like a hawk.

The universities were still quite wealthy in the 60s and 70s – and we had money to get writers over – Sam Selvon, George Lamming, Shiva Naipaul, Wilson Harris. It was so exciting ... suddenly my students realized that all these writers were people – were alive! And of course they were a different colour and that was very unusual at that time in Denmark. Wilson Harris was the catalyst for the press and he has been the greatest influence on my critical thinking, there's no doubt about that. When he was lecturing in Aarhus, we used to roll up each day – we weren't sure exactly at times what he was saying, but Kirsten Holst Petersen and I decided it was too good to let go so we thought we'd have a press. I knew nothing about publishing – not a thing – but that didn't deter me – and I decided to form Dangaroo press. We had arranged everything for the launch of our first book, *Enigma of Values*: the people, the food, the wine ... and the book didn't turn up ... and this has in some ways been the pattern. The first major triumph was the publication of David Dabydeen's first book, *Slave Song*, which was the first book written in creole to win the Commonwealth Poetry Prize. In the early days of the press David and I would backpack the books around the bookshops of London – hawking our wares! But you could say in terms of publishing we have gone from strength to strength. Our publications have ranged from the Outer Hebrides to the Antipodes. There have been good moments and bad moments, and there have been books that I've been excited about and books that haven't made me so excited. Perhaps one of the most exciting moments was the launch of *Unbecoming Daughters of Empire* – it reads like a Who's Who. I know most of the writers I've published and most are my personal friends. Another point that I suppose I would want to make is that writers put their life-blood into their writing and my aim has always been to produce beautiful books – perhaps it is the source of some of my greatest satisfaction ... and of course, the press is a radical press – what would you expect from me!

I should also say that I had the support of writers from around the world who became well known and who would write and say, yes you may have this piece because I got my first chance in a small magazine, and I know how important they are.

AC: But there must have been a certain amount of difficulty, at least in the early days, making contacts and gaining access to cultures not your own – what were your credentials, or what was it about you and your attitudes that opened up hearts and minds – lasting friendships and loyal allies?

AR: To gain access ... most people would say I was a friendly gregarious person – and I listen, and I guess you could say I'm colour blind – so when I'd meet a person who said I've got a manuscript for you to read, I'd say alright I'll look at it. I spent most of my time when I wasn't teaching, and mostly at my own expense, travelling in the different countries of the world.

AC: As all teachers do, you must have found some texts that could be depended upon to 'work' in every new class context and configuration ...could you tell us something about those texts, what the nature of their working was and why they worked? Maybe you could tell us something about Sam Selvon's A Brighter Sun *– I know it's one of your favourites – a text that you have said always works and a text that you come back to again and again.*

AR: *Brighter Sun* is certainly one of the texts that I would take with me to a desert island – it's the first book written entirely in dialect, but that's not what grabbed me – what grabbed me and always grabbed my students – it's never failed – never – is the understanding and sympathy – it's a funny book and it's a sad book – a bit like *Muriel's Wedding* or *Secrets and Lies* – it's a book that gives hope. I think *A House For Mr. Biswas* is Naipaul's best book, but in the finish, even though he has his house, it's a jerry-built house and one doesn't feel it will last, whereas *A Brighter Sun* for me is a forerunner of *Myal* (by Erna Brodber), because it shows the growing awareness of the central character, Tiger, of the nature and effects of colonialism, and that there is good and bad in black and white and brown; and so when he builds his house, his house stands – stands for a sense of common purpose, of shared humanity – he stays on to build the nation. I think it's just as sophisticated as Myal, but I don't think it's as complicated.

AC: I know that one of your priorities as a teacher was to maintain contemporaneity and currency in terms both of the creative and the critical texts you worked with ...

AR: How did I keep up? I am a voracious reader and I was also a reader for Macmillan, Longman and Heinemann, and Routledge asked me to be General Editor for their post-colonial series, which I thought about for a while and then turned down. And on top of that were all the manuscripts that came for *Kunapipi* – I was able to keep up with what was going on – and pass it on to my students; and it changed their views and mine, sometimes radically, as when I read a short story by Alice Walker. I've always had a great admiration for Scarlett O'Hara – and I can remember when she stood on Tara's Hill and it was all burnt, and she said, 'I'll never be hungry again'. Alice Walker's story is set in a university college and focuses upon two friends, one black and one white. There is a fancy-dress ball to which the white girl goes dressed as Scarlett O'Hara. Her black friend comes up to her and says, 'This is the end of our friendship'. Her friend asks why, to which she replies, 'Have you ever noticed how Scarlett O'Hara treated her servants?' I had never noticed. It was something I used to point out to my students

– who certainly when I first went to Denmark must have been the most homogeneous group on earth.

AC: So how do you get round the problem of these literatures being seen as just exotic and other but not us?

AR: Somehow or other I tried to make them not exotic – they weren't exotic – they were just writers from another country, and I tried to point out that there were different points of view. In terms of teaching, I was always determined not to teach in the way that I had been taught in my own Australian childhood where we learned by rote. I would say, 'You may not think the same way as I do, but that's perfectly alright as long as you can argue for your own point of view'. I can remember one student asking me, 'Which forty pages shall we read for next week?' and I said, 'You're in the wrong class, it's not how I work'. I have the advantage these days of videos, I've brought back artifacts – I used every possible means to make them understand. One of the issues that I stressed perhaps more than any of the others – or two – was that of decolonizing the mind – how relatively easy it was to become independent economically and yet how difficult it was to change the mind: I had a copy of *Drum* magazine and on the cover it had a picture of a beautiful black girl, subtitled 'black is beautiful', and on the back cover it had an advertisement for skin lightening cream. ... The other issue is language – first of all the imposition of a foreign language on a group of people so that they were led to believe that only good things come through English and nothing good could come through their own language – Ngugi related how if you did well in English you got to the top of the class and if you didn't do well in English you had to wear a sign around your neck saying 'I'm stupid'. Then I pointed out the difficulty of learning 'a for apple', 'b for bat', 'c for cat' if you had never seen an apple; and I would say to my students '"a for ake", "b for brumby", "c for Carib", "d for dunny" ... what does it mean to you?' I encouraged my students to travel .... I sent them to Zimbabwe, to Australia, to New Zealand, and particularly when they went to Zimbabwe I said, 'Now you'll find out what it's like to have the wrong coloured skin'. I said to my students that perhaps after taking my class they might think in another way. Some didn't, but I think most did.

AC: So this was actually the basis behind the 'Anna's Canon' course, wasn't it? – A course based on texts that had changed your thinking, your perception of the world.

AR: Yes, changed me. There is a direct correlation between colonialism and feminism – nearly all the texts were by women writers – Doris Lessing, Shirley Hazard, Buchi Emecheta ... .[2] When I first came to Aarhus I taught the general English literature course – although I must admit the Romantics didn't get much of a look in, because, well, they'd never really appealed to me. I didn't throw the baby out with the bath-water. And then of course I did the rewrites of the canonical texts, but I pointed out that the Manichean reversal was not an answer, and that's why Wilson Harris's works, and later on, Erna Brodber's *Myal*, have been books that have influenced me very deeply. One of my students has just written her dissertation on *Myal* and it's my intention to publish it as a book.

AC: Myal is interesting because the reader goes into it in a state of almost complete confusion and you have to work your way through – feeling your way to some kind of understanding ...

AR: My students didn't know what to make of it, except a few very bright ones, and they read it two or three times, and then it was the joy of having cracked it ... and my own joy ... my students were my joy ... I loved teaching ... I was probably one of the 5% of people who had a job they loved. To be honest, my last few years at Aarhus were not very happy years, but I suppose some of that unhappiness was made up for by the loyalty of certain members of staff, many of my students, and in particular, Lars, Mette and Ruth. This loyalty was perhaps turned into triumph when the University of Gothenburg granted me an honorary Doctorate. When the fanfare sounded and I stood before the cream of Scandinavia's academics, I could not help thinking what a long way I had come from my first school, a weather-board shed, technically St. John's Catholic School but known to all as 'Snake Gully'. But my most rewarding moment came when I was presented with the wonderful *Festschrift* at the EACLALS conference in Oviedo. It was and always will be one of the most moving moments of my life, when Hena Maes-Jelenik, who had organized it all, presented it to me, when a representative from each of the five continents said their piece and when the whole audience stood for a fantastic ovation. The whole event wiped away the blood of the battles and the sadness, and I'll never forget it.

AC: That was indeed a very moving occasion, and perhaps now is the time to think about the present and the future. If you think about Selvon's Brighter Sun and being ultimately optimistic, do you still feel optimistic about what's happening – can you see real changes happening – do you see real decolonizing taking place – after having been involved for over thirty years?

AR: I think my answer unfortunately would have to be no. I have come back to my own country, which I thought was the most successful of multi-racial societies that came into existence, and I've come back to what I can only describe as a racist society. I find it more than offensive, the phrase that goes around, 'pick the Australian, pick the Aussie'. Who's the Aussie? The Aussie is the aboriginal – so my answer unfortunately has to be, no. You asked earlier about the battle, the

28

blood, the glory. Well of course there were battles and some blood was shed but bearing grudges has never been something I have gone in for so I'll leave the first two alone. There was a lot of hard work and not much glory but to end on a positive note, one of the nicest things is when you get feedback from writers or students who say thank you for publishing me, or thank you for helping me change, and I suppose I was very moved by Olive Senior's tribute in her most recent collection of short stories, where she said, 'For Anna Rutherford who helped us to sing our songs'.

Notes

1. Grethe Hjort is known in the English-speaking world as Greta Hort.
2. Primary texts for the course included: (Australia) Shirley Hazard, *The Transit of Venus* (New York : Viking Press, 1980); (New Zealand) Janet Frame, *Owls Do Cry* (Melbourne: Sun Books, 1967); (South Pacific) Albert Wendt, 'The Coming of the White Man', in *Flying-fox in a Freedom Tree* (Auckland: Longman Paul, 1974); (Caribbean) Sam Selvon, *A Brighter Sun* (Trinidad: Longman Caribbean, 1971); (South Africa/Rhodesia) Doris Lessing, *The Grass is Singing* (London, 1950; reprinted e.g. New York: Penguin, 1991); (Africa) Buchi Emecheta, *The Joys of Motherhood* (New York: G. Braziller, 1979); (India) Githa Hariharan, *The Thousand Faces of Night* (New Delhi: Penguin Books, 1992); (Canada) selected short stories by Alice Munro and by Stephen Heighton.

Teaching African Literature in Denmark

Kirsten Holst Petersen

A long time ago (1979) at a conference in Kent I was asked by an incredulous English teacher 'Why on Earth do you teach African literature in Denmark?' His utter amazement reflected the prevailing attitude at the conference, which saw the teaching of African and Caribbean literature primarily as a tool for teaching African and Caribbean immigrant children about their home culture. Seen in that light, African literature in Denmark is indeed amazing. Until the seventies Denmark must have been one of the most homogenous countries in the world. We have an unbroken history of self government since our beginning (apart from the Second World War), constitutional and social change at a comfortable speed since the Vikings, a shared and unthreatened language despite our small number (just over five million), a national literature, enough won and lost wars to create enough national monuments, and a state religion, shared by virtually everybody. This uniformity was only broken by the Greenlanders, whom we colonized and treated as second class citizens, but they remained mainly on Greenland and were not incorporated into the society in Denmark.

On this mono-cultural background, which in many cases amounted to ignorance about the difficulties of multi-cultural living, Danes built an image of themselves as a country with clean hands, ethically and morally concerned with global injustices, in the forefront of the battle against apartheid in South Africa and internationally indignant about racial injustices in the world. Denmark set aside a larger than average percentage of the GNP for aid to the Third World.

It was this self image which fired the students when teaching of African literature was started in the early seventies. They were enthusiastic in their defence of Third World rights *vis-à-vis* the old world. Their (our) enthusiasm was often emotional rather than based on any actual knowledge of the countries or cultures involved. The 1968 students' revolt in Paris affected Danish university life, and students revolted against the strict and steep university hierarchy. In the battle against the power of the professors students saw themselves as dispossessed underdogs, fighting an unjust system to gain the power over the direction and content of their own education which was theirs by right. The parallel to the Third

World's battle for survival may seem ludicrous today, but then it was self evident and felt natural. We were on a crusade together, to save the world, and it was nothing less than global.

My point is that the level of motivation was high, and high-minded, if a touch philanthropic. Our revolt was based on a Marxist analysis of society, and Marxism was seen as the remedy, both on a national and a global level, but the revolt also included an almost modernist sense of a crisis of values in our technological society. This explains how a Marxist-inspired movement could include romantic notions about finding meaningful differences and values in foreign cultures to oppose our materialistic, capitalist, individualist and exploitative world view. African literature was approached as one possible source of such enlightenment. The expectations were high.

At Aarhus University the 1968 student revolt provided the liberalization of the curriculum structure and made the inclusion of new subjects possible, and it also generated the 'enthusiasm-without-which', but these essential ingredients had a base to build on. African literature entered the Danish university system under the umbrella of Commonwealth literature, and Commonwealth literature entered the university mainly in the shape of Australian literature. This is, of course, an absurdity, but new beginnings are not always planned.

Commonwealth literature, including Australian literature and some New Zealand and Indian literature, was established at Aarhus university in 1966, during the period of the power of the professors, by an eccentric and brilliant Dane, Grethe Hjort. After a period as the first principal of Women's college, Melbourne University, she returned to Denmark as professor of English at Aarhus University, which she considered an outpost of civilization. She combined an imaginative and more comprehensive view of other cultures than prevailed in Aarhus at the time with excessive cultural snobbery. She was a true Girton graduate; Virginia Woolf would have liked her. The Danes weren't very enthusiastic.

The exclusion of African and West Indian literature from the curriculum of her new course was not a deliberate choice. She just did not happen to know those cultures, to have travelled to those places, so they were outside her ken. That's all. She employed an Australian lecturer, Anna Rutherford, who after Grethe Hjort's death took over the embryonic department and expanded it. She went to a conference in Leeds, and as a result of that experience she embarked on the first African literature course in 1972, 'Visions of Africa'. She had a full and dedicated class (I was one of them), and we were soon referred to as 'the visionaries'. The reading list was an ambitious fourteen novels, and because of the cost of the books this was classed among students as a 1,000 kroner (approximately £100) course – which made us hopelessly idealistic in the eyes of the more level-headed.

That year, as a result of much lobbying, Commonwealth literature was made a compulsory subject at Aarhus university. But the absurdities continued. The order of study included compulsory drama and poetry, both notoriously unpopular

31

genres, and I, who soon graduated into teaching the African literature course, offered African poetry and drama as an incentive to join the African course. It worked, and as a result some student generations from Aarhus base their knowledge of drama and poetry in the English language mainly on Soyinka and Okigbo.

Apart from such tactical considerations, the choice of texts was governed by the search for alternative values. Texts which demonstrated cultural difference and specificity were the most popular: Chinua Achebe, *Things Fall Apart* and *The Arrow of God;* Elechi Amadi, *The Concubine* (which was translated into Danish along with Achebe's novels) and The Great Ponds; Okot p'Bitek, *Song of Lawino* and *Song of Ocol;* and Gabriel Okara, *The Voice,* and his poetry, particularly 'The Fisherman's Invocation'. We sat in our classroom in Denmark, actively willing African cultural nationalism. Edward Said would probably maintain that we created it.

Interesting as those texts are, it soon became clear that they did not contain the answers to our problems, and we widened our scope to include the novels of disillusion and the novels about the fight against colonialism, particularly Ngugi's early novels.

The most immediate problem with teaching those texts in Denmark was – and remains – the students' ignorance of the African historical and cultural background. Before you can teach a novel like *Things Fall Apart* you have to fight your way through a vast amount of history and sociology. This is often uphill work, but it can also be very rewarding. In discussions about concepts like 'tribe', 'traditional African religion', 'orature', 'African history' or 'essentialism', you as a teacher can occasionally find yourself, if not changing lives, then at least challenging firmly-held convictions or clarifying diffuse opinions based on ignorance or plain prejudice, mostly as a result of inadequate newspaper reporting. This situation is still true to day, even though the students are less idealistic and more knowledgeable about multi-cultural living. Within the subject of English it seems to me that only feminist studies offer a comparable platform for combining academic work with a debate about issues of vital importance.

Unlike feminist studies, however, African literature (African culture) studies can come up against insurmountable difficulties. They appear mainly in the area of religion and various forms of magic. Danes are exceptionally rational; the Lutheran Church does not include the possibility of miracles after Jesus in its creed. It looks for a rational explanation, and if that is not possible it (and we, in general) incorporate the inexplicable as something symbolic, psychological or in some other way capable of an explanation. Magic realism is a problem. Once, when teaching Ben Okri's *The Famished Road,* I went to great length to dissuade a student from writing his term paper on the novel as an expression of madness and mental breakdown. He was interested in schizophrenia, he said. I suggested Bessie Head's *A Question of Power,* but he persisted. The problem was the concept of the *abiku*, which Ben Okri borrows from Yoruba mythology. Its symbolic value and its explanatory potential in a situation of a high infant mortality rate were accepted, but the *abiku* as a reality, unexplained and a fact of life! never. After many discussions about the difference or non-difference between religion and superstition we settled for a term paper about the *abiku* as a metaphor for the artist in *The Famished Road*. This maintained the distance to reality without relegating the concept to the realm of madness.

This is a long way from the original aspiration of finding new values to save a degenerate civilization. The focus has changed under the impact of Danish, not African, developments. In the seventies Denmark, like other industrialized countries in Europe, imported foreign labour to underpin the economic boom, and the Danish foreign worker was born. She was at first Yugoslavian, then Turkish, then Iranian and Pakistani. Not African, so the new experience is not of a direct contact with African people, rather it is an experience of the difficulties of multi-cultural living. Faced with the reality of otherness Danes discovered to their surprise that they (we) are as racially and culturally prejudiced as the rest of Europe. The country went through a rapid development, separating the frankly racist from the quietly prejudiced from the naturally intolerant from the open-minded from the idealists, bending blackwards, or perhaps brownwards. Political correctness appeared on the scene, along with born agains. The role of African literature was reshuffled. It was at the mercy of two somewhat opposite developments.

Within the universities it was strengthened. It now comes under the umbrella of Post-colonial Literature, and the difference between that and the former Common-wealth literature is a theory of its own, and this gives it academic legitimacy. It is now taught at four out of a total of five Danish universities. On the other hand, the social experience of multi-culturalism deprived it definitively of the attraction of the exotic and the otherness. African literature courses became less popular and they ran into the danger of becoming bastions of political correctness. This took – and takes – the form of Dane-bashing. In post-colonial theory, European culture is not only responsible for slavery and imperialism, but it is also seriously warped at the root. Orientalism can be an empowering insight, leading to greater self-awareness and a changed perspective, but it can also be paralysing; in some post-colonial readings anything the students say will automatically be discredited by an orientalist reading of it. This casts the students as enemies in the discourse of the subject, and that creates anger and resentment rather than positive interest. As post-colonial literature has by now become a compulsory subject at several universities I (we) now face antagonistic students, objecting to being cast in the role as villains, or the sons and daughters of villains. The tables are turned completely. I now find myself telling the students that as Europeans they do have a right to an opinion; that there is a difference between a European and a Euro-centric point of view. Instead of students eager to save the world I am now faced with students concerned with saving themselves – from post-colonial anger at one end of the scale and self-denigrating political correctness at the other. *Things Fall Apart* suddenly becomes a very complicated text to read in these circumstances. Despite its difficulties I see a progression in the student response to African literature: from naively idealistic to realistically sceptical or even oppositional. Either way the course is a challenge to the students, and it is still an eye-opener to a surprisingly large number of them. I hope, however, that this present stage is only a temporary one, and I have a clear idea of where I would like African literature – and the other post-colonial literatures – to settle: as individual subjects (as national literatures), not as adjuncts to English literature; and as such, on the syllabus, ordinarily, like French or German or Japanese, to be studied by students and scholars because they find them particularly interesting or important. This can, however, only be realized when the heavily charged ideological atmosphere which surrounds the subject has settled at a less controversial level. This would indicate a normalization of our relationship to the post-colonial world. And within that structure there is plenty of scope for changes and new directions which, thank God, I cannot foresee.

The Definition of African Literature Revisited

S.A. *Dseagu*

1. Introduction

The issue of what constitutes African literature has been controversial ever since the emergence of modern African literature written in the metropolitan European languages.[1]

The controversy is in a way related to the uniqueness of the phenomenon. Whereas in all the other continents literatures are classified on national and linguistic lines which invariably are identical, in Africa alone the literatures of the diverse linguistic, racial, cultural, social, and political groups, some of which are large and complex enough to have been regarded as nation-states should they have been elsewhere, are all classified together into a single continent-wide basket as African literature.

This anomaly was caused by the historical factors of the Atlantic slave trade and colonialism which engendered an idea in Europe that Africans were inferior and were lacking in complex institutions. Hegel has often been cited as the most systematic exponent of that negative view of the continent.

> Africa proper, as far as history goes back, has remained for all purposes of connection with the rest of the world shut up ... The Negro ... exhibits the natural man in his completely wild and untamed state ... Africa ... has no historical part of the world. It has no movement or development to exhibit.[2]

Regarding that negative view as the dominant colonialist discourse, African writers and writers of African descent as well as all others sympathetic to the condition of all colonized peoples then presented a common counter discourse to refute and denounce that colonialist discourse. That counter discourse was to become the basis of African literature as the following extract from Aimé Césaire's poem 'Cahier d'un retour au pays natal' illustrates:

> my negritude is not a stone,
> nor deafness flung out against the clamour of the day
> my negritude is not a white speck of dead water

on the dead eye of the earth
my negritude is neither tower nor cathedral

....

Heia for those who have never invented anything
those who never explored anything
those who never tamed anything.[3]

It is noteworthy that the persona defines his personality in terms of an assertion of negatives ('is not'; 'nor'; 'neither'; 'never') to proclaim his strength in those very attributes for which he is denounced. ('Heia for those who have never invented anything.')

As is illustrated by the passage, the counter-discourse is framed in the parameters of the colonialist discourse. Put crudely, the colonialist discourse states 'All of you African are inferior' and the anti-colonialist counter-discourse replies 'We Africans are not inferior'. The assertion and the counter-assertion both assume the validity of the principle of grouping together ('all of you') the disparate and multitudinous linguistic, cultural, racial, economic, and political communities of the continent into one common basket. The concept of a continent-wide African literature therefore emerged in the context of larger political and ideological issues. Since then most discussions of the definition have remained anchored to those larger issues of politics and ideology.

2. Aim

My aim is to try to show that, in the present post-colonial and multi-cultural era, many of the original political and ideological assumptions underlying the concept of African literature are no longer current and valid and should therefore be abandoned in favour of a more objective and formal definition of the literature.

3. Critical standpoints

2.1 Pan-Africanism

The conceptualization of the literature as creative writing by colonized Africans as well as by colonized and segregated people of the African diaspora in the Caribbean and the USA was the first consistent definition. The definition was founded on the notion that the Atlantic slave trade and colonialism were the most significant factors in the psyche of black people. This common denominator, defined as 'Negritude' between the two world wars, was an idea created in France by a movement of Francophone writers from various continents drawn together and united by the common concern of all colonized peoples for freedom. Having come under the influence of communism, many of these writers perceived the issue of race and colonialism in dialectical terms as having to do with the universal struggle between capital and labour.

It is worth noting that during that era between the two world wars no particular distinction was made between the colonial situation of Africa, the race problem of the USA, and the colonial problems in the Caribbean and Asia. All were regarded as intertwined global commotions caused by world capitalism. One of the achievements of these scholars and writers from the colonized and disadvantaged regions of the world was the creation of the world-wide black movement, the Pan-African Movement.

The idea of a purely African literature was then therefore incongruous because the aim of most of the writers of the time was to seek a global end to colonialism and its underlying capitalism. As Jean-Paul Sartre remarked, 'It is no mere chance that the most ardent poets of the negritude movement [were] also militant marxists'.[4]

2.2 Black-African nativism

Between 1950 and 1960, serious cracks began to emerge in the Pan-African Movement because the Africans began to adopt a different approach toward the struggle for liberation. For instance, in contrast to the celebration of nonentity illustrated in the above-quoted extract from Césaire, African writers were seeking valorization for the struggle for political and cultural liberation in the glories of their ancestral past; a recourse denied to the blacks of the diaspora. The idea of literature as a tool was maintained as before but the technique changed in the hands of the African writers. Chinua Achebe's aim in novel-writing is illustrative: 'I would be quite satisfied if my novels ... did no more than teach my readers that their past ... was not one long night of savagery'.[5]

As the technique changed so also did the conception of the literature. Thus emerged not only the idea of an African literature but also that of a committed African literature using the past as a technique of valorization and as a functional tool for African liberation and empowerment. Hence was born also the idea of African literature as having to do solely with black Africa. Professor Mphahlele's *The African Image,* published in 1962, when Southern Rhodesia was still under racist rule, is a vivid example of the mode of thinking then on the subject: 'Africa refers to independent *Black* Africa which excludes Southern Rhodesia'.[6]

2.3 Continental Pluralism

By the end of the 1960s such a massive collection of creative compositions had emerged that academics and scholars could initiate courses on them. The practical requirements of classification and course-content description to avoid overlapping and thinning of courses meant that the academics and scholars had to re-evaluate many of the concepts and standpoints of the definition.[7] In 1962 at a conference of academics and scholars at the University of Ibadan a resolution was adopted to make the following the standard definition of African literature: 'creative writing in which an African setting is authentically handled or to which experiences originating in Africa are integral'.[8]

The resolution reflected the diversity of opinion and background of the participants who were native African and expatriate academics on the staff of English and Modern Language departments of universities in West Africa, East Africa and Britain as well as inspectors of schools and heads of international examinations syndicates. For the pragmatic reasons of pedagogy, the definition was made broad enough to encompass the writings of white Africans such as Olive Schreiner, Laurens van der Post, Doris Lessing, and Nadine Gordimer as well as even Joseph Conrad's *Heart of Darkness*.

This pluralist definition is echoed in Nadine Gordimer's definition of African literature as creative writing 'in any language by Africans themselves and by others of whatever skin colour' who share the African experience or Africa-centred consciousness.[9]

2.4 Linguistic Indigenism

Meanwhile, the immense publication of creative works around the theme of the glory of Africa's ancestral past had by the end of the 1970s engendered another conception of definition largely among militant black African academics and scholars. The idea was first propagated in print by Obianjunwa Wali in an article entitled 'The Dead End of African Literature'.[10] Mr. Wali's argument was that as literature has always been classified on the basis of the language in which it is written,[11] African literature should be literature written in the African languages. Under that proposition, we went on to argue, African literature in the metropolitan European languages is neither wholly within the African languages classification nor within the European languages classification and was therefore at a 'dead end'.

This formidable argument has since been re-formulated into a variety of standpoints. First, it can be identified in the standpoint of Edgar Wright[12] that the African literature written in the metropolitan European languages should be classified as part of those languages. Second, it can be identified in the standpoint to which Ngugi has become attached:[13] that it is only literature in the African languages that can validly express the sentiments of black Africa. Third, it can be identified in the standpoints of Professor Mphahlele[14] and Chinweizu and others[15] that it is only literature composed in a style appropriate to the standard of the ordinary African that can adequately reflect the situation of the majority of the African people.

2.6 Terraced Classification

As if to reconcile all the different definitions, the grand old man of African *belles lettres*, Chinua Achebe,[16] has proposed a three-tier conception of African literature comprising firstly indigenous literature, which he calls 'ethnic literature'; secondly 'national literature written in the national language of [a] nation'; and finally African literature, being 'the sum total of all national and ethnic literatures of Africa'.

2.7 Fact-of-Life Approach
Since the 1980s, there has been the proposition that African literature is now a fact and does not therefore need any definition just as, for instance, English or French literature does not need a definition.

3. Discussion

Jean-Paul Sartre appears to have been the first to have systematically analyzed the definition of African literature which he discussed in the course of his critique of negritude poetry: 'la poésie noire n'a rien de commun avec les effusions de coeur: elle est fonctionnelle; elle réponde à un besoin qui la définit exactement'.[17]

To the extent that the literature was concerned with putting up a counter-discourse on black and African values against the dominant colonialist discourse, Jean-Paul Sartre perceived the goal as 'anti-racist racism'. As the original scope of negritude poetry was pan-African rather than Africa-centred, the literature is therefore relevant to the present study only to the extent to which it served as a precursor to the emergence of the African literature proper.

The same charge of anti-racist racism can be laid against some of the later standpoints of definition. There is a certain syllogism in equating the black skin with the continent of Africa and also with sympathetic affiliation with the well-being of Africans. Although the continent is inhabited predominantly by black Africans, since the dawn of history there have also been fair-skinned Africans. Moreover, there has been such extensive miscegenation over the centuries among the various races that any classification of Africa by race must be attempted with extreme caution.

Besides, there is no guarantee that a black-skinned person of African descent living, for instance, in Europe or America will automatically have any sympathy and affiliation with black Africans or write 'African' books. One other fallacy in the black-nativism definition is the assumption that even if such a writer has never been to Africa or has never even seen himself as African, his skin colour will nevertheless pass him.

Apart from the charge of racism, the black-nativism definition is fraught with contradictions. Where do we place writers from North Africa? What about children born to lightskinned Africans married to 'pure' whites? And what about the children of those children? Clearly, the definition lacks logical consistency.

The continental pluralism definitions suffer from vagueness through their all-inclusiveness. If the primary yardstick is authenticity *of African setting presentation,* one would be unnecessarily bogged down in deciding, for instance, whether or not Laurens van der Post is more authentic and therefore more African than Amos Tutuola or Bessie Head. Similarly, if *sympathy with Africa* were to be the primary yardstick, one would be hardpressed to decide whether or not Yambo Uouloguem or Wole Soyinka was more sympathetic and therefore more African than Olive Schreiner.

In spite of their vagueness, the continental pluralism definitions have the advantage over the previous definitions of drawing attention to the formal aspects of the literature. That advantage is also shared by the linguistic indigenism definitions.

The weakness of the linguistic indigenism definitions is that they are too narrow to encompass the heterogeneity of Africa's languages. For instance, if Swahili, a hybrid of Arabic and Bantu languages, is accepted as an indigenous language, why not Creole or even Afrikaans? Moreover, there is now a sizeable proportion of Africans who speak no so-called indigenous language but only English or French or Portuguese or Afrikaans as their first language. If one of these were asked to write in his indigenous language, surely he would write in the language of his tongue. Moreover, Arabic, the language of North Africa, is not in fact indigenous to the region nor is it even African.

The problem with the three-tier classification is that African literature will then become for all practical purposes a remote and even foreign literature as it will not be the literature of first recourse to most people.

It can be seen from the brief outline above that apart from the 1962 working definition, which appears to have been based more on expediency than on formal considerations, there has never been any widespread, not to say unanimous, support for any particular definition. In that respect, the present-day proposition that African literature should be regarded as a fact that does not require definition rather tends to freeze the controversy. Moreover, the proposition is logically unsound. Everybody knows what a horse is but that has never prevented biologists from defining it. Besides, it is incorrect to claim that English and French literature are not defined because they are assumed to be there. Throughout the nineteenth century, critics made it their habit to define and re-define those literatures. Even in this century, one such definition appears in E.M. Forster's *Aspects of the Novel.*

The problem is that since the 1930s discussion of the definition of the literature has often been guided by politics and ideology rather than by formal textual considerations. In the colonial era, those larger political and ideological concerns were, of course, significant. Now, however, in this era of post-colonialism, the situation has changed. Several of the writers who in the 1960s thought political independence would usher in individual liberty and national development are now disillusioned.

Wole Soyinka, for instance, has since the 1960s been calling for a revaluation of the counter-discourse so that 'the African's concern for international humanism' is anchored in a domestic and local confrontation with 'the problems of [national] power, of a national army, of education, the arts, law and house ownership, poverty, and medical use'.[18]

Similarly, Ousmane Sembene is insistent upon a revaluation of earlier standpoints.

> I also know, and so do you, that in the past, as well as in the present, there have been many anonymous heroic actions among us. But not everything we have done has been heroic ... The debility of the AFRICAN MAN – which we call our AFRICANITY, our NEGRITUDE, and which, instead of fostering the subjection of nature by science, upholds oppression and engenders venality, nepotism, intrigue, and all those weaknesses in which we try to conceal the base instincts of man (may at least one of us shout it out before he dies) – is the greatest defect of our time.[19]

Two urgent factors have now made it imperative that the issue of the definition of African literature be raised once again for discussion: first, the present intellectual climate of post-colonial criticism, and second the rapid political changes in South Africa that have rendered obsolete many of the long-held ideological standpoints on politics and culture in Africa. In the event, the reflection which Jean-Paul Sartre made almost fifty years ago on the political function of African literature has become very relevant today.

> What will happen if the Negro despoils his negritude for the sake of the revolution and only wishes to be taken for a member of the proletariat? What will happen if he allows himself to be defined only by his objective condition ... Will the source of his poetry run dry?[20]

4. Toward an objective definition

What is needed is a definition that is based mainly on the formal characteristics of the literature; that is to say, a definition based on the morphology. As in all scientific morphological studies, it should be possible in African literature to isolate the recurrent elements from the variables.

Even a cursory examination of the literature can reveal that certain features occur repeatedly in spite of the diversity of language, religion, culture, and politics. Jahnheinz Jahn has not only meticulously noted some of those recurrent features but has even traced their diffusion to other continents.[21]

One of such features can be found in African music. The essential factor of African music is now generally recognized as the rhythm.[22] What makes the rhythm so obviously different and peculiar to the Westerner is the absence of harmony as it is known to the West. Whenever traditional African music is played by a group or even by an individual, any casual listener notices that the melody tends to have a different beat from the accompanying hand-clap, ululaying, foot-stamping, or instrument. 'Whatever be the devices used to produce them, in African music there is practically always a *clash of rhythms*'.[23]

This divergence of beats, called polyrhythm, in a single musical performance is the fundamental feature of African music. So far no other indigenous society elsewhere in the world has been found with a similar system of rhythm. Significantly, it has been reproduced only in areas of the African diaspora. The syncopated music so characteristic of Black Americans, as Janheinz Jahn has forcefully demonstrated in his *Muntu*,[24] is actually an expression of that indigenous African form. Anywhere such crossed-rhythms are played, anyone would readily identify them as *African* music.

Some African poets are experimenting with the indigenous traditional cross-rhythm in their poetry. Atukwei Okai of Ghana has been at the forefront of that movement. The following extract is illustrative:

> And God I know
> And Serikin Zongo too I know
> Adolf Hitler I know
> And Aaleyngoy too I know
> Kweku Ananse I know
> Adode Akaibi I know
> Napoleon Bonarparte I know
> And Sitting Bull I know
> But who are you?
> ('Aayalolo Concerto')[25]

In the African novels also there are clearly discernible features of the traditional indigenous African forms in characterization. Critics have consistently remarked the blandness of characterization in the African novel.[26] What is however not realized is that the deficiency is not as much due to poor craftmanship as it is to sheer interference from the indigenous tradition.

In the folk tales characters are hardly ever presented and described copiously; very often the barest description of appearance is given. That bare physical description is often coupled with the name which almost invariably suggests the character to present the character. The following extract from *The Forest of the Lord*, a traditional novel by D.O. Fagunwa of Nigeria, is typical:

So my father went on his way singing and whistling and striding along like a soldier. He had not long started on his way when helooked in f ront and saw two women coming along the road talking and laughing and slapping their hands as is the habit of countless women ... One of them was light in colour and was tall and stout, with the appearance of a married woman, but the second was somwhat slender and not very tall. She was dark in colour and her teeth were white like fresh maize.[27]

42

As always happens in the tradition, the two women are contrasted through their polarization: one is stout; the other is slender. Moreover, their physical appearance symbolizes their social and moral situation. One is stout and is therefore obviously a married woman; the other is slender and is therefore unmarried. The actions of the two women clearly affirms and confirms their symbolic physical representation.

As in the traditions so also in the modern novel characters are given bare descriptions which in fact turn out to be symbolic representations. Even Ayi Kwei Armah, often cited as the most un-African in his techniques of presentation, turns out to be typical in his characters. All the characters of his novels are functional: their names suggest their character and their character is revealed in their appearance. Take the oft-quoted description of the corrupt timber merchant in *The Beautyful Ones Are Not Yet Born:* 'In through the door came a belly swathed in kente cloth. The feet beneath the belly dragged themselves and the mass above in little arcs, getting caught in angular ends of heavy cloth'.[28] Similarly, the following description of a Ghanaian returning home from abroad contended with his cargo symbolizes the character: 'The black man in the wool suit made several trips to the rear of the plane and back to his seat, his movements as well as the smile on his face exuding an irrepressible happiness'.[29]

The phenomenon is widespread; it is there in all the African novels in the length and breadth of the continent. A close examination of other elements such as setting and discourse in the novels and drama reveals a similar situation of cross-over peculiar to the African continent. It is all the more remarkable when such *avant garde* writers as Ayi Kwei Armah unconsciously demonstrate it.

It is therefore valid to conclude that indigenous traditional African forms are carried over into the modern literature written in the Euoropean metropolitan languages. What is needed now is the necessary critical application to be made from that commonplace.

For categorization purposes, such constants could be used as elements of a purely African form of literature. Like African music and African art, African literature will then be identified universally with objective formal characteristics and the degree of African-ness of individual texts assessed in consonance with universally recognized features. The question of who is or who is not a national would then be left to the politicians into whose sphere the issue legitimately falls.

Notes

1. When one considers the African language compositions since the nineteenth century which were screened by missionaries and governments on concepts of what should be valid as *African* compositions, the issue can in fact be said to pre-date the emergence of modern African literature.
2. Cited by Ngugi in 'The African writer and his past', *Perspectives on African Literature,* ed. Christopher Heywood (London: Heinemann, 1971), 6.
3. Aimé Césaire, *Return to my Native Land.* Translated John Berger and Anna Bostok (Basingstoke, Berkshire: Penguin 1969)
4. Cited from Claude Wauthier, *The Literature and Thought of Modern Africa* (Washington, D.C.: Three Continents Press, Inc., 1979), 170.
5. Chinua Achebe, 'The Novelist as Teacher', *African Writers Talking,* ed. G.D. Killam (London: Heinemann, 1973), 1-4, 1. Also Ngugi: 'What the African novelist has attempted to do is restore the African character to its history', *Perspectives,* 7.
6. (London: Faber & Faber, repr. 1974), 20, footnote 1.
7. Also, Theo Vincent, 'Designing a Course in African Literature: The Case of the University of Lagos' *Research in African Literatures* 5/1 (1974), 60-66. For instance, recently in the Department of English of the University of Ghana-Legon attempts were made to introduce courses on Ghanaian Literature and West African Literature in addition to courses on the African Novel, African Poetry, and African Drama. A question that was persistently raised was: is it possible to teach Ghanaian Literature or West African Literature to students who had already taken courses on the African Novel, Poetry, and Drama without thinning the courses or duplicating key texts such as the Works of Ayi Kwei Armah and Wole Soyinka?
8. Quoted in Emmanuel Ngara, *Stylistic Criticism and the African Novel* (London: Heinemann, 1982), 3.
9. Nadine Gordimer, *The Black Interpreters* (Johannesburg: Raven Press, 1973) 3. Also Abiola Irele: 'Our writers are recognizably African only in the sense in which they give an African character to their works' ('The criticism of modern African literature', in *The Critical Evaluation of African Literature*, ed. Edgar Wright (London: Heinemann, 1973), 15.
10. *Transition* 3/10 (1963).
11. The argument on classification according to language has been exhaustively presented in Janheinz Jahn's *A History of Neo-African Literature* (London: Faber & Faber, 1968).
12. *The Critical Evaluation of African Literature* (London: Heinemann, 1973).
13. Ngugi wa Thiong'o, *Homecoming* (London: Heinemann Educational Books, 1972); Ngugi wa Thiong'o, *Decolonising the Mind* (London: James Currey & Heinemann, 1986).
14. *Voices in the Whirlwind* (London: Macmillan, 1973); *The African Image*; 'Facts on reading for pleasure', *New Nation* (Johannesburg, 23 September, 1994).
15. *Towards a Decolonization of African Literature* (Enugu, Nigeria: Fourth Dimension, 1980).
16. Chinua Achebe, *Morning Yet on Creation Day* (London: Heinemann Educational Books, 1975), 56.
17. Jean-Paul Sartre, 'Orphée Noir, *Anthologie de la nouvelle poésie nègre et malgache de langue française*, ed. Leopold Sedar Senghor, Paris: Presses Universitaires de France. Translated from the French as 'Black Orpheus' by S.W. Allen (Paris: Présence Africaine, 1963), ix.
18. Edgar Wright: 36; also 'The Writer in a Modern African State' in *The Writer in Modern Africa,* ed. P. Wastberg (Uppsala: 1968).

19. Sembene Ousmane, *The Money Order with White Genesis*. Translated Clive Wake (London: Heinemann, 1972), 5-6. Also Ngugi, *A Grain of Wheat,* Ayi Kwei Armah, *The Beautyful Ones Are Not Yet Born* (London: Heinemann Educational Books, 1968).
20. 'Black Orpheus', xliv.
21. Muntu: *An Outline of Neo-African Culture*. Translated Marjorie Grene (London: Faber & Faber) 1961.
22. A.M. Jones, 'African Music', in *African Affairs* 48/193 (October 1949), 290-97; A.M. Jones, *Studies in African Music* (London: Oxford University Press, 1959); Rose Brandel, *The Music of Central Africa: An Ethnomusicological Study* (New York: Da Capo Press, 1984).
23. A.M. Jones, 'African Rhythms', *Africa: Journal of the International African Institute* XXIV (1954), 26-47, 27.
24. Muntu, *An Outline of Neo-African Culture*. Translated by Marjorie Grene (London: Faber & Faber, 1961).
25. John D.A. Okai, *The Oath of the Fontomfrom and Other Poems* (New York: Simon and Schuster, 1971), 81-82.
26. Notable are Gerald Moore, 'English Words, African Lives', *Présence Africaine* No 54 (1965), 94-95; Charles R. Larson, *The Emergence of African Fiction* (Macmillan: London, 1978).
27. W.H. Whiteley, *A Selection of African Prose. Vol II, Written Prose* (Oxford: Clarendon Press, 1964), 81.
28. Armah, chapter 3.
29. Ayi Kwei Armah, *Fragments* (London: Heinemann Educational Books, 1970), chapter 3.

Teaching Literature under the Rubric of 'Decolonisation' in South Africa

M.J. Daymond

There is a dissatisfaction with aspects of post-colonial literary theorising amongst some South African critics, and so my understanding of what they see as problematic accompanies my account of how I think the issues in 'post-coloniality' can be taught here. The tensions to which I point arise from the need to understand our writing in relation to our history, and they reflect debates within local literary studies as well as between international and national approaches.

As a first indication of questions about the term 'post-colonial' I should say that in this place and time it seems to me more appropriate to work under the rubric of decolonisation rather than accept the stasis suggested by post-coloniality/ism (Lionnet 1995:3-4).[1] In the South African context the process that this choice enables one to keep in view is that of 'unlearning [the] historically determined habits of privilege and privation' (Mohanty 1995:110) and, I would add, of oppression, that derive from our history. The emphasis on process also enables one to deploy analytical terms in a way that challenges rather than rehearses the centre-margin configuration of colonialism. Secondly, my choice is made so as to question the accuracy of both parts of the word 'post-colonial' for South Africa: is an undifferentiated use of 'colonisation' the best identifying term for the kinds of conquest and oppression that have been practised here, and do we really find ourselves after/beyond that process? Thirdly, my choice of 'decolonisation' comes from the point stressed by Benita Parry: amongst students of

> Colonial Discourse Analysis and Postcolonial Theory ... there has been a tendency ... to forget that the critique of colonialism did not begin with the academic discussions of the last decades ... [rather] it was the thinking of theorist-activists engaged in liberation struggles which inaugurated the interrogation of colonialism and imperialism as projects of, and constitutive forces in, western modernity. (1995:85)

Parry's insistence that we remember the role of liberation struggles and that they belong within the larger context of modernity is also a reminder that the need for resistance has not ended. As South Africa is frequently being hailed by Europe and the US as the gateway to trade with sub-Saharan Africa, our understanding of our present relationship to the colonial past must extend to the neo-imperial pressures that come from being part of the global economic system.

If 'decolonisation' serves some if not all of these purposes and questions, the issue within it which seems to divide South African criticism is whether a discursive and a materialist analysis of the process can find common ground, or even inform one another, in literary studies. Inasmuch as this involves asking whether and to what extent a distinction between 'history' and 'literature' (and their study) is operative, the debate is not a new one. And inasmuch as that distinction is both real and false (because 'history' can signify both events in the real world and our constructed understanding of them), the terms in which I am reflecting the debate are an over-simplification of the positions taken up by its proponents. Nevertheless, one of the charges against the discursive approach has been that its analytical categories carry too generalising a tendency: it has often seemed, for example, as though the binaries of race and gender can be uniformly applied to suggest that they have structured colonial thinking and actions in the same way in all contexts; or as though the scope for mimicry and/or resistance that lies in all signifying systems, even in the language of the oppressor, will manifest itself in the same way; or as though *metissage* can be revealed to function consistently in all contexts.

Against the universalising inclinations of discourse analysis, many materialist commentators have pointed out that South Africa's history has specific features that should not, if we wish to understand and contest our present, be elided into general patterns.[2] If one accepts the longstanding argument that apartheid has been 'colonialism of a special type' (Wolpe 1988:29-30), the 'internal colonisation' to which it points was, it should be remembered, produced by several waves of invasion, conquest and settlement in the course of which those who were once invader-settlers were themselves colonised. In this way Afrikaner resistance to British colonial occupation and control was part of the origins of apartheid. That it was an internal white nationalism that took up the colonisers' oppression of indigenous people in South Africa means that this racism cannot readily be discussed in the terms which have emerged from, say, the British control of India. Nor can the resources of local liberation struggles be understood directly through the analytical categories developed from the experiences of the peoples of India in their resistance to British occupation.

Similarly, the patterns of land appropriation in South Africa are not simply those of colonial invasion. The movements of pastoral peoples on the subcontinent (the Bushmen being ousted by the Khoi and then by Nguni peoples) seem to demand a different understanding from those which followed the arrival of Europeans.[3] And even seventeenth and eighteenth-century settlement at the Cape for the purposes of trade and then farming (the Dutch) or military control of sea routes (the British) does not seem to have produced a will to control indigenous peoples and their claims to land that is comparable to that which followed the discovery of diamonds and gold in the nineteenth century. As Olive Schreiner's *The Story of an African Farm* recognises, it was the discovery of mineral wealth that brought industrialisation and modernity and subjected the region to the serious interest of international capital; and it was then that something like a modern nation state began to be formed. The Land Act of 1913 which followed Union in 1910 is generally regarded as the first of the many pieces of legislation which served white nationalism by systematically disempowering the indigenous peoples.

The particularities of our history are producing in many South African scholars a wariness of imported grand narratives of all kinds – marxist, poststructuralist, feminist and post-colonialist (Currie 1990; Johnson 1994) – which are seen as having hegemonic tendencies. In particular, a wariness of a generalised discourse analysis in post-colonialism has been expressed by Kelwyn Sole, who accuses it of working with

> a theoretical armoury consisting of vague conceptions of 'transgression', 'subversion', 'subalternity', 'insurgency', 'filiation', 'affiliation' and the like; concepts which can prove as unwieldy and inappropriate as any sweeping generalisations of class and race they strive to supplant. (Sole 1994:19)

While he grants the cogency of a critical endeavour to recover identity and resistance in the work of marginalised people, Sole argues that in its attention to interstitial being, for example, post-colonial criticism cannot adequately engage with the realities of power in South Africa (or any emergent state) as they have been shaped by interacting local and global forces. But Sole is arguing partly so as to sustain 'class' as an important general category of analysis; it is therefore interesting to note that a similar wariness may come from a quite different quarter. Teresa Dovey recently declared that although she has worked with Lacanian aspects of 'postcolonial theory in relation to South African literature since the mid-1980s' she has, since 'the recent changes in the country', found herself increasingly concerned by 'the inadequacies of the theoretical discourse that academics outside South Africa apply to this part of the world' (1995:1048-9).

Dovey's use of 'outside' is not a parochial objection to metropolitan appropriation of a now fashionable terminology; she is concerned by the real but seldom acknowledged power of the international academic and publishing circuit to recentre in the west what is fundamentally the concern of its marginalised others. The general case is that the authority which comes with western economic power has a neo-colonial effect that will sustain the very othering which post-colonialism seeks to challenge and can, in the process, deny or sweep aside the agency of those whose struggle post-colonial writing seeks to celebrate. Dovey's declaration comes in response to a discussion by Rosemary Jolly (1995) of the relation of post-colonial discourse to social change in South Africa – an article in which, incidentally, there is not a single reference to a journal of literary criticism published in South Africa. The structural contradictions (ironies, at least) in a critic's taking up a post-colonial cause from the centre are demonstrated in this exchange, for Jolly's own concern is with the danger that metropolitan attention to a resistance form such as protest theatre may encourage its 'tropes of dissidence' (1995:18) to atrophy into stereotypes.

Defence against metropolitan power cannot, however, lie in proprietary attitudes to local history and questions of identity, for this would lead to a new form of isolation. It would also encourage a preoccupation with origins, cultural purity and authenticity that would soon produce hierarchies and new forms of oppression. An impulse to assert exclusive ownership was, however, understandably present in the 1970s when black South Africans sought to recover a sense of pride and identity. Guided by the writing of Steve Biko (1979), the Black Consciousness Movement demanded that black people should be the ones to represent themselves to themselves. Although he was influenced by Frantz Fanon, Biko, in countering his people's history of deprivation, argued that the starting point had to be a return to the cultural concepts through which black people had traditionally understood themselves. He placed his emphasis on the collective values and psychology of *ubuntu*. He was criticised by some for separating cultural discourse from material matters because this indicated that he sought to have little real impact on the economic interests which underpinned white domination. For discourse critics, the problem has been that Black Consciousness tended simply to reverse and so perpetuate racist binaries. But the recovery of identity in which culture is regarded as the starting point for resistance to oppression has a distinguished history in Africa (Senghor, Cabral and Fanon – in their various ways); recently it has received indirect support from as anti-essentialist a critic as Gayatri Spivak. She is careful not to comment directly on South Africa, but she clearly has an analogy in mind when she says that undergraduate literary courses in the US need in the first instance to be 'national-origin validation courses' (de Kock 1992:43) and that it is at postgraduate level that the work of establishing 'transnational literacy' (44) can begin.

Another reason why there is a strong will to resist merging into the bland internationalism of much post-colonial criticism is that while a new constitution is being written and debated, nation-building has properly been our major preoccupation. It is a concern which runs somewhat counter to the strongly anti-nationalist drive of post-colonial studies in *The Empire Writes Back* (Ashcroft *et al.* 1989). It is not that South Africans are rushing to form another strong, centralised nation-state; rather it is that we need to create ways of cohering within which 'difference' can be contested and our multi-cultural identities recognised. This is why A.E. Voss, in order to give the devolution occurring in this country its context, refers to Simon During's observation that 'nationalism has effects and meanings in a peripheral nation different from those in a world power' (Voss 1992:6). We remind ourselves of what Ngugi wrote more than a decade ago:

> A study of African literature, culture and history, starting from a national base, would ... be linked with progressive and democratic trends in world literature, culture and history .... the quest for relevance is not a call for isolationism but a recognition that national liberation is the basis of an internationalism of all the democratic and social struggles for human equality, justice, peace and progress. (Ngugi 1986:103)

Tensions remain, therefore, between specific and generalising perspectives and, within that tension, between a discursive and a materialist emphasis (Slemon 1994:22). Nevertheless, all of these lines of criticism manifest a shared sense of purpose. A decade ago, Ketu Katrak, taking her line from Wole Soyinka, argued that criticism needs to work from 'the concept of social responsibility' (Katrak 1989:157). Recently, reflecting on the discontents of post-colonial criticism, Stephen Slemon still recognises a common sense of purpose in 'the messy productivity of working intellectually towards genuine social change' (Slemon 1995:10). Seeking the mind-set needed for this work, Satya P. Mohanty has argued that to effect our freedom from past and current forms of colonisation we have to break out of a static, polarised understanding of 'difference' (the binaries of race, gender, culture, etc.), and that to recover an appropriate 'postpositivist' sense of agency we need to move away from the nihilistic relativism found in some aspects of postmodernism: 'what emerges as an alternative to relativism and skepticism is ... [a] conception of objectivity as a goal of inquiry that includes in it the possibility of fallibility, self-correction, and improvement' (1995:115). In this way, Mohanty argues, 'the conditions and resources of effective (moral) agency' (116) may be achievable by all those (ourselves and our others) engaged in the decolonising process.

This sense of fostering agency as well as identity is what I think the teacher of literature should undertake in the teaching of all texts – metropolitan, colonial and neo-colonial. It would, however, be mistaken to think that in South Africa the task of analysing cultural representations is one for which we are all equally equipped, for our history has seen to it that students do not come with similarly developed access to their cultural heritages. History as constructed and agreed-upon knowledge does not yet match history as a shaping force in this country. What this uneven cultural positioning brings to the fore in a multi-cultural classroom is that students are likely to feel themselves on a more equal footing when meeting texts from other cultures. This complements my own view that what is important is not simply teaching the texts of writers who can be called colonial or post-colonial, but the teaching of writing of all provenances and all periods from a post-colonial perspective which would differ according to one's locality. In my case it would be South Africa's continuing decolonisation which shapes the point of view from which I teach.[4]

In my own department we go some way towards this approach; for example, we select for a course in nineteenth-century British fiction, texts (*Hard Times* and *Mary Barton*) which grapple with the economic forces and socio-political changes in a Britain that was rising to her imperial zenith. And we teach this fiction in relation to Karl Marx's global outlook and Matthew Arnold's more parochial, strictly European sense of culture. We have also taught eighteenth-century writing through courses in which the issue of slavery is central; like much of the British Empire, the Cape was a slave-owning society until 1838-40, and this institution shaped the colonists' expectations of labourers in general. As Michelle Cliff points out in *Abeng*, 'slavery was not an aberration – it was an extreme' (1995:28) and 'slavery-in-fact' and 'veiled slavery' form a continuum.

The comparisons which can be made explicit through such courses represent one way of bringing local and world literature written in English into a relationship that does not just subsume the local into a generalised array of discursive concepts. The problems of Gaskell and of Dickens in depicting industrialisation offer a way of bringing home to students what might be entailed in a local representation of comparable if historically differently shaped events. The discursive choices made by Alan Paton in depicting the bus boycott in *Cry, the Beloved Country* or the realist mode in Phyllis Altman's handling of union activity in *The Law of the Vultures* would be cases in point here. But, perhaps because there has as yet been too little enquiry into the inter-cultural relationships that are *internal* to our own literary production (and which work across oral and written forms), such inter-regional, historicised comparisons are not yet widely established in South African criticism and teaching.[5]

Since the 1980s, the dominant thrust in local criticism has been to move away from decontextualised, western models of literary form and value and to establish more appropriate ways of understanding black literary production. It has been one which should encourage informed comparisons of interacting traditions within our literature(s), but even this work has further to go. Part of the reason why may be sketched in from views expressed in two critical anthologies from the 1980s – *Literature and Society in South Africa* (White and Couzens 1984) and *Rendering Things Visible* (Trump 1990). In the first of these collections, the editors ask:

> Is there, then a single South African 'literature'? Are there not at least five literatures operating alongside each other, each with its own traditions and conventions, even its own audience, and achieving only the most rudimentary of contacts and mutual influences? (1984:1)

and the essayists themselves do not seek to get beyond that 'rudimentary' cultural contact. As the editors see it, politically enforced cultural divisions had been sustained because of what they term a Leavisian focus on aesthetic matters rather than on the common historical context of South African writing: in their terms, 'literature' and 'society' do not meet. In the later collection the problems of cultural diversity are more openly recognised. One critic, Karen Press, is prepared to bridge divisions by marshalling artists to the creation of a single, anti-ethnic, indigenised 'national culture' that will serve liberation politics by fostering a 'non-racial, national consciousness within the ranks of the black working class and its allies' (Press 1990:24). She does argue that the understanding of the 'relationship between the psychological and the social' that art offers should not be either 'collapsed into some other type of knowledge' or seen as 'a production-line for ideas moulded elsewhere' (37), but she remains uneasy about the degree of diversity (and freedom) which the task of creating a coherent national culture can allow to artists: 'What I am arguing for is a situation in which artists have the right to produce what *they* believe to be of use to the liberation struggle ... a democratization of the relationship between artists and their audience'. (37) Press takes her line from Amilcar Cabral, arguing that a new culture cannot be imposed on people and its creation must begin from 'the cultural practices at present valued by those classes' (30).[6] In the same anthology, however, David Attwell reflects on J.M. Coetzee's decidedly anti-solidarity view of the novelist's role, and he enlarges the debate beyond the question of contact between cultural traditions to that of whether reciprocity should occur under or beyond the state's shadow. Coetzee's is a view which, as Attwell demonstrates, emerges from venerable western intellectual traditions and it indicates the philosophical problems in working for a future cultural cohesion (let alone a co-optable tradition). Coetzee's 1987 argument is well known: 'in times of intense ideological pressure ... the novel ... has only two options: supplementarity or rivalry' (Coetzee 1998:3) and rivalry must be chosen on the grounds that there is a need for 'the freedom to decline – or better, rethink – the oppositions ... out of which history and the historical disciplines erect themselves' (3). Attwell's explanation of Coetzee's 'emphasis on discursiveness' in the task of re-thinking history – that it 'is not necessarily an indication of the belief that history does not exist, so much as the conviction that since no discourse has unmediated access to history, any utterance, but the novel in particular, can claim a qualified freedom from it' (Attwell 1990:103) – brings us back to one of my opening points. A tension between a materialist and a discursive emphasis in our criticism is one of the factors inhibiting internal cultural comparisons as well as a productive relationship between a discursively based, international post-colonialism and local inquiry.

The possibility that historically oriented materialism and a discursive approach are not necessarily mutually exclusive can, however, be seen in Attwell's use of 'qualified' when speaking of 'freedom'. It can be taken as pointing to the task of the critic-teacher to explore, after the event, exactly the discursive relationship between itself and received history (and here I mean the fullness of its material and ideological context) that a text seems to claim, and to understand the significance, both for its material context and for that of the present reader, of such a claim. Such a critical practice would not legislate for artists, not even in order to use culture to promote justice and equality, and the practice is reflexive in that it requires the critic-teacher to question her own historical positioning and her purposes in invoking history in relation to art. It is when texts are allowed to interrogate their readers in this way that we attain the means of fostering mutual understanding in a country that has been as divided as this. A single critical article is unlikely to demonstrate all of what I have claimed, but in Brenda Bosman's and Anthony Chennels's responses to Tsitsi Dangarembga's novel, *Nervous Conditions*, can be seen the critical awareness of positionality and the willingness to interrogate the novelist's relation to historical events that I am advocating. Bosman's (1996) concern is with consciously accepting and resisting the identity constructed for white settlers (and readers?) by the text, and the relationship between the depicted life on the rural homestead and the larger context of the war of liberation. What Chennels takes up is the novel's implicit challenge to the view that all African writing posits and resists colonial oppression in the same unproblematised way. He points, for example, to certain passages presenting women's 'cultural displacements' in which the 'shocking idea' that 'British culture is healing and liberating, [while] the classic [Shona] culture [is] ... damaging and constraining' (1996:66) is explored. In seminar discussion, Dangarembga's decision to explore these issues in a *bildungsroman* could be set beside another novel in this genre which represents comparable questions of subjectivity, such as Michelle Cliff's *Abeng* and *No Telephone to Heaven*. Through such a comparison, the significance of formal choices such as narrative mode could be been seen in their relation to historical context.

Before I indicate further how a comparative approach would establish the historical particularities of a work and set them in relation to more general, transnational matters, I would like to add that the start of an internally comparative approach has been made by Michael Chapman in his recent study *Southern African Literatures* (1996), in which he eschews 'the general practice in most existing literary surveys and histories of balkanising the literature into discrete ethnic units; units that can be unwitting reminders of the divide-and-rule tactics of the colonial legacy'. Instead, he pursues the common preoccupations evident in writing of the nineteenth and twentieth centuries from Zimbabwe, Angola, Mozambique, Namibia and South Africa, claiming that matters such as oppression and liberation, tradition, urbanisation and memory, inform the writing 'beyond any stronghold of language, race or nationality' (1996:xvi). In a section entitled 'The Xhosa Legacy from Ntsikana to Mandela', Chapman goes further than thematic similarities, and argues that:

> it is unhelpful to separate Xhosa literary history from the history of European settlement. Both are defined by a process of acculturation .... Just as writing by British settlers can be grasped properly only in relation to the conditions of colonialism operating at the Cape, so the function and forms of Xhosa literature bear the marks of frontier politics in the eastern Cape. (1996:103)

This wish to find a similarity in the bearing of political contexts on literary responses may be a basis from which inter-national comparisons which retain the specifics of our history *and* recognise the general paradigms of post-colonial enquiry can proceed.

In opening my teaching to 'cultural-validation' in a multi-cultural classroom, and in order to enquire into fiction's imagined possibilities for subjectivity and agency in the processes of decolonisation, I concentrate on writing by women in South Africa in relation to other countries in Africa (sometimes including the African diaspora), and particularly on the ways in which women represent the functioning of gender in their lives and their writing. While it is obviously not women alone who are gendered, the purposes of control and the relationships of power which inform gendering are experienced differently by them. When women attempt the understanding that is needed for the representation (as distinct from the mere reflection) of these processes, then the result is likely to be disruptive; when women also draw on the operations of racial oppression in their work, then their representation of 'difference' is doubly disruptive of political and historical certainties, and particularly of the pressures towards uniformity in nation-formation. Few students find it comfortable to have life's questions written back to them, but it is through these texts that I believe I can further the 'working intellectually towards genuine social change' that is the declared objective of post-colonial criticism.

My comments so far have suggested some of the issues which teaching the fictional representation of gender in African contexts will bring to the fore: women and gender in relation to the homogenising and centralising forces of nationalism; women's function in the new national economy; gender in a multicultural society; gender and the representation of history. To these I add the issues around women and language; women and literacy; women and writing. In the brief comments and suggestions about teaching texts which follow, I have not expanded systematically on particular texts in relation to these headings, especially as each text raises several issues at once.

1.   Autobiographical writing by women is, as with the *bildungsroman*, invaluable to an enquiry into the cultural construction of subjectivity, cultural positioning and the attainment of agency. I have found the most successful teaching texts to be Ellen Kuzwayo's *Call Me Woman* and Sindiwe Magona's two-volumes, *To My Children's Children* and *Forced to Grow*. While I have not yet attempted it, I imagine that an exciting comparison would be with Maxine Hong Kingston's account of discovering and resisting her cultural heritage in *The Woman Warrior: Memoirs of a Girlhood Among Ghosts*.

In the 1970s, it was customary for readers of African writing to ignore what western theorists had to say of writing as mediation, and to practise an historical/anthropological reading of texts such as *Things Fall Apart*. In this vein, Buchi Emecheta's *The Joys of Motherhood* could be presented as completing the picture given by Chinua Achebe.[7] Similarly, much South African autobiography has been mined as though its content were factual – as history from below (Daymond 1995). Now, however, the influence of post-structuralist narratology and reception theory is being extended to African texts and things are changing. Now, Noni Jabavu's account, in *The Ochre People*, of returning to her Xhosa family's Christian and pagan cultural traditions at the point of their near-destruction by apartheid invites the critic to set its mediation of subjectivity alongside the more obvious matter of cultural interaction, and to do so under the rubric of hybridity. This is a condition which Jabavu exemplifies but which, in many respect, she fails to interrogate. (Similar questions arise about Bloke Modisane's *Blame Me On History*.) As hybridity has become something of a comfort blanket in post-colonial studies, Jabavu's recognitions and avoidances are challenging to theory as well as to historical enquiry. They are useful too to set alongside Caribbean novelists such as Jamaica Kincaid and Michelle Cliff who look at the complexity of the cultural ingredients of identity and particularly at the staying-power of racism in a nominally free society. In these contexts, Snead's pointing, through the term 'contagion', to the touching together of cultures whose effects are felt to have 'already erupted without cause or warning' (1990:245) is a useful reminder that in our reading we and the writers we study are engaged in a retrospective recognition of such a process.

2. Western critics' generalising glosses on 'Africa' (Snead 1990; Chennels 1996) make it particularly important to consider how novelists from different parts of this continent (including north Africa) represent the various ways in which gender works in their societies. Equally we have to recognise that all women writers have experienced similar problems in writing fiction at all, and then of getting due recognition at home for what they have achieved. Miriam Tlali (1989) has written about this in South Africa; Bessie Head's writing life was a qualified triumph over rejection (Eilersen 1995; Mackenzie 1990); Ama Ata Aidoo has given similar testimony from Ghana (James 1990). But, as critics' debates around 'womanism' and 'feminism' as responses to 'differ-ence' in the context of national liberation struggles suggest, literary analysis cannot take its categories directly from western feminism (Ogunyemi 1985; Lockett 1996; Wicomb 1966; Ward 1990). Critics' power and influence is at stake in contests between Africanist and feminist approaches; it is important therefore to take students directly to the intricacy of women's writing as they depict gender oppression as either/both an instrument of colonialism and a continuation of traditional patriarchy – writing such as the short stories of Miriam Tlali and Bessie Head (Daymond 1996), Lauretta Ngcobo's novel *And They Didn't Die*, Mariamma Ba's *So Long a Letter* and Zoe Wicomb's story

55

cycle *You Can't Get Lost in Cape Town* (Driver 1996). These novelists' representations of how women struggle to utter problems of gender are interesting to set besides Ezekiel Mphahlele's admiring depiction of strong women in *Down Second Avenue*. In the 1950s he depicted women as vulnerable both to the cruelty of their men and the forces of white racism, but in narratives of the 1970s, such as Serote's *To Every Birth Its Blood*, racism has come to be the only oppressor. By the 1980s, in Ellen Kuzwayo's autobiography, the complexity of oppression is reappearing and Sindiwe Magona, in the 1990s, is even less likely to identify a single force against which women struggle.

3. One of the temptations in nurturing multi-culturalism has been to deploy the 'each to her own' kind of relativism which may barely conceal patronage or indifference. In this regard I find it valuable to teach texts whose anti-colonial anger makes it impossible to respond in comfort: Aidoo's *Our Sister Killjoy*, with its varied textual strategies, compares well with Ncgobo's *And They Didn't Die*. Similarly Bessie Head's treatment of the unravelling of cultural conflict (including attitudes to sexual passion and polygamy) in *The Collector of Treasures* compares well with Mariamma Ba's *So Long a Letter*. And all of these texts demand that we attempt to understand, perhaps in relation to oral story-telling, why some writers vigorously declare their narrative strategies while in other more realistic texts the act of mediation needs to be defamiliarised before it is evident.

4. Both of the relationships to a coloniser's language that obtain in the context of decolonisation operate in South Africa: there are writers who still possess but do not write in their first language and there are writers whose language of origin has recently or long since been denied them and so they use a conqueror's language. The question of language and power has been well canvassed here (Ndebele 1991) in the debate that led to the recognition of eleven official languages, but multicultural issues such as translation and creolisation have surfaced for discussion only comparatively recently. Many writers, again ahead of their critics, have found ways of signalling that they are either engaged in translation or are reflecting a polyglot world – Magona and Tlali are particularly interesting in this respect. And the first story, 'Bowl Like Hole', in Zoe Wicomb's *You Can't Get Lost in Cape Town* is, like Marlene Nourbese Philip's poem 'Discourse on the Logic of Language', a wonderful representation of the coercive power of language. In this context, the narration of Daphne Rooke's *Ratoons* is historically significant. She writes, in 1953, of an earlier time when a sugar farm in Natal was something of a community of English, Indian and Zulu people, and she works through a first-person narrator, Helen Angus, but she seldom signals the role of a

language mix in the tensions as well as the sympathies of the world of 'difference' that she represents.

5. On the question of women writers and the representation of history, it has to be said that as yet we have nothing like Toni Morrison's *Beloved*. One of the reasons may be seen in the ending of Nadine Gordimer's *Burger's Daughter*: Rosa, her protagonist, has achieved an understanding of her positioning in and by history but is prevented (perhaps temporarily) from acting on what she understands. Another kind of waiting on events, or abeyance, is conveyed by the ending of *Nervous Conditions*. Dangarembga does not show her protagonist, Tambu, as entering the world on new or on sanctioned terms. Instead she depicts her as entering writing: 'something in my mind ... [is] bringing me to the time when I can set down this story' (1988:204). In the temporal context of the liberation struggle in Zimbabwe, in the literary context of Fanon's writing (declared in the title), and given the novelist's deliberate turning to 'the story of four women whom I loved' (204), this ending has a significance for women and post-coloniality that we have not yet begun to explore.

In conclusion: the value of a comparative approach such as I have tried to suggest should not be new in social experience (although reading habits may be different) for, as Mohanty reminds us, 'developing this shared epistemic and social space ... is hardly peculiar to cross-cultural encounters .... it characterizes the everyday practice of cooperative inquiry within the most homogeneous of social groups' (1995:115).

Bibliography

1. Primary Texts
Achebe, Chinua. 1958. *Things Fall Apart*. London: Heinemann.
Aidoo, Ama Ata. 1977. *Our Sister Killjoy*. London: Longman.
Altman, Phyllis. 1987. *The Law of the Vultures*. Johannesburg: Ad Donker.
Ba, Mariamma. 1982. *So Long A Letter*. London: Virago.
Biko, Steve. 1979. *I Write What I Like*. London: Heinemann.
Cliff, Michelle. 1995. *Abeng*. New York: Plume.
Cliff, Michelle. 1989. *No Telephone to Heaven*. New York: Vintage Books.
Dangarembga, Tsitsi. 1988. *Nervous Conditions*. London: Women's Press.
Emecheta, Buchi. 1980. *The Joys of Motherhood*. London: Heinemann.
Gordimer, Nadine. 1979. *Burger's Daughter*. Harmondsworth: Penguin.
Head, Bessie. 1971. *Maru*. London: Heinemann.
Head, Bessie. 1977. *The Collector of Treasures*. London: Heinemann.
Head, Bessie. 1984. *A Bewitched Crossroad: An African Saga*. Johannesburg: Ad Donker.
Jabavu, Noni. 1982. *The Ochre People*. Johannesburg: Ravan Press.
Kingston, Maxine Hong. 1977. *The Woman Warrior*. New York: Random House.
Kuzwayo, Ellen. 1985. *Call Me Woman*. London: Women's Press.

Magona, Sindiwe. 1990. *To My Children's Children*. Cape Town: David Philip.
Magona, Sindiwe. 1992. *Forced to Grow*. Cape Town: David Philip.
Modisane, Bloke. 1986. *Blame Me On History*. Johannesburg: Ad Donker.
Mphahlele, Ezekiel. 1971. *Down Second Avenue*. London: Faber and Faber.
Morrison, Toni. 1987. *Beloved*. London: Picador.
Ngcobo, Lauretta. 1990. *And They Didn't Die*. Johannesburg: Skotaville.
Paton, Alan. 1958. *Cry, The Beloved Country*. London: Penguin
Rooke, Daphe. 1990. *Ratoons*. Cape Town: Chameleon Press.
Schreiner, Olive. 1986. *The Story of an African Farm*. Clayton, Cherry (ed). Johannesburg: Ad Donker.
Serote, Mongane. 1981. *To Every Birth Its Blood*. Johannesburg: Ravan Press.
Tlali, Miriam. 1989. *Footprints in the Quag*. Cape Town: David Philip.
Wicomb, Zoe. 1987. *You Can't Get Lost in Cape Town*. London: Virago Press.

2. Critical Texts
Aidoo, Ama Ata. 1990. Interview, in Adeola James, *In Their Own Voices: African Woman Writers Talk*. London: James Currey; Portsmouth, N.H.: Heinemann; 8-27.
Ashcroft, Bill; Gareth Griffiths and Helen Tiffin. 1989. *The Empire Writes Back*. London and New York: Routledge.
Attwell, David. 1990. 'The Problem of history in the fiction of J.M. Coetzee', in Martin Trump (ed.), *Rendering Things Visible*. Johannesburg: Ravan Press; 94-133.
Benson, Eugene and L W Conolly (eds.). 1994. *Encyclopedia of Post-Colonial Literatures in English*. 2 vols. London and New York: Routledge.
Bosman, Brenda. 1996. 'A correspondence without theory: Tsitsi Dangarembga's *Nervous Conditions*', in M.J. Daymond (ed.), *South African Feminisms: Writing, Theory, and Criticism 1990 – 1994*. New York: Garland Press; 301-11.
Brown, Duncan and Bruno van Dyk. 1991. *Exchanges: South African Writing in Transition*. Pietermaritzburg: University of Natal Press.
Chapman, Michael. 1996. *South African Literatures*. London and New York: Longman.
Chennels, Anthony. 1996. 'Authorizing women, women's authoring: Tsitsi Dangarembga's *Nervous Conditions*', in Emmanuel Ngara (ed.), *New Writing From Southern Africa*. London: James Currey; Cape Town: David Phillip; Harare: Baobab Books; Nairobi: EAEP; Portsmouth, N.H.: Heinemann; 59-75.
Coetzee, J.M. 1998. 'The novel today'. *Upstream* 6/1; 2-5.
Currie, Iain. 1990. Review of *The Empire Writes Back*. *Pretexts* 2/1; 105-10.
Daymond, M.J. 1996. 'Inventing gendered traditions: The short stories of Bessie Head and Miriam Tlali', in M.J. Daymond (ed.), *South African Feminisms: Writing, Theory, and Criticism 1990 – 1994*. New York: Garland Press; 223-39.
Daymond, M.J. 1995. 'Class in the discourses of Sindiwe Magona's autobiography and fiction'. *Journal of Southern African Studies* 21/4; 561-72.
de Kock, Leon. 1992. 'Interview with Gayatri Chakravorty Spivak: New Nation Writers conference in South Africa'. *Ariel* 23/3; 29-47.
de Kock, Ingrid and Karen Press (eds). 1990. *Spring is Rebellious*. Cape Town: Buchu Books.
Dovey, Teresa. 1995. 'Letter: Colonialism and the postcolonial condition'. *PMLA* 110/5; 1048-49.
Driver, Dorothy. 1996. 'Transformation through art: Writing, representation, and subjectivity in recent South African fiction'. *World Literature Today* 70/1; 45-52.
Eilersen, Gillian Stead. 1995. *Bessie Head: Thunder Behind Her Ears*. Portsmouth, N.H.: Heinemann; London: James Currey; Cape Town: David Phillip.

Gray, Stephen. 1979. *South African Literature: An Introduction*. Cape Town: David Phillip, London: Rex Collings.

Johnson, David. 1994. 'Importing metropolitan post-colonials'. *Current Writing* 6/1; 73-85.

Jolly, Rosemary. 1995. 'Rehearsals of liberation: Contemporary postcolonial discourse and the new South Africa'. *PMLA* 110/1; 17-29.

Katrak, Ketu H. 1989. 'Decolonizing culture: Towards a theory for postcolonial women's texts'. *Modern Fiction Studies* 35/1; 157-79.

Lionnet, Francoise. 1995. *Postcolonial Representations: Women Literature Identity*. Ithaca and London: Cornell University Press.

Lockett, Cecily. 1996. 'Feminism(s) and writing in English in South Africa', in M.J. Daymond (ed.), *South African Feminisms: Writing, Theory, and Criticism 1990-1994*. New York: Garland; 3-26.

Mackenzie, Craig (ed). 1990. *Bessie Head, A Woman Alone: Autobiographical Writings*. London: Heinemann.

Mohanty, Satya P. 1995. 'Epilogue, colonial legacies, multicultural futures: Relativism, objectivity, and the challenge of otherness'. *PMLA* 110/1; 108-18.

Ndebele, Njabulo S. 'The English language and social change in South Africa'. *Rediscovery of the Ordinary*. Johannesburg: COSAW.

Ngugi wa Thiong'o. 1986. *Decolonising the Mind: The Politics of Language in African Literature*. London: James Currey; Nairobi: Heinemann Kenya; Portsmouth N H: Heinemann.

Ogunyemi, Chikwenye Okonjo. 1985. 'Womanism: The dynamics of the contemporary black female novel in English'. *Signs* 11/1; 63-80.

Parry, Benita. 1995. 'Reconciliation and remembrance'. *Pretexts* 5/1-2; 84-96.

Press, Karen. 1990. 'Building a national culture in South Africa', in Martin Trump (ed), *Rendering Things Visible*. Johannesburg: Ravan Press; 22-40.

Slemon, Stephen. 1994. 'The scramble for post-colonialism', in Chris Tiffin and Alan Lawson (eds.), *De-scribing Empire: Post-colonialism and Textuality*. London and New York: Routledge; 15-32.

Slemon, Stephen. 1995. 'Introductory notes: Postcolonialism and its discontents'. *Ariel*. 26/1; 7-11.

Snead, James. 1990. 'European pedigrees/African contagions: Nationality, narrative and communality in Tutuola, Achebe, and Reed', in Homi Bhabha (ed.), *Nation and Narration*. London and New York: Routledge; 231-49.

Sole, Kelwyn. 1994. 'Democratising culture and literature in a "New South Africa": Organisation and theory'. *Current Writing* 6/2; 1-37.

Stratton, Florence. 1994. *Contemporary African Literature and the Politics of Gender*. London and New York: Routledge.

Tlali, Miriam. 1989. Interviewed by Cecily Lockett, in Craig Mackenzie and Cherry Clayton (eds.), *Between the Lines*. Grahamstown: NELM; 67-85.

Voss, A.E. 1992. 'Reading and writing in the new South Africa'. *Current Writing: Text and Reception in Southern Africa* 4; 1-9.

Ward, Cynthia. 'What they told Buchi Emecheta: Oral subjectivity and the joys of "Otherhood"'. *PMLA* 105/1; 83-97.

White, Landeg and Tim Couzens (eds). 1984. *Literature and Society in South Africa*. Cape Town: Maskew Miller Longman.

Wicomb, Zoe. 1996. 'To hear the variety of discourses', in M.J. Daymond (ed.), *South African Feminisms: Writing, Theory, and Criticism 1990-1994*. New York: Garland; 45-55.

Wolpe, Harold. 1988. *Race, Class and the Apartheid State*. London: James Currey.

Notes

1. Please refer to the Bibliography for references to both primary texts and critical works.
2. Resistance to a reading of our literature which incorporates it in an international collectivity was signalled by Stephen Gray who declared: 'Of all the attempts to classify Southern African English literature, perhaps the ... least successful have been those which view it as a part of the literature of the British Commonwealth of Nations' (Gray 1979:10).
3. As Bessie Head in *A Bewitched Crossroad* indicates of the country we now call Botswana, land seems to have been a component of pastoral peoples' identity in a way that is different from those living in bounded nation states.
4. While the teaching I advocate does not depend on the 'writing back' that has been celebrated, past educational practices have resulted in metropolitan classics such as Shakespeare playing a directly discernible role in the work of many South African writers – Sol T Plaatje, Can Themba, etc.. And there is at least one recent example of a local appropriation of Shakespeare. *Umabatha* is a loose translation of *Macbeth* into a Zulu setting; the production had great success at two World Theatre seasons in London in the 1960s and has just been revived here. A conference, 'Postcolonial Shakespeares', was held in July at the University of the Witwatersrand and another, 'Dickens, Empire and Children', will soon take place at Rhodes University.
5. It is significant that in the South African contributions to the *Routledge Encyclopaedia of Post Colonial Literatures*, there was little evidence of the comparative approach that the editors had suggested (Benson and Conolly 1994).
6. Since then, the debate about artists' freedom prompted by Albie Sachs (de Kock and Press 1990; Brown and van Dyk 1991) has indicated that Press's programmatic view is unlikely to gain even party acceptance.
7. On the occlusion of women's point of view in Achebe's early novels, see Stratton 1994.

'Buttered scones at 4 p.m. on Sundays': Configuring English in Colonial India[1]

Prem Poddar

1. Introduction

The issue of 'English' in the post-colonial 'nation', especially in India, is not just a simple question of legacy. The binarism of the colonizer and the colonized was never sutured to the extent that 'local' epistemologies, whether in the form of religious traditions or schools, had no space to exist or even to resist modes of domination.

Although British presence on Indian territory goes back to the late sixteenth century, English achieved official language status only in the mid nineteenth century. Charles Grant's proposal of 1792 that English be made the language of instruction at all levels became an actuality on March 7, 1835. Lord Bentick, the Governor General in Council, passed a brief resolution for the 'promotion of European literature and science among the natives of India'. The Minute made English the medium of instruction in government-subsidized schools and, in effect, made English the official language of British India. The rationale put forward at the time was derived from the largely influential view of the utilitarian James Mill who found nations such as India 'tainted with the vices of insincerity, dissembling, treacherous, mendacious to an excess which surpasses even the unusual measure of uncultivated society' (quoted in Kopf 1980:504).

The decision to promote English and the study of English literature in India was a result of a network of configurations, but was primarily determined by the pressing need for an effective strategy of containment. Though there was protracted debate over issues of language and the mode of instruction, the specific appeal of western education was twofold. First, to maintain and consolidate British supremacy in India (which was of paramount importance to the policy-makers) and secondly, because of the need for a palisade against 'the proneness of the period to movements subversive to the established order of things' (Marshman, in Sinha 1964:5). Of all the interpellative apparatuses or regimes of truth, western secular education was seen by the British administration as the most convenient and effective means to establish 'the foundation for a stability that "even a political revolution will not destroy and upon which after many ages may rest a vast superstructure"' (from an 1826 *Asiatic Journal,* cited in Viswanathan 1989:117).

2. 'The Necessary Furniture of Empire'

The transformation, with the Diwani in 1765, from a mercantile power to a revenue collecting agency was of great import. The trading organization in effect became the sovereign power in Bengal. Warren Hastings, the Governor-General from 1774 to 1785, was faced with the job of organizing an elaborate bureaucracy as the maintenance of law and order gradually entered the purview of the Company's activities in addition to assessing and collecting revenue. Hastings remonstrated acridly in his letters to the company directors about the ineptitude of the Company servants and implored for the induction of a training programme. His aim was to produce a service of orientalized elites well-versed in Indian languages and responsive to local traditions and customs. The equation between an acculturated civil servant and administrative efficiency provided the *raison d'etre* for Hastings' enthusiasm for understanding Indian culture.

The pragmatic side of his orientalism was tempered and instituted through his admiration of Indian cultural heritage. His orientalism was that of 'positive geography and history' as opposed to 'imaginative geography and history' (Said 1979:55). The cultural relativism that he brought to bear on his project is evident from his comments on *The Bhagavat-Geeta*: 'Might I, an unlettered man, venture to prescribe bounds to the latitude of criticism, *I should exclude, in estimating the merit of such a production, all rules from the ancient or modern literature of Europe* (quoted in Marshall 1970:185; emphasis added). He showed no inclination to interfere in 'native' affairs and worked predominantly through the existing governmental machinery. The replacement of Hindu and Muslim legal systems by English law was unacceptable to him and explains his patronage of oriental scholarship. Hastings was opposed to the extension of British law (under the Regulating Act of 1773) to Indians as well as the Company employees because he also 'regarded the Supreme Court as a possible threat to his own freedom of government and a rival to the Company's own system of policing' (Musselwhite 1986:83). His encouragement of the study of Islamic and Hindu codes of law coincided with the British Parliament's increasing alarm at the 'depravity' of the administrators and merchants in these far-flung shores. As Edmund Burke remarks, the British government was motivated to 'form a strong and solid security for the natives against oppression of British subjects resident in Bengal' (Stokes 1959:2).

But the paradox of Hastings' position is that the idea of codifying 'Hindu' and 'Muslim' law *was* realized during his time and proved a significant intervention. Law in pre-colonial India was not a fixed, immutable body of knowledge (Derrett 1968). The Warren Hastings Plan of 1772 (which was later to become *The Administration of Justice Regulation of April 11th, 1780*) proclaimed that the *sastris* (learned pundits of Hindu law) would be consulted on matters relating to caste, religious usages, marriage, etc. (Derrett 1968:232-33). Thus began the project of codifying Hindu (and later Muslim) law by British administrators and jurists with the help of local pundits. This patronage of the *sastras* (sacred Hindu texts) is embodied in the funding of the Sanskrit College at Benaras and in Calcutta. This nexus with the *sastris* insured that a more Brahmanical mode emphasizing the immutability of native religious axioms was imposed on the society (Cohn 1987). Validation of the caste system and the *varna* theory of social order were also thus carried out. These groups outside the sphere of the Brahmanical precepts thus became subject to its scriptural dictates (Washbrook 1981; Cohn 1987). Domination was deeply inscribed within pre-colonial India and colonialism, for its own purposes, helped reconstitute earlier dominations.

The British political position was far from consolidated, and Hastings desperately sought to win over the governed. In a letter to Nathaniel Smith, Chairman of the Court of Directors, he wrote that 'every accumulation of knowledge and especially such as is obtained by social communication with people over whom we exercise a dominion founded on the right of conquest is useful to the state; it is the gain of humanity' (Kopf 1969:18). Colonial knowledge was inextricably bound with power (Cohn 1985) but to attribute positive design to all of Hastings' efforts in the encouragement of oriental scholarship is not only unjust, but also restrictive; as Foucault has shown, power cannot be analysed in terms of conscious intentions. The dominant themselves are contained within power matrices, although their rationales are important data.

Lord Cornwallis, who succeeded Hastings as Governor General in 1786, was faced with deteriorating standards in government (including a corrupt system of administration) and serious financial problems. He faced an immediate imbroglio over the creation of an efficient administrative machinery providing the company with a regular surplus revenue. Veering away from Hastings' orientalist predilections, Cornwallis strongly promoted the Europeanization of the service. Cornwallis was anxious 'to make everything as English as possible in a country which resembles England in nothing' (cited in Aspinall 1931:173). The fulcrum of the financial conundrum for Cornwallis lay in what he considered to be the official indulgence towards oriental forms of governmental organization. 'I think it must be universally admitted that without a large and well-regulated body of Europeans, our hold of these valuable dominions must be very insecure' (quoted in Thompson and Garrat 1958:174).[2]

The Charter Act of 1813 renewed the East India Company's privileged trading status. This produced two historically significant effects: a relaxation of controls over missionary work in India, and the undertaking of responsibility by the state for Indian education. This was enforced by the British Parliament and was a curious occurrence since at this stage education was not the responsibility of the state in England. Although drawing from moral discourse, political considerations were distinctly more important. The conflict between Parliament and the East India Company had partly to do with the rise of the free trade era and subsequent demands for demonopolising the company's trade in India (see Bowen 1991). Perhaps, more importantly, Parliament was becoming increasingly threatened by the political power the company wielded. Pitt's India Bill of 1784 specifically rejected the unconditional subordination of the Company to the Crown. A specious reason to intervene in the affairs of the company was provided by the criticisms of the excesses committed by the English Nabobs (or gentlemen-capitalists who had amassed wealth in India). Disguised as concern for the well-being of the natives, Parliament's expanded involvement by the end of the eighteenth century marked the weakening of the company and its subsequent demise.

The thirteenth resolution of the 1813 Charter stated unequivocally that England was responsible for promoting the 'interests and happiness' of the Indian people and that educational measures ought to be adopted 'as may tend to the introduction among them of useful knowledge, and of religious and moral improvements' (*Parliamentary Debates* 1813: 562). Section 43 of the East India Company Act of 1813 specifically set aside a lakh of rupees annually to be spent on education, 'for the revival and improvement of literature ... and for the introduction and promotion of a knowledge of the sciences' (*Selections from Educational Records* 1965: 22). This mandate triggered off an explosion of discourse around education, in particular the debate over the implementation and implication of the mandate which was to be sorted out only by Lord William Bentick's 1835 resolution.

3. 'The Best Part of the English Nation'

The future governance of India was largely debated by the powerful lobbies of the Anglicists and the Orientalists. Although the Anglicists succeeded in bringing round the Parliament in 1835 to the view that western education would be well-suited for India, the Orientalists' arguments for Sanskrit and Arabic education were taken, for some time, to be persuasive. The Orientalists maintained that a 'revival' of literature, as inscribed in the Charter, could only refer to Sanskrit and Arabic literature. The Anglicists converged on the term 'useful learning' avowing that 'it was worse than a waste of time' to teach or be instructed in the sciences 'in the state in which they are found in the oriental books' (Trevelyan 1838:75).

It was the fruits of oriental scholarship that paradoxically helped the Anglicists to become victors. Hastings, William Jones and their orientalist heirs were concerned with the culture and languages of India and their ambitious explorations of the cultural legacy of the East produced an assembly of scholarship grounded in what was considered unprejudiced knowledge (Dirks 1992). If there was rediscovery as a result of Orientalism's inquiry into classical Indian history, it also fashioned a cultural past. Whatever we know of Indian history is thus entrapped in a 'major contradiction' in that our 'understanding of the entire Indian past' is 'derived from the interpretation of Indian history made in the last two hundred years' (Thapar 1966:3). The project for the development of the vernaculars included the production of grammars, lexicons, translations, and similar texts (cf. Dharwadker 1993; Pollock 1993). Western philology was directly embroiled in the undertaking of Orientalism. In the work of Ernest Renan, as Edward Said observes, 'what comes to replace divine authority is the textual authority of the philological critic' (1983:47). The ensemble of codified information was far from ideologically neutral; it provided material for the Anglicists' call for a transformation of premodern Indian society.

The Anglicists opposed any policy that advocated the use of native languages and literature in education as they did the hiring of native officials in any positions of power. To buttress their claims, they gestured to the failure of Hastings' administration in maintaining order. Indian traditions, it was felt, produced political dissidence and near-anarchism. Macaulay, one of the foremost Anglicists, cited the body of scholarship now available as material proof of the minor status of oriental cultures:

> We have to educate a people who cannot at present be educated by means of the mother tongue. We must teach them some foreign language. The claim of our language is hardly necessary to recapitulate. It stands pre-eminent even among the languages of the west. (1952:354)

Though formally in conflict, there was little difference between the Orientalist and Anglicist projects. Through both projects, strategies and tactics oriented toward the consolidation of power and the continuation of the colonial enterprise were manifest. Hastings, the first orientalist administrator of note, was to defend himself thus before the House of Lords on charges of 'High Crimes and Misdemeanours' alleged to have been perpetrated during his term of office in India:

> To the Commons of England, in whose name I am arraigned for desolating the provinces of their dominion in India, I dare to reply, that they are, and their representatives persist in telling them so, the most flourishing of all the States of India– it was I who made them so. The valour of others acquired, I enlarged and gave shape and consistency to the dominion which you hold there; I preserved it: I sent forth its armies with an effectual, but an

65

economical hand, through unknown and hostile regions, to the support of your other possessions; to the retrieval of one from degradation and dishonour; and of the other, from utter loss and subjection. I maintained the wars which were of your formation, or that of others, *not of mine.* I won one member of the great Indian Confederacy from it by an act of seasonable restitution; with another I maintained a secret intercourse, and converted him into a friend; a third I threw off by diversion and negotiation, and employed him as an instrument of peace.– When you cried out for peace, and your cries were heard by those who were the object of it, I resisted this, and every other species of counteraction, by rising in my demands; and I at least afforded the efficient means by which a place, if not so durable, more seasonable at least, was accomplished with another. I gave *you all,* and you have awarded me with *confiscation, disgrace, and a life of impeachment* (quoted in Musselwhite 1986:91).

If Hastings advocated familiarization of the resident British with Indian customs and the induction of Indian officials in the service, the Anglicists showed a dispensation toward the 'spirit of English literature' which would inculcate certain virtues and make the 'Indian youth almost cease to regard us [as] foreigners' (Trevelyan 1838:192). In the *Despatch to Governor-General in Council, Bengal, dated 18th February, 1824,* the Court of Directors of the Company condemned support for oriental institutions as 'organically and fundamentally erroneous', deeming that the object of education is the advancement of 'useful knowledge' and not 'obscure and worthless knowledge' (*Selections from Educational Records* 1965:91).

Since the identity of the colonizers could only be defined in relation to the colonised, they were both ensnared, in Bhabha's model of mimeticism, within a Lacanian mirror-image. Thus, 'British civil servants in India, schooled in the "best part of the English nation" [which for Macaulay meant English], would success-fully *impress* the natives with the glories of their colonial masters' (Azim 1993:13).

4. The Cross and the Flag

The relaxation of strictures apropos of missionary work in India was another momentous outcome of the Charter. It was not surprising that groups normally opposed to each other forged alliances in their common zeal to demonstrate that eastern religions were not, or were less, rational. Clapham Evangelists among other denominations had been frantically trying to build up a presence in India. An alliance between them and the Utilitarians and Liberals was understandable based as it was on the commonality of their eagerness to bring about a metamorphosis in the fabric of Indian civilization. Consensus emerged on the issue and the urgent need of overhauling Indian society and in particular, changing the 'Indian character' (see Stokes 1959).[3]

The British could not realize these goals alone without the support of indigenous forces. The effacement of the old aristocratic ruling class under Cornwallis and the ascent of the recruits of power and wealth, created a new business class who were only too keen to collaborate, and thus realized the British dream. This new class derived their capital not through inheritance but by trade with the East India Company (see Chandra 1987-88). This located them well for purposes of what would later be called 'filtration theory'.

This theory, which derived from the idea that cultural values percolate downwards from a site of power, was deployed enthusiastically for dissemination by the Anglicists. The archetypal Anglicist Macaulay strategised to form an elite group of Indians steeped in Anglocentrism who could promulgate western philosophies and discourse. He hoped, in what is fast becoming one of the most quoted sentences in colonial discourse, to originate a class who 'may be interpreters between us and the millions whom we govern, a class of persons Indian in blood and colour but English in taste, in opinion, in morals and intellect' (1952:359).

Macaulay was not alone in his desire: he articulated the attitudes and opinions prevalent in the third and fourth decades of the nineteenth century concerning the medium of instruction and curricular content.[4] Indians in places of influence and authority, and critical of their traditions, spurred the government to displace Sanskrit education. Its persistence, wrote Raja Rammohun Roy in a letter to William Pitt dated 11 December, 1813, would be 'the best calculated to keep this country in darkness' (Roy 1945-58, Part 4: 108).

The main preoccupation among Anglicists from the 1820s on involved the problematic of curricular composition that would achieve the result of creating a subject race capable of promoting the imperial project. The curriculum introduced by the British was at first centred on language studies. Horace Wilson, a pupil of the Indologist Sir William Jones and a Sanskrit scholar, among others criticized this pedagogical mode on the premise that 'mere language cannot work any material change'. It was his conviction that exclusively at the moment when:

we initiate them into our literature particularly at an early age, and get them to adopt feelings and sentiments from our standard writers we make an impression upon them and effect any considerable alteration in their feelings and *notions* (*Parliamentary Papers* 1852-53, vol. 32: 266).

The missionaries, in contrast, contended that European education might help to demolish 'heathen' superstition; yet 'moral' instruction was indispensable for well-rounded schooling of the native. The teaching of the Bible instead of a secular syllabus in their view was a responsibility of the British educators. The teaching of religion to the poor in Britain had traditionally been seen as a telling means to siphon off social disquiet. Ian Michael, for example, writing on the compilers of anthologies used in British schools in the nineteenth century, comments: 'The compilers do not discuss, or seem to recognise, any difference between religious poetry and versified doctrine'. He cites the hope harboured by one compiler ('one of Her majesty's Inspectors of Church Schools')

> that the 'children of the peasantry and artisans' would come to understand and 'sympathise with sentiments and principles by which well educated persons are influenced' and 'to understand and sympathise with the views of the superiors'. Because such children 'are frequently at a loss to understand the forms, which persons of cultivated minds are accustomed to use in expressing their thoughts' they are open to persuasion by the 'socialist infidel'. (1987:221)

The domestic education policy that advocated instruction in Christian principles seemed to be oriented toward control – echoing unwittingly Marx's description of religion as the opium of the masses. The impulse to moralise the poor and the project of education were intimately connected in that hegemony, in Gramsci's sense, which underlay the educational objectives of the Victorian 'experts' (see Johnson 1977; also Stallybrass and White 1986). An educational curriculum tailored on these lines in the colonies would, the missionaries argued, have the double advantage of expanding the market for trade. 'Wherever our principles and our language are introduced', Charles Grant suggested in an amazingly overt manner disregarding the supposed opposition between the spiritual and the material, 'our commerce will follow' (1797: 220).

The spectre of native insurgency always provided the backcloth for any policy, especially educational policy for the colony. Missionary thinking consistently showed signs of cathectation on 'moral improvement' (by which was meant Christian religious education) as the only forestalling antidote against native insubordination. The fear that the introduction of Christian values itself might provide the stepping stone and make Indians aspire toward self-rule was vehemently rejected by Charles Grant in 1832:

> The establishment of Christianity in a country does not necessarily bring after it a free political constitution. The early Christians made no attempts to change forms of Government;... Christianity seeks moral good, and general happiness. It does not, in the pursuit of these objects erect a peculiar political system; it views politics through the safe medium of morals, and subjects them to the law of universal rectitude (quoted in Hutchins 1967:13).

Yielding to such contentions was out of the question for the powers that controlled the East India Company. That the moralizing and civilizing missions would lead to the institutionalization of church edification was an anxiety connected to the fear of subaltern insurgency. The avoidance of insurrections, like the one in Vellore in 1806, had become one of the main priorities of the administration.

Viswanathan's pioneering work on the beginnings of English literary studies in India relates the imposition of literature to the double-faced momentum of missionary insistence on hegemony in education and disquietude over subaltern restiveness:

Provoked by missionaries on the one hand and fears of native subordination on the other, British administrators discovered an ally in English literature to support them in maintaining control of the natives under the guise of a liberal education. With both secularism and religion appearing as political liabilities, literature appeared to represent a perfect synthesis. (1987:17)

The policy makers were cautious in including only those texts into the curriculum which would be conducive to 'moral' pedagogy. With this in view, Addison's *Spectator* papers, Adam Smith's *Moral Sentiments* and some of the works of Bacon, Locke, and Shakespeare appeared on the syllabus.

These and other canonized texts were used to serve as an example of English Literature, an exalted mode of intellectual production, in contrast to indigenous texts in Indian languages. 'English' as 'an accepted canon of works in a clearly defined national language' (MacCabe 1985:5) of course never existed until the gradual consolidation in Britain of literature as body of knowledge. As a repository of objective and universally valid knowledge culled with the tools of rationalism, English literature, it was claimed by these educators, prepared the intellect for the tasks of rationality (like Latin before it) and sagacious argument. The new education policy was intended to produce students that could approach subjects in a detached, rational manner. Questions set in the examinations demanded analyses but left little room for unfettered conclusions The following fairly regular essay topics display a tortured sort of rationality at best: 'On the Internal Marks of Falsehood in the Hindu Shastras'; 'On the Merits of Christianity and the Demerits of Hinduism'; 'The Advantages India Derived in Regard to Commerce, Security of Property, and the Diffusion of Knowledge from its Connexion with England' (*Parliamentary Papers 1852-53*, vol. 29: 452-53; 491-617).

The educational system not only actively took on the propagation of English as the medium of instruction, it gradually valorized English literary studies. Thus, the Bengal government's proposal to build up Hindu and Muslim colleges and bolster the publication of Indian classical works was rejected on arrival for approval at the India House in London. James Mill, whose views wielded immense power and was critical of the Orientalist glorification of Indian tradition, put forward the case for western education in India:

> The great end should not have been to Hindu learning or to Mohammedan learning, but useful learning .... In professing to establish seminaries for the purpose of teaching mere Hindu or mere Mohammedan literature, you bound yourself to teach a great deal of what was frivolous, not a little of what was purely mischievous.... (*Parliamentary Papers 1831-32*, IX: 488).

Oriental scholarship was devalued and all patronage of it withdrawn. All that was meant (or desired) to be known had already congealed in comfortable stereotypical knowledge; any need for further scholarship was at best an appendage and at worst redundancy. The Government, in a Resolution dated 7th March 1835, categorically stated that no portion of the fund set aside for educational purposes might be used in printing oriental works (Trevelyan 1838:14). Thus, extensive plans for the publication of Arabic and Sanskrit works were immediately suspended as were medical classes held in Indian languages.

5. Local Intellectual Responses

In a sense, the strategic aims of the project were realised, and more extensively than the planners would have expected. That the British mission of self-representation as an even-handed, upright and moral rule succeeded to a large extent is borne out by the testimony of some notable Indians. Keshabchandra Sen, for instance, held that 'it is not a man's work but a work which God is doing with His own Hands, using [the] British nation as His instrument' (1938:90).

This is reminiscent of what Fanon calls the assimilative phase, the first phase, when the native intellectual responds to the colonial presence in a certain way which

> gives proof that he has assimilated the culture of the occupying power. His writings correspond point by point with those of his opposite numbers in the mother country. His inspiration is European and we can easily link up these works with definite trends in the literature of the mother country. This is the period of unqualified assimilation. (1967:178-79)

Defined within the parameters of bourgeois-liberal ideology, the intellectual community in colonial India was fascinated by the prospect of a future fashioned by the liberalism (it was not before the first quarter of the twentieth century that some leaned towards marxism) of Mill, Spencer, Rousseau and Thomas Paine (see Pannikar 1987:2117). It was in this context that Dadabhoy Naoroji characterized colonial rule as unBritish. Ram Mohan Roy labelled England as a nation of people 'blessed with the enjoyment of a civil and political liberty but [who] also interest themselves in promoting liberty and social happiness, as well as free inquiry into literary and religious subjects among those nations to which their influence extends' (quoted in Pannikar 1985:415).

The chief architect in the implementation of educational policy in India, C.E. Trevelyan, maintained that the finest desire of the natives was to catapult themselves to the cerebral and moral rank of the rulers. His inference in 1838 was that 'we have gained everything by our superior knowledge; that it is this superiority which enabled us to conquer India, and to keep it'.

British educational policy produced individuals who were alienated from their own culture and the masses of Indian society. This awareness of a denationalised middle class is present in periodicals, such as the *Tattvabodhini Patrika* and *The Bengal Spectator*, of that time: '[we] blindly imitate what others have done' (quoted in Pannikar 1987:2119). A pundit from South India in 1866, Lingam Lakshmaji Pantlu Garu, had unlimited faith in English knowledge and what it could do for India. 'A man that has received a thorough English education is fit for everything that is good and laudable' (1866:20). His only complaint was that the British 'look upon us as beings of an inferior order' which surely 'tend[s] to demoralize us and to estrange us' (35). Ambivalent about these demoralizing effects, he attributes them, like his masters, to India's own past: 'We lie; we steal; we desire; we commit rape ... and then early in the morning we bathe in the Ganges, whose filthy waters wash away our sins' (28). The English-educated minority drawn from the middle classes became collaborators or 'native informants' crucial to the day-to-day functioning of the Empire (Dirks 1993). This middle class was on the ascendancy particularly after the revolt or national uprising of 1857, which marked the demise of the indigenous ruling class.

Attempts to produce a sense of inadequacy and a dependency complex in the minds of the colonized was largely effected through a certain kind of educational discourse[5] (see Walsh 1983). Examinations manifestly designed to teach students to consider 'objectively' such themes as the 'Demerits of Hinduism' could lead to a debasement of inherited cultural traditions. K.N. Pannikar, among other historians, observes that 'the colonizer created and propagated several myths about the character and capacity of the colonized which in course of time [some of] the colonized themselves began to believe' (1985:420). Deception, untruthfulness, undependability, and similarly negative characteristics imagined as common Indian attributes became an integral element of the self-image of India (or of certain classes) in this era. The legacy of that self-representation persists in that 'today the English-educated elite readily ascribes these qualities to the masses' (1985:420).

A generation after the institution of English as the official language in India, literary activity in the colonizers' language emerged. The Indian novel in English began as a colonial venture vaguely aspiring to continue the English tradition. The literary models of Bankim Chandra Chatterjee's *Rajmohan's Wife* (1864) and Toru Dutt's *Bianca* (1878) were European and the authors clearly aspired to be what Michael Madhusadan Dutt characterized as 'gents who fancy that they are swarthy Macaulays and Carlyles and Thackerays'. Dutt himself was scarcely less complicitous, attempting an epic on the Miltonic model: 'Nothing can be better than Milton. ... I don't think it impossible to equate Virgil, Kalidas and Tasso. Though glorious, still they are mortal poets. Milton is divine' (cited in Gupta 1963:146).

There was, of course, considerable variation among nineteenth century intellectuals in their opinions about European culture. It ranged from the cultural chauvinism of Pandit Sasadhar Tarkachudamani (who certified the 'scientific' basis of Hinduism) and Haji Muhammad Hashim to the anglophilia of the Derozians. Ambivalence towards tradition and modernity can be seen in Rammohun Roy's mix of reform and compromises with orthodoxy (see Sarkar 1985) and the assertive Hinduism of Bankimchandra who drew from such disciplines as 'comparative philology, sociology, the study of myths, Christian higher criticism and the methodology of "scientific history"' (Raychaudhuri 1988:148). Bhudev Mukhopadhyaya and Vivekananda, for instance, were both products of western education but preoccupied with the projection of a Hindu way of life and whose 'perceptions of Europe became part of the region's [Bengal's] cultural heritage and even influenced popular stereotypes' (Raychaudhuri 1988:xiii).

But Bankim, especially, is too complex a figure to sum up and place in such a neat way. Recent studies by Chatterjee (1986), Kaviraj (1995), and others suggest the ambivalence in his attitudes.[6] Bankim typifies, writes Chatterjee, the unresolved contradiction in nationalist thought which, on the one hand, emphasises the modern and thus seeks tutelage and 'collaboration' with the West, and yet, on the other hand, sets itself ideologically to strongly espouse what is distinctly national (1986:80-81). Bankim is a case of that part of the native intelligentsia which 'certainly cannot be dismissed easily as *either* revivalist or "native informant"' (Loomba 1991:181).

Fanon's second phase in which 'we spew ourselves up' (1967:179) arrives with the native intellectual's assimilated identity rupturing and the beacons of the pre-colonial past re-emerging in the lived and living experiences of the colonised. As Ahmad notes:

Rare would be a text of our canonical nationalism (witness, for example, the agnostic, socialist Mr Nehru's *Discovery of India*) which did not assume that 'spirituality' was the special vocation of the Indian in World history. Positivist kinds of secularism and modernism which grew during the same period often found it difficult to withstand these pressures for identifying Indian cultural nationalism with metaphysics and revivalist tendencies (1992:276).

One example of this kind of stimulus was Rabindranath Tagore's work which, in terms of mimeticist poetics, showed mystical elements and tensions between modernity and the attractions of the feudal order. Tagore indeed was later to testify to the dominance of English literary culture in Indian education:

Our literary gods then were Shakespeare, Milton and Byron. ...The frenzy of Romeo's and Juliet's love, the fury of King Lear's impotent lamentation, the all-consuming fire of Othello's jealousy, these were the things that roused us to enthusiastic admiration (1921:181-82).

Tagore was, of course, the archetypal *bhadralok* with an ambivalence about his own identity: 'when in the village I become an Indian. The moment I go to Calcutta I become a European. Who knows which is my true self?' (quoted in Moorhouse 1983:203).

Bhadraloks like Tagore and even Ram Mohan Roy can be placed in a Eurocentric-Orientalist bind aspiring to evolve an indigenous modern culture but, in the words of an historian who has studied the cultural formation in nineteenth century Bengal, also inherit[ing] from the two schools their common socially exclusive attitude of total indifference to certain socio-economic and historical factors – the unequal access among the indigenous population to western education, which was bound to make 'European thoughts and literary forms' a jealously guarded preserve of the privileged few; the hierarchical features of the indigenous traditional culture separating courtly culture from folk culture, the esoteric from the popular in the religious and ideological movements from the past; the occupational division of labour in nineteenth century Calcutta which gave birth to two separate streams of culture (Bannerjee 1989:7).

Nationalism as an oppositional discourse and the construction of nationalist intellectuals occurred primarily through the repressive and discursive state apparatuses of the empire. Nationalism in the post-colonial state can still be seen as dependent on imperial forms as a continuation of anti-colonial nationalism against the imperial state (Chatterjee 1986). The problem with Fanon's three-phase genealogy is that it imposes a reading of Indian nationalism as a diachronic evolution, as an apprenticeship for the elites negotiating (with an aborted third phase displacing the subaltern) to carry on the complex machinery of colonialism. The success of the Raj ideology is apparent not only in departments of English and in the production of fictions that are specifically targeted for a 'western' readership, but is even more powerfully evident in intellectual histories of colonial India. Only in the last two decades or so have historians challenged the notion that European thought and knowledge, specifically English education, were the catalysts that brought about a socio-cultural regeneration in India.

Governmental and developmental discourses constitute the notion of 'discipline' that ambiguously serves both sides of the power-knowledge equation in Foucault: a procedure of correction and control as well as a branch of knowledge. In the context of colonial India, as I have discussed above, the procedures of control are partly constructed through the discipline of English Studies as is the constitution of a particular discipline, both narrowly and widely: India and English literature. The discursive effects of creating subjects in a form of self-government (submitting to an idealized self) is at the very heart of a disciplinary mechanism, which in turn is part of larger cultural apparatuses. Such power-relations allow a subject to come into being but not without the capacity to resist. Witness this remark from a student in a college in India: 'When the last Englishman with the thoughts of empire has perished, Enid Blyton will still be around converting a few more colonials, who will forever dream of potted meat sandwiches and buttered scones at four p.m. on Sundays, to the Christian universe' (quoted in Rajan 1992:82). The danger, of course, is of a simple substitution of terms such that a nationalist agenda keen to revert to a certain tradition, or even a modernist programme that seeks to re-imagine the nation, rules out the claims of a productive hybridity. 'Pedagogic' narratives (which claim to instruct us as to who we are) co-exist with 'performative' counter-narratives (Bhabha 1990), which issue from the nation's margins and are articulated by cultural hybrids who live at the restless junction of several cultures. Such a hybridity invokes and at the same time blots out the totalizing boundaries of the nation.

One of the questions for a post-colonial pedagogy then is: can we *do* English literature post-colonially *without* an idea of the history sketched above?

References

Ahmad, Aijaz. 1992. *In Theory: Classes, Nations, Literatures*. London: Verso.

Aspinall, A. 1931. *Cornwallis in Bengal: the Administration and Judicial Reforms of Lord Cornwallis in Bengal, together with Accounts of the Commercial Expansion of the East India Company, 1786-1793, and the Foundation of Penang, 1786-1793*. Manchester: Manchester University Press.

Azim, Firdous. 1993. *The Colonial Rise of the Novel*. London: Routledge.

Bannerjee, Sumanta. 1989. *The Parlour and the State: Elite and Popular Culture in Nineteenth Century Bengal*. Calcutta: Seagull Books.

Bayly, C.A. 1988. *Indian Society and the Making of the British Empire*. Cambridge: Cambridge University Press.

Bhabha, Homi K. 1990. 'Dissemination: Time, narrative, and the margins of the modern nation', in Homi Bhabha(ed.), *Nation and Narration*. London and New York: Routledge.

Bowen, H.V. 1991. *Revenue and Reform: the Indian Problem in British Politics 1757-73*. Cambridge: Cambridge University Press.

Chandra, Bipan. 1987-88. *India's Struggle for Independence*. New Delhi: Viking.

Chatterjee, Partha. 1986. *Nationalism and the Colonial World: A Derivative Discourse?* London: Zed Books.

Cohn, B.S. 1985. 'The command of language and the language of command', in Ranajit Guha (ed.), *Subaltern Studies IV*. Delhi: Oxford University Press.

Cohn, B.S. 1987. *An Anthropologist Among Historians and Other Essays*. Delhi: Oxford University Press.

Derrett, J. 1968. *Religion, Law and the State in India*. London: Faber & Faber.

Dharwadker, Vinay. 1993. 'Orientalism and the study of Indian literatures', in C. Breckenbridge and P. van der Veer (eds.), *Orientalism and the Postcolonial Predicament: Perspectives on South Asia*. Philadelphia: University of Pennsylvania Press.

Dirks, Nicholas. 1992. *Culture and Colonialism*. Ann Arbor: University of Michigan Press.

Dirks, Nicholas. 1993. 'Colonial histories and native informants: Biography of an archive', in C. Breckenbridge and P. van der Veer (eds.), *Orientalism and the Postcolonial Predicament: Perspectives on South Asia*. Philadelphia: University of Pennsylvania Press.

Fanon, Frantz. 1967. *The Wretched of the Earth*. Harmondsworth: Penguin.

Garu, L.K.P. 1866. *The Social Status of the Hindus*. Benares.

Grant, Charles. 1797. *Observations on the State of Society among the Asiatic Subjects of Great Britain, particularly with respect to Morals; and on the means of Improving it*. London: privately printed.

Gupta, Kshetra. 1963. *Kabi Madhusudan o tār Patrabali*. Calcutta.

Hutchins, Francis, G. 1967. *The Illusion of Permanence*. Princeton: Princeton University Press.

Johnson, Richard. 1977. 'Educating the educators: "Experts" and the state 1833-9' in A.P. Donajgrodzki (ed.), *Social Control in Nineteenth Century Britain*. London: Croom Helm.

Kaviraj, Sudipto. 1995. *The Unhappy Consciousness, Bankimchandra Chattopadhyay and the Formation of Nationalist Discourse in India*. Bombay: Oxford University Press.

Kopf, D. 1980. 'Hermeneutics versus history'. *Journal of South Asian Studies* XXIX/3.

Kopf, David. 1969. *British Orientalism and the Bengal Renaissance.* Berkeley & Los Angeles: University of California Press.

Loomba, Ania. 1991. 'Overworlding the third world'. *Oxford Literary Review* 13.

Macaulay, T. B. 1952. *Selected Speeches.* London: Oxford University Press.

MacCabe, C. 1985. 'English literature in a global context', in Randolph Quirk and H.G. Widdowson (eds.), *English in the World: Teaching and Learning the Language and Literature.* Cambridge: Cambridge University Press.

Marshall, P.J. (ed.). 1970. *The British Discovery of Hinduism in the Eighteenth Century.* Cambridge: Cambridge University Press.

Michael, Ian. 1987. *The Teaching of English from the Sixteenth Century to 1870.* Cambridge: Cambridge University Press.

Moorhouse, Geoffrey. 1983. *Calcutta: the City Revealed.* Harmondsworth: Penguin.

Musselwhite David. 1986. 'The trial of Warren Hastings', in Francis Barker *et al.* (eds.), *Literature, Politics and Theory.* London: Methuen.

Pannikar, K.N. 1985. 'The intellectual history of Colonial India: Some historiographical and conceptual questions', in S. Bhattacharya and Romila Thapar (eds.), *Situating Indian History.* Delhi: Oxford University Press.

Pannikar, K.N. 1987. 'Culture and ideology: Contradictions in Intellectual transformation of colonial society in India'. *Economic and Political Weekly of India,* December 5.

Parliamentary Debates. Vol. 26: 1813. Great Britain.

Parliamentary Papers (Reports from Committees): East India Company's Affairs. Vol. IX: 1831-32. Great Britain.

Parliamentary Papers (Reports from Committees): East India Sixth Report. Vol. 29: 1852-53. Great Britain.

Parliamentary Papers: Second Report from the Select Committee of the House of Lords, Together with the Minutes of Evidence. Vol. 32: 1852-53. Great Britain.

Pollock, Sheldon. 1993. 'Deep orientalism: Notes on Sanskrit and power beyond the Raj', in C. Breckenbridge and P. van der Veer (eds.), *Orientalism and the Postcolonial Predicament: Perspectives on South Asia.* Philadelphia: University of Pennsylvania Press.

Rajan, Rajeswari Sunder (Ed.). 1992. *The Lie of the Land.* Delhi: Oxford University Press.

Raychaudhuri, Tapan. 1988. *Perceptions of the West in Nineteenth Century Bengal.* Delhi: Oxford University Press.

Roy, Rammohun. 1945-58. *The English Works of Rammohun Roy.* 6 parts. Eds. Kalidas Nag and Debajyoti Burman. Calcutta: Sadharan Brahmo Samaj.

Said, Edward. 1979. *Orientalism.* New York: Vintage.

Said, Edward. 1983. *The World, the Text, and the Critic.* London: Vintage.

Sarkar, Sumit. 1985. *A Critique of Colonial India.* Calcutta: Papyrus.

Selections from Educational Records. Compiled by H. Sharp, 1965 (reprint), Delhi: National Archives of India.

Shayer, David. 1972. *The Teaching of English in Schools 1900-1970.* London: Routledge & Kegan Paul.

Sinha, D. P. 1964. *The Educational Policy of The East India Company in Bengal to 1854.* Calcutta: Punthi Pustak.

Spear, Percival. 1963. *The Nabobs: A Study of Social Life of the English in the Eighteenth Century.* London: Oxford University Press.

Stallybrass, P. and Allon White. 1986. *The Politics and Poetics of Transgression.* London: Methuen.

Stokes, Eric. 1959. *The English Utilitarians and India.* Oxford: Clarendon Press.

Tagore, Rabindranath. 1921. *Reminiscences*. London: Macmillan.

Thapar, Romila. 1966. *A History of India*. Vol. 1. Harmondsworth: Penguin.

Thompson, Edward and Garrat, G.T. 1958. *Rise and Fulfilment of British Rule In India*. Central Book Depot: Allahabad.

Trevelyan, C.E. 1838. *On the Education of the People of India*. London: Longman, Orme, Brown, Green and Longmans.

Viswanathan, G. 1989. *The Masks Of Conquest: Literary Study and British Rule in India*. London: Faber & Faber.

Walsh, Judith E. 1983. *Growing Up in British India: Indian Autobiographers on Childhood and Education under the Raj*. New York: Holmes and Meier.

Washbrook, David. 1981. 'Law, State and Agrarian Society in Colonial India'. *Modern Asian Studies* 15/3.

Notes

1. This article is a shortened version of a chapter from Prem Poddar *English Studies and the Articulation of the Nation in India*, unpublished D.Phil. thesis (University of Sussex: 1996).
2. Citing from Cornwallis's minute dated 18 September 1789 (in G. Forrest (ed.), *Selections from the State papers of the Governors-General of India. Lord Cornwallis* (London, 1914), ii, 79) C.A. Bayly writes: 'dispensing with "native agency" and its replacement by a disciplined cadre of European collectors of revenue and judges would hasten the demise of what Cornwallis saw as 'Asiatic tyranny' and 'the corruption of public office' (1988:65-66).
3. The theme of the 'Indian character', as one might expect, was a favourite one. I will restrict myself to just one citation from Lord Wellesley on the Indian people: 'vulgar, ignorant, rude, familiar and stupid' (quoted in Spear 1963:145). Qualities such as these in Indian character could be traced to, it was argued, ancient Indian literature. This literature instructed that 'revenge is to be cherished, and truth is not to be rewarded as a virtue, or falsehood as a crime' (*Parliamentary Papers 32*: 29).
4. 'Macaulay had said little that was new', Stokes writes, 'everywhere his speech rings with ideas which the older Charles grant and Wilberforce had uttered forty years before' (1959:54).
5. Viswanathan (1989), for instance, cites the case of Nobinchunder Dass, a student of Hooghly College, Calcutta, who internalised, like Lingam Garu cited above, all the aims of British education to the extent that he can refer to his fellow Indians as 'the natives'.
6. 'Imprisoned within the rationalist framework of his theoretical discourse and powerless to reject its dominating implications, Bankim lived out his dreams of liberation in his later novels. In form, *Anandmath* (1882), *Devi Chaudhurani* (1884) and *Sitaram* (1887) are historical romances, but they are suffused with a utopianism which, by the power of the particular religious semiotic in which it was expressed, had a deep emotional influence on the new intelligentsia' (Chatterjee 1986:79).

Teaching Post-colonial Literature in Sri Lanka

Rajiva Wijesinha

Sri Lanka has claims, which I suspect no other former colony would contest, to being the most brainwashed of former British possessions. These claims, it should be emphasized, are those of its establishment, which prides itself on speaking English with a proper accent such as would be readily understandable in London, centre of all authority, unlike the strange accents of say Indians or Africans. Indeed the country is perhaps unusual in that upper class Sri Lankans would tend to talk to each other exclusively in English, and not engage in the bilingualism a similar stratum would employ in the rest of the subcontinent; and only in Sri Lanka is tremendous stress laid on pronunciation, so that rural children learning English for the first time are reprimanded for not producing vowel sounds that do not exist in their own languages.

Similarly the literary establishment, at all levels, used until recently to pride itself on maintaining traditions of which, it assumed, Britain herself would be proud. There were of course dissenting voices; but it was often a matter of luck as to whether innovations were accepted. Thus, when literature was reintroduced to the Ordinary Level Examination a few years ago, the proposed syllabus was challenged on the grounds that it did not include Shakespeare. On that occasion the educational authorities held firm. However, just a few years before that, an innovatory syllabus at Advanced Level had been thrown out in favour of one that was thought to provide a thorough introduction to the great tradition of English Literature. The syllabus that was reimposed, and which is still being followed ten years later, began with poems by Thomas Lodge and Thomas Campion and included no living poets; indeed the only living writer prescribed, apart from Arthur Miller (offered only as a rarely taken up alternative to Shakespeare), was Alan Sillitoe. Expunged from the syllabus were the Sri Lankan and other Commonwealth writers to whom students had responded very positively in the few years they had been taught.

One reason preferred for the change back to earlier practices was that teachers had complained that there was no secondary material on contemporary writers. The fact that such a reason could be advanced accorded with the belief, which still holds sway in many quarters, that studying literature is a matter of learning and regurgitating notes, without the necessity of actually reading the given texts to which they refer. This reaches its most ridiculous level with regard to Shakespeare: many students even at degree level are unable to understand or paraphrase passages from the plays, but are nevertheless expected to answer complex general questions often based on quotations from critics (whose views, or rather simplified versions of them, have been studied at second hand through age-old notes). The argument, though, as put by the head of one English department, was that Chaucer and Shakespeare had to have pride of place on the university syllabus because graduates from the university had to be fit to go on to do postgraduate work at Cambridge.

Despite the strength of traditional views, however, a number of innovations have been introduced over the last couple of decades into university departments in English. There are in fact three universities in Sri Lanka that now offer honours degrees in English Literature; and though all of them still prescribe aspects of the great tradition, all have interesting programmes in what might be termed modern literatures in English. The different ways in which these have been developed, however, are worth looking at, particularly in terms of the various preconceptions that are apparent in catering to a clientele that is still fairly exclusive. After describing these programmes, I will also deal with a new syllabus introduced at a university that tried to offer a degree in English for students for whom the language is quite clearly a second language, unlike those belonging to the elite who use it in daily discourse.

The oldest English department in the country, that of the University of Peradeniya, did in fact introduce post-colonial literatures into its programmes a couple of decades ago. These were generally options, but more recently it introduced a complete paper in *New Literatures*, which features writers who have established themselves over the years, i.e. Raja Rao, Mulk Raj Anand and Narayan representing what might be termed Indian classics, Achebe, Ngugi, Soyinka and Fugard for the Africans, Naipaul and Patrick White, and in addition a range of predominantly Indian poets. Peradeniya has also always been quite strong on Sri Lankan writers, though its syllabus still addresses a canon formulated in the early eighties. Some latitude however has been permitted recently, and a number of younger academics deal with contemporary material too.

The University of Kelaniya functioned for a long time in the shadow of Peradeniya, though it has in fact had comparatively large numbers of students both because of its proximity to Colombo and also due to the fact that it offers other subjects in the English medium for students from Colombo schools who studied, say, French or Greek and Roman Civilization. It has traditionally inclined towards greater fidelity to the English canon, though when the canon worldwide moved towards post-colonial material it followed suit. Its approach, therefore, governed perhaps also by its adoption of a course unit system, was to include post-colonial material in courses that deal with what are seen as top-quality representatives of particular genres. Thus Leonard Woolf's *Village in the Jungle*, still thought of at Kelaniya as the quintessential Sri Lankan novel, figures in an *Introduction to Literature* course together with *Othello*, *Oliver Twist*, 'The Charge of the Light Brigade' and various other select hits. Again two Sri Lankan poems and one each by Soyinka and Ezekiel appear in a course entitled *Blake to T.S. Eliot and After* while *Midnight's Children* appears together with *Ulysses*, *Women in Love* and so on in *New Directions in Fiction*.

These courses, it should be noted, are targeted primarily at students taking a general degree, i.e. one that includes two other subjects in addition to English. Those taking a special degree do go much deeper into the field, albeit still within the framework of the study of the highlights of a great tradition.

It is Colombo university that offers the most innovative programme in post-colonial literatures, though it should be noted that this is a recent development. It had for a long time been the smallest of the English departments in the country, having initially been concerned mainly with language teaching, and perhaps for this reason when it first offered English for an honours degree it had seemed even more conservative in its approach. Recently, however, given the presence of a couple of young lecturers not long returned from Kent and Columbia, it has developed a thoroughgoing programme that introduces a range of texts as well as a large dose of theory. Understandably enough, African drama and Spivak figure largely in the programme, but students can also engage with Black American writers and Feminists and various others in courses with titles such as *Discourses of Modernity: Diasporas* (Naipaul, Rushdie, etc.) / *The Empire Writes Back* (Rhys, Walcott, etc) / *Discourses on Power* (Said, Fanon, etc.). It is worth remarking, however, that Sri Lankan writers are barely represented on the syllabus. This may be because they are considered inferior, but such a view is in itself indicative of a perspective that gives primacy to a canon formulated in the West.

The courses described above are for honours students, of whom there are comparatively few. Courses leading towards a general degree include some short stories, some Sri Lankan poetry and a play by Soyinka in the first year; but there is nothing post-colonial in the second year, and only some contemporary poetry as well as plays by Walcott and Fugard in the third and final year. It should also be noted that honours students tend to be those with a good command of English to begin with; given a syllabus that is extremely sophisticated by Sri Lankan standards, it is understandable that academics at Colombo are less than enthusiastic about students allowed into university on what is termed a special intake, whereby students who have taken English at Advanced Level can get into university with lower marks than their peers.

The reason for this provision, as also that whereby teachers of English who pass the first year university general degree examination externally are thereafter accommodated as internal students, was that the government felt that potential and actual teachers of English should be given concessions that would help them in their profession. The scheme was in fact ill thought out, because the courses had been designed for what were virtually first language speakers (possibly with Cambridge in mind, as noted above), and the expertise gained was totally irrelevant to teaching English in the rural schools where teachers were in short supply, and where it was basic communication skills that were required rather than the capacity to analyse Shakespeare or even Wilson Harris.

It was for this reason that the University of Sri Jayawardenepura, which had for some years been offering English for the general degree to students predominantly from rural schools where English was not always available (and certainly not at Advanced Level), moved to set up an English department whilst also overseeing English programmes at Colleges which offered a diploma.

The syllabuses were designed primarily to increase familiarity with the language amongst those who could become English teachers in their home regions, but who would also be able to use the language actively in a context in which economic opportunities were more readily available to those with a fair command of English. The programme therefore was concerned mainly with language skills; at the same time it was held that literature was essential, both to develop reading skills and encourage extensive reading, and also to stimulate analysis and critical discrimination in the medium of English.

The programme is still being developed, so the description below deals with future proposals as well as with what has already been implemented over a few years. However, the general principles followed will be sketched out, and the sort of text prescribed will be noted. The appendix that follows the article was initially based on this syllabus, though it includes several other texts that may also be of interest to a wider audience.

It was thought imperative in designing the course to introduce students initially to material that would hold their attention and engage them in issues of immediate concern to them. The focus in the first year therefore was on contemporary Sri Lankan writing, through collections of poetry, prose and drama that contained material on political and social issues likely to involve students who had grown up accustomed previously to thinking of English as a language of alien concerns. Luckily there has been an efflorescence recently of Sri Lankan writing that serves the purpose admirably. Poets such as Jean Arasanayagam, Suresh Canagarajah, Basil Fernando and Kamala Wijeratne, short story writers such as Vijita Fernando, Nirmali Hettiarachchi, Maureen Seneviratne and Punyakante Wijenaike, and dramatists such as Thiagarajah Arasanayagam and Ernest MacIntyre have produced work that can be profitably studied. Certainly some of these writers are not as accomplished as others, but the view was that students could respond to them freely, and should be encouraged to make discriminating judgments.

As their command of the language developed, students were to be introduced to more complex material. Poets from what had earlier been seen as the canon in Sri Lanka, namely Patrick Fernando, Anne Ranasinghe and Lakdasa Wikkramasinha, were read as major literary figures, while novels or novellas by Punyakante Wijenaike and James Goonewardene were also prescribed. At the same time the syllabus was always intended to be open to new material, and amongst writers suggested for inclusion recently are Carl Muller and Shyam Selvadurai.

The programme also envisages introducing students from the first year onwards to literature in English from other Commonwealth countries, though the range must necessarily be limited, for in addition students are also studying British and American writing. Since accessibility is still important, there is a bias towards Indian writing. The first Commonwealth writer prescribed for study is Narayan, while others to be introduced over the years include, as well as Naipaul, Desai, Rushdie, Seth and Sidhwa from the subcontinent, and Achebe, Gordimer, Ngugi and Soyinka from Africa. Poetry suffers from comparative neglect, in part because of the difficulty of finding individual writers with a body of work that would be both accessible and interesting. Kamala Das and Michael Ondaatje have been suggested, but selections from a range of writers would perhaps be preferable. However, given the problem of ready access to texts, it will be necessary to produce an anthology dealing with particular themes.

Access is of course a major problem for all the universities. The established departments have managed so far largely because the number of students they have is limited, so that departmental libraries that have perhaps two or three copies of prescribed texts have sufficed. In addition academics are generous with loans of their own books or photocopies, while a few at least of the students are able to afford books of their own even at the exorbitant prices arising from unfavourable exchange rates. This is another reason for the Sri Jayawardenepura programmes laying such stress on Sri Lankan writing, and also promoting the production of anthologies that bring several writers together in an economical format. The student intake for honours programmes at the other universities almost never rose above single figures in any given year, whereas colleges offering diplomas took in between fifty and a hundred students each. Ensuring an adequate supply of books for these students was essential; otherwise the new programmes too would have resulted merely in the regurgitation of second hand notes – a recourse to which many teachers who now seek to obtain English degrees externally must unfortunately turn.

To sum up, then, it can be seen that the teaching of post-colonial literatures in Sri Lanka springs from two essentially different principles, even though in practice there is a great deal of overlap. The first is the assumption that the study of literature is concerned primarily with literary qualities, and particular texts are prescribed because of their excellence; such excellence was earlier attributed to an established British tradition, but such a concept has always been elastic and now it has been stretched to include a great deal of writing from former colonies – and also, I think significantly, from the former colonized now settled in the West and therefore the more quickly absorbable into the great tradition.

The other viewpoint is that the study of literature is intended to develop awareness of particular issues as well as the potential of language. On this assumption initial study would be largely of material that is readily accessible, though both for balance and to widen perspectives, texts from different areas would also need to be studied. Both approaches seem to me valid; given the very different target groups we have in Sri Lanka, as a legacy of the initial colonial presence, both approaches seem essential.

Appendix: Suggestions for study of Sri Lankan Literature in English

(Some of the earlier books mentioned are out of print, but they have been included because of their significance at the time they were published. With regard to the poetry, a large selection from the publications of individual writers may be found in the first anthology cited. The most significant books that would also be of interest to a wider audience have been highlighted, as have the anthologies that provide a basic but thorough introduction to the state of the art in Sri Lanka at present.)

Poetry
Goonetilleke, D.C.R.A. (ed.). 1988. *Modern Sri Lankan Poetry in English*. New Delhi: Sri Satguru.
Wijesinha, Rajiva (ed.). 1993. *An Anthology of Contemporary Sri Lankan Poetry in English*. Colombo: English Association of Sri Lanka.

Arasanayagam, Jean. 1984. *Apocalypse 183*. Kandy.
Arasanayagam, Jean. 1993. *Shooting the Floricans*. Kandy.
de Zoysa, Richard. 1990. *This Other Eden*. Colombo: EASL.
Fernando, Patrick. 1984. *Selected Poems*. New Delhi: OUP.
Ranasinghe, Anne. 1985. *Against Eternity and Darkness*. Colombo.
Wikkramasinha, Lakdasa. 1976. *The Grasshopper Gleaming*. Colombo.

Fiction
Fernando, Dinali and Rajiva Wijesinha (eds.). 1993. *A Selection of Sri Lankan Short Stories In English*. Colombo: EASL.
Halpe, Ashley (ed.). 1990. *An Anthology of Contemporary Sri Lankan Short Stories in English*. Colombo: EASL.

Arasanayagam, Jean. 1995. *All is Burning*. New Delhi: Penguin.
Gooneratne, Yasmine. 1995. *The Pleasures of Conquest*. New Delhi: Penguin.
Goonewardene, James. 1976. *The Awakening of Dr. Xirth: L*. Colombo.
Goonewardene, James. 1985. *An Asian Gambit*. New Delhi: Navrang.
Muller, Carl. 1993. *The Jam Fruit Tree*. New Delhi: Penguin.
Muller, Carl. 1994. *Yakada Yaka*. New Delhi: Penguin.
Muller, Carl. 1995. *Colombo*. New Delhi: Penguin.

Rambukwelle, P.B. 1985. *The Desert Makers*. Colombo.
Selvadurai, Shyam. 1994. *Funny Boy*. London: Jonathan Cape.
Wijenaike, Punyakante. 1963. *The Third Woman*. Colombo.
Wijenaike, Punyakante. 1966. *The Waiting Earth*. Colombo.
Wijenaike, Punyakante. 1971. *Giraya*. Colombo.
Wijenaike, Punyakante. 1994. *Amulet*. Colombo.
Wijesinha, Rajiva. 1985. *Acts of Faith*. New Delhi: Navrang.
Wijesinha, Rajiva. 1995. *Servants*. Colombo: McCallum's.

Drama
Arasanayagam, T. 1988. *The Intruder,* in The British Council, *A Selection of English Drama*. Colombo.
MacIntyre, Ernest. 1991. *Ramanayagam's Last Riot*. Sydney.

English Studies in Pakistan

Alamgir Hashmi

'I doubt any work is being done at the moment.'

'No. But the works will be there. I only want to see something our men from Aiyero have helped build in Cross-river, something to reassure me that all that is happening now cannot add up to zero.'

(Season of Anomy)

When the present writer began his university teaching[1] career in Pakistan in 1971, the Departments of English were much the same as they had been in the 1950s and 1960s. Not much had changed since Independence, except that there were fewer British or American individuals on the faculty as we had become, it was commonly said, more English than the English; implying, to a degree, the redundancy of that personnel and of any earnest preaching to the converted.

The leading Departments were structured along British lines, modelled on the Universities of Oxford, Cambridge, and London. Part of the reason for this was that many Pakistani members of the faculty had been trained at those places, only sometimes at others; and part of it, less obvious, too, was embedded in the history of educational development since the mid 19th century; the colonial university existed largely to create an unquestioning mind that otherwise possessed the requisite skills. The syllabi and the teaching methods, besides the *style,* also conformed to the practice in those places. Here, with a vengeance though, it was an elite subject for the aspiring elite; it was not uncommon at all in those days that many pursuing a subject area in the humanities and the social or natural sciences had first been turned away by the English Department. Most of those with a degree in English would join the Civil Service and become (or at least be treated as), in the words of Maulvi Farid Ahmed (a member of parliament in the 1960s from the then East Pakistan), 'the ruling princes of Pakistan'; the rest in any case formed the entourage. They also formed the higher cadres of the military, manned the modern professions while serving to large feudal or mercantile interests, competently managed various departments of life, and often served the country with fair distinction, cutting a figure in society. 'Git-git' and the degree in English had a lot to do with it. Lord Macaulay[2] was correct – up to a point. But his main idea had proved infructuous: fashioned as bureau gentlemen, these sahibs rarely made it to the pinnacle – to become scholars; in more slovenly dispositions, these products proved to be neither 'gentlemen' nor 'sahibs', just babus.[3] There were very few 'ladies' to speak of; little industry or organised labour – just the depressed peasantry; no media consciousness; hardly sufficient or precise information; and minimal academic contact with the world at large. Towards the end of the 1960s the system was crumbling.

The denouement came rather quickly when the link (with English as the link language) with East Pakistan snapped (c. 1971). The Bengali language movement in the former East Pakistan, increasing regional rumbling in the then West Pakistan, the constitutional reshuffles, industrialisation, the wars with India and the Bangladeshi secession, the attempts at land reforms in the rural areas, and the impact of international intellectual movements – as well as the youthful optimism of the times – particularly in the urban centres were phenomena that left a deep mark on society. They produced the social formations and the sensibility which were to have a profound influence on all walks of life. Literature (in all languages of Pakistan) and the institutions, as well as the professions, were to reflect this altered state of things to a significant degree.

The English Departments had until then taught the medieval-to-modern survey courses, with a particular focus on the Greats, while the students were generally expected to fill in the blanks themselves and read up on the lesser lights on their own. It was the pre-Xerox era, so there were no unread photocopies to be seen lying around the desk. They read hardbound volumes mostly, as the paperback revolution had not yet hit the shores of the Arabian Sea, and they wrote their 'tutorials' and 'sessionals' with fountain-pens, often with an ink-stained hand. (The other hand, usually with a white handkerchief, worked as a wiper on the sweating brow). Questions set in examinations demanded wide reading and appeared to address a far more comprehensive syllabus and rigorous reading regime than was evident from the University calendar or any other official document. Very few actually tried the medicine not provided in the test prescription; still fewer ventured outside the course list and other much-tried inventory. The invisible syllabus was much larger than ever expected. The Honours Course through to the M.A. was both intensive and exhaustive, and allowed specialisation. To go any further than that, to examine the original archives for example, required transportation (though not for life) to Europe or America.

The medium of instruction and the language accepted for all written or oral assignments, *viva voce*, etc., was and has remained English. But the country remained aloof – and probably was deliberately kept isolated – from developments in the discipline worldwide; despite the occasional noise issuing from it, there was a refusal to move past the neo-colonial status as a decolonised state towards an equivalent national intellectual/imaginative reference and post-colonial[4] culture. The situation was an ironical if adequate illustration of Fanon's theory (apropos *Black Skin, White Masks*, 1952; *The Wretched of the Earth*, 1961), as it went against the grain and threatened for a while to undermine our value system. Colonial disparities had trained those colonised not to accept anything of their own and its dynamic transformations as respectable, whether words or objects. Besides, the *vieux jeu* fare made no new academic or intellectual demands; classroom notes were passed on as heirlooms. 'English Literature' meant British literature. There was a smattering of Old English for the extra-keen and diligent; other developments, particularly following Chaucer and Shakespeare, usually highlighted the various crises and achievements of the Nineteenth Century – on the outskirts of the Twentieth Century, the student barely got past the hem of the Edwardian or Georgian mores. So it was not exactly like the situation at inter-war Oxford, where the latest poet taken seriously since Wordsworth was Matthew Arnold.[5] Sir Arthur Quiller-Couch's *The Oxford Book of English Verse* did not then seem very old; in fact Q's anthology was quite good enough. Dame Helen Gardner's *The New Oxford Book of English Verse* had yet to appear. We could rest content largely with the treasures selected up to 1900. Whether poetry or drama and prose, full-length works were read, or selections made, to match the criteria outlined there, with courtly caution and with Victorian generosity as to the genres – and lengths.

Critical and pedagogical methods also generally conformed to the period. Q and his generation were still influential as critics, though we did witness the glancing blows they had with their younger contemporaries. Overall, Leavis held sway. The New Critics were too new. There was to be an unwritten law later against structuralist *goondas*. If the *biography* of authors and works – and Shakespeare's laundry bills written up by some local *dhobin* – exacted over-valuation, courses were still guided by horse sense and Cambridge-style reading, leading to worthy samples of 'Practical Criticism'. The objective and the subjective moieties could be neatly separated, and then each part could be found to have a logical, integral relationship with the other. Cartesian assumptions could be elaborated by Hartley, and the two got along fine together: in the body of the text, reason made sense. The faculty orientation, albeit never so embattled or influential as in England or America, was more liberal than imperial. The classroom could have existed anywhere in England (if not Ruritania or Spookystan), and ostensibly had nothing much to do with the life around; hence what (if anything) happened there never went beyond the academy; and later cultural and national developments (or disasters) – with so many English-educated individuals in command at all levels – proved its functional incapacity to keep the civil society from collapse, let alone promote or sustain it. There was no holocaust. Language knew no silence. World War II never took place. It was a good world that way.

English *teaching* in particular has been affected by specific, though bovine, policies adopted by successive governments mainly to assert Independence and, at the same time, measure up to some very dated and imperfect European notions of nationhood. They have all been generally negative and restrictive *vis-a-vis* the role of English in Pakistan and have supported its replacement with the country's lingua franca, Urdu. As the government of the late General Zia-ul-Haq, for example, attempted to transit democracy to Afghanistan during the 1980s, while suspending the fundamental rights of his own countrymen in Pakistan, it found in certain pseudo-religious political lobbies and Urdu enthusiasts a ready ally to appeal to nativism and a phoney nationalism that denied the same status not only to English but also to all other languages of Pakistan. Status apart, the standards of English underwent a major change during the 1970s and 1980s as a result of such policies. The subject was defined by these decades as even more elitist (and a marker of social mobility) than before, and its demand increased manifold for this reason besides the privatisation of education, the power of the English media, and the general pull towards a global economy. Thus, a main feature of the 1980s pretentious regime was a grudging Yes to language (English) but a definite No to literature (English) as a cultural reservation. The University Grants Commission at this time became the main conduit for creating the new cadres, convinced that literature was to be done away with. Such coyness in a time of the country's complete absorption in the Cold War economy, as a frontline state against the Soviet Union, offered a remarkable gloss on the Orientalism of the Orient. Western agencies involved in planning with Pakistani officials even relished the smirk as a *modus vivendi*, as it seemed to promise a greater spread as well as wider engagement of the educated unemployed in Britain and the USA. Higher English studies in the country had to pay the price of that Oriental affectation and Occidental complicity as no other sector of life. Such stringency and larger cultural developments which impinged on the subject caused the decline of English literature teaching, on the one hand; but, on the other hand, the jolt received caused the discipline to reconsider what it was all about, and this was salutary: the process helped to relocate the classroom in the post-colonial state of Pakistan.[6] As the medium of instruction itself became a subject of debate, language studies and language-teaching matters also became substantial areas of research. It coincided with generational succession to leadership, whereby a large number of those involved in the teaching of English had been trained in Pakistan and also in the United States or Britain, or another Commonwealth country.

But the factors responsible for this development were not just internal or anterior to present professional configuration. There had been the sharp recognition that, alongside epochal progress within its known culture, the language, widespread as it was, had also current literary usage and weight in many cultures; that the objective situation had already superseded the colonial rationale as well as the colonial inhibitions about the subject, which now required different approaches. This writer was part of the first committee in Lahore in the early 1970s which took steps to mend the postgraduate English syllabus of the University of the Punjab and its affiliated colleges. The 'Commonwealth Literature/American Literature' option was introduced at that time. His association with the Pakistan Broadcasting Corporation also led to an on-going lecture series on air in British, American, and Post-colonial literatures, as well as to a broadcast English literary journal, which was Pakistan's first outside print. The academic work begun in Lahore was continued during his years of exile, in the West, where he taught British, American, and Commonwealth/Post-colonial literatures, and writing. In the meantime, student intake of the universities in Pakistan was also changing, with students from more diverse social and academic backgrounds, as well as improved gender ratios confirming a 1970s trend. The increasing popularity of the A Level and O Level courses, particularly since the 1970s, generally underlined the British and Commonwealth aspects of the discipline, raising the awareness at crucial starting-points. Language and linguistics became nearly as strong as in the 1960s. It was realised that comparative studies involving the literatures of Pakistan, other less well-known literatures in English, and European literatures in addition to that (not those, indeed) of the British Isles were more pertinent areas of study within English Departments. Thus, the Government College and the Forman Christian College in Lahore[7] – premier seats of learning in Asia since the nineteenth century – and some other institutions were engaged in developing programmes along these lines already in the 1970s. Their impact was unmistakably conducive to revisions elsewhere. By 1980s, the Departments of English all around the country were planning specialisations in the areas of their choice.

From the south up to the north, the picture across the universities was kaleidoscopic. Karachi already had a programme in British and American literature and linguistics – it kept to that and added ELT. The Department of English in the University of Aza Jammu and Kashmir, under the headship of the present writer, wrote out a syllabus with concentrations in British, post-colonial, and language studies. Multan found language-teaching studies and British and Commonwealth literature to be of particular interest. Quetta continued with British literature and expanded its language programme. Peshawar, under the headship of the late Daud Kamal, had planned a re-designed M.A. and M.Phil. programme in English, Commonwealth, and post-colonial literature shortly before his sudden death in 1987 (Kamal had requested the present writer to be an external examiner for this programme). In the mid-1980s the present writer founded a larger but similar programme within the ambit of English and Comparative Literature at the Quaid-i-Azam University (University of Islamabad); it offered specialisations at the M.Phil./Ph.D. levels in such areas as Canadian, US, African-American, Caribbean, Latin American, and African literatures. There was a further plan afoot to commence studies of Asian and Pacific literatures (as this writer had been teaching these elsewhere since the early 1970s, starting with Mansfield, Moraes, Slessor, and Peter Cowan). Bahawalpur and Sindh continued with their mix of British and American courses and, from time to time, expressed an interest in Pakistani literature, as have some training institutes and academies for the professional and administrative cadres. Progressively, as such, the approaches have been post-colonial rather than antediluvian. There is no Department of Post-colonial Literature(s), nor as yet a place for film and media studies to look into the increasingly important interactions and permutations between the verbal and the visual texts. However, post-colonial studies, initially imported into most English Departments under the 'Commonwealth' or the 'Comparative' rubric, are here to stay[8] – even though they are sometimes placed on the official guest list.

But the formal academy of today is extremely weak, anyway, and its intellectual lethargy is further cushioned by the limited or irrelevant membership of its advisory bodies. A shortcoming of the university apparatus has been that only teachers and serving government officials hammer out the syllabi and examine the candidates for degrees; they have little contact with other universities or with current scholarship or writing outside the academy, an academy which still largely persists in its neo-colonial posture. The moral bankruptcy of the institutional structure is another major issue; the man who abrogated the constitution of Pakistan in the late 1970s was awarded the degree of Doctor of Laws (*honoris causa*) shortly after the perpetration of the deed. Both acts were symptomatic of a deeper malaise: John Stuart Mill's *On Liberty* was *externed* from the syllabus in the 1970s; Yeats's 'Leda and the Swan' was considered too tempting in the 1980s and 'deleted from the syllabus'; Byron's *Don Juan*, Lawrence's *Women in Love*, and Russell's *In Praise of Idleness* were treated likewise; and the Government of Pakistan followed suit by proscribing Walter Scott's *Ivanhoe* (fortunately for Scott and his heirs, more than a century and a half after its publication in the United Kingdom). These are but a few examples of the whim indulged – more than that, fanaticism[9] had a free rein and constrained good sense. Frequent changes of educational policy in the country and the 1980s crisis in the universities have resulted in some major setbacks to earlier development. By now, several English Departments have gone under with faint hopes of a recovery, and yet several others float on aided by a raft or two left from the olden times. The journals have gone down, too, and all that we have published here, since the 1970s, can now be found in the back files. Hence, the role of *The Journal of Commonwealth Literature* and *Kunapipi* in our context, and also of *World Literature Today*, can hardly be overemphasised; these journals have continued to promote, worldwide, a sustained scholarly interest in post-colonial literatures, including Pakistani literature. As guardians of *cordon sanitaire* we have the responsibility – to reorganise and start off again, and again. In twenty-five years' teaching, this writer is glad to say that he has learnt to be hopeful about the least bit there: anon – *inshallah*.

Reading List: Pakistani Literature

A. Poetry
Ghose, Zulfikar. 1991. *Selected Poems*. Karachi: Oxford University Press.
Hashmi, Alamgir. 1992. *The Poems of Alamgir Hashmi* (Collected Poems). Islamabad: National Book Foundation.

Hashmi, Alamgir. 1992. *Sun and Moon and Other Poems*. Islamabad: Indus Books.
Kamal, Daud. 1995. *Before the Carnations Wither*. Peshawar: Daud Kamal Trust.
Rafat, Taufiq. 1985. *Arrival of the Monsoon*. Lahore: Vanguard.

B. Novels
Ali, Ahmed. 1994. *Twilight in Delhi*. (1940) New York: New Directions.
Ali, Ahmed. 1986. *Rats and Diplomats*. Karachi: Akrash Publishing.
Ali, Tariq. 1992. *Shadows of the Pomegranate Tree*. London: Chatto and Windus.
Aslam, Nadeem. 1993. *Season of the Rainbirds*. London: Andre Deutsh.
Ghose, Zulfikar. 1967. *The Murder of Aziz Khan*. London: Macmillan.
Ghose, Zulfikar. 1992. *The Triple Mirror of the Self*. London: Bloomsbury.
Kureishi, Hanif. 1990. *The Buddha of Suburbia*. London: Faber and Faber.
Sheikh, Farhana. 1991. *The Red Box*. London: The Women's Press.
Sheikh, Nazneen (Sadiq, Nazneen). 1988. *Ice Bangles*. Toronto: Lorimer.
Sidhwa, Bapsi. 1980. *The Crow Eaters*. London: Jonathan Cape.
Sidhwa, Bapsi. 1988. *Ice-Candy-Man*. London: Heinemann.
Zameenzad, Adam. 1987. *The Thirteenth House*. London: Fourth Estate.

C. Drama
Ali, Tariq (with Howard Brenton). 1990. *Moscow Gold*. London: N. Hern Books.
Kureishi, Hanif. 1981. *Borderline*. London: Methuen.
Kureishi, Hanif. 1983. *Outskirts and Other Plays*. London: John Calder.

D. Anthologies
Hashmi, Alamgir (ed). 1987. *Pakistani Literature: The Contemporary English Writers*. 2nd ed. Islamabad: Gulmohar Press (first published New York, 1978).
Hashmi, Alamgir (ed). *Pakistani Short Stories in English* (forthcoming).

E. Criticism
Afzal-Khan, Fawzia. 1991. 'Bapsi Sidhwa: Women in History', in Robert L. Ross (ed.), *International Literature in English: Essays on the Major Writers*. New York: Garland Publishing, 271-81.
Ali, Hina Babar. 1988. 'Alamgir Hashmir's Wandering Soul'. *Journal of South Asian Literature*, 23/1, 146-50.
Anderson, David D. 1975. 'Ahmed Ali and the Growth of a Pakistani Literary Tradition in English'. *World Literature Written in English*, 14/2, 436-49.
Benson, Eugene and L.W. Conolly, eds. 1994. *Encyclopedia of Post-colonial Literatures in English*. 2 vols. London & New York: Routledge. See contents for Pakistan-related articles.
Coppola, Carlo. 1980. 'The Poetry of Ahmed Ali'. *Journal of Indian Writing in English*, 8/1 & 2, 63-76.
Coppola, Carlo. 'Recent English Poetry from Pakistan'. *The New Quarterly*. New York, 3/1, 102-12; also in Alamgir Hashmi (ed.), *Pakistani Literature: The Contemporary English Writers* (see anthologies).
Coppola, Carlo. 1979. 'The Short Stories of Ahmed Ali', in Muhammad Umar Memon (ed.), *Studies in the Urdu Gazal and Prose Fiction*. Madison, Wisconsin: South Asian Studies, University of Wisconsin-Madison, 211-42.
Gemmill, Janet Powers. 1981. 'Hashmi's Poetry of Double Roots'. *New Literature Review*, 8, 60-62.
Gowda, H.H.A. 1981. 'Ahmed Ali's *Twilight in Delhi* (1940) and Achebe's *Things Fall Apart* (1958)'. *The Literary Half-Yearly*, 21/1, 11-18.

Hamilton, Ian (ed). 1994. *The Oxford Companion to Twentieth-Century Poetry in English*; contains short notes on Zulfikar Ghose, Alamgir Hashmi, Daud Kamal, and Taufiq Rafat.

Hashmi, Alamgir. 1983. *Commonwealth Literature: An Essay Towards the Redefinition of a Popular/Counter Culture*. London & Lahore: Vision Press.

Hashmi, Alamgir. 1988. *Commonwealth, Comparative Literature and the World*. Islamabad: Gulmohar Press.

Hashmi, Alamgir. 1990. 'Ahmed Ali and the Transition to a Postcolonial Mode in the Pakistani Novel in English'. *Journal of Modern Literature*, 17/1, 177-82.

Hashmi, Alamgir. 1992. '"A Stylised Motif of Eagle Wings Woven": The Selected Poems of Zulfikar Ghose'. *World Literature Today*, 66/1, 66-69.

Hashmi, Alamgir. 1993. 'Prolegomena to the Study of Pakistani English and Pakistani Literature in English' in *Major Minorities: English Literatures in Transit*, ed. Raoul Granqvist. Amsterdam/Atlanta, GA: Rodopi, 99-110.

Hashmi, Alamgir. 'Current Pakistani Fiction'. *Span*, 33, 126-33.

Hashmi, Alamgir. 'Hanif Kureishi and the Tradition of the Novel'. *The International Fiction Review*, 19/2, 88-95.

Hashmi, Alamgir. 1990. 'Poetry, Pakistani Idiom in English, and the Groupies'. *World Literature Today*, 64/2, 268-71.

Ibrahim, Huma. 1994. 'Post-Colonial Literature in Africa and Pakistan'. *The Nation: Friday Review*. (Lahore & Islamabad), 12 August, 5 and 14.

Imam, Hina Faisal. 'Romance and Religion in Hashmi's Kentucky'. *Crosscurrent* (NZ), 1/1, 61-62.

Kanaganayakam, Chelva. 1993. *Structures of Negation: The Writings of Zulfikar Ghose*. Toronto: University of Toronto.

King, Bruce. 1988. 'Alamgir Hashmi's Poetry: Pakistan, Modernity and Language'. *JIWE: Writing in English from Pakistan, Sri Lanka & Bangladesh*, 16/2 July, 55-68.

King, Bruce. 1986. 'From *Twilight* to *Midnight*: Muslim Novels of India and Pakistan', in Alamgir Hashmi (ed.), *The Worlds of Muslim Imagination*. Islamabad: Gulmohar, 243-59.

Mann, Harveen Sachdeva. 1994. 'Cracking India: Minority Women Writers and the Contentious Margins of Indian Nationalist Discourse'. *Journal of Commonwealth Literature*, 29/2, 71-94.

Marowski, Daniel G. & Roger Matuz (eds). 1987. 'Zulfikar Ghose' (Critical excerpts by various hands). *Contemporary Literary* Criticism, 42. Detroit: Gale Research, 176-86.

Matuz, Roger (ed). 1992. 'Ahmed Ali' (Critical excerpts by various hands). *Contemporary Literary Criticism,* 69 Detroit: Gale Research, 19-32.

Niven, Alistair. 'Historical Imagination in the Novels of Ahmed Ali'. *Journal of Indian Writing in English*, 8/1&2, 3-13.

Raffel, Burton. 1994. 'The Poems of Alamgir Hashmi'. *The Literary Review* (Madison, NJ), 37/4, 705-10.

Rahman, Tariq. 'English Prose by Pakistanis'. *The Journal of the English Literary Club 1987*, 97-105.

Rahman, Tariq. 'Linguistic Deviation as a Stylistic Device in Pakistani English Fiction'. *The Journal of Commonwealth Literature*, 25/1, 1-11.

The Review of Contemporary Fiction: Milan Kundera/Zulfikar Ghose Number, 9/2 1989, 108-237.

Sharkey, Michael. 1988. '"Let's Celebrate": Alamgir Hashmi's *My Second in Kentucky*'. *New Literature Review*, 15, 33-9.

Sirajuddin, Shaista Sonnu. 1991. 'Three Contemporary Poets: A Study of Their Use of Language'. *Explorations*, 14/1 Summer, 51-63.

Stilz, Gerhard. 1988. 'Live in Fragments No Longer: A Conciliatory Analysis of Ahmed Ali's *Twilight*'. *Journal of Indian Writing in English*, 16/2 July, 69-88.

Yearly critical surveys in *The Journal of Commonwealth Literature*, 1965-.

Yearly critical surveys in *Kunapipi*, 1981-.

Notes

1. The universities in Pakistan no longer conduct undergraduate teaching, which is mostly carried out at the affiliated undergraduate colleges and colleges which also offer graduate studies. Some universities admitted students for the B.A. Honours Course until the early 1970s, while the (B.A.) Pass Course was taught entirely at the colleges. That practice has been discontinued since the general abolishment of the Honours Course. Thus, in terms of the Western university system, the universities and the colleges affiliated to them together form our system of tertiary or higher education.

2. 'Minute on Indian Education' (1835), *Thomas Babington Macaulay: Selected Writings*, edited by John Clive & Thomas Pinney (Chicago: University of Chicago Press, 1972).

3. Shuaib bin Hasan many years ago invoked the pedigree traits of the neocolonialists in the Dickensian formulation of 'baboos and/or baboons', reversed, excepting the anomalous category of writers. See his 'Pakistani Practitioners of English Verse', *The Ravi*, 65/2 (April 1974), 53-71. It can be argued, though, that the neocolonial state never allowed much scholarship – the genuine scholarship in any case.

4. In the precise sense, this writer quite agrees with Edwin Thumboo that Britain is a post-colonial state (and so is the USA then), certainly one that proceeds to discuss or allude to itself centrally in order to describe the world, or any part thereof. The coloniser (British, French, Portuguese, Dutch, etc.), as such, also experiences post-coloniality, both from chronology and condition. The progression/regression is conceived here as given above: colonial, neocolonial, post-colonial. For Thumboo's views on the subject, see his 'Essential Space and Cross-cultural Challenges', paper presented at the Crossing Cultures conference, Canberra, 6-9 November, 1995.

5. See F.W. Bateson, *Essays in Critical Dissent* (London: Longman, 1972).

6. See the first chapter of *The Commonwealth, Comparative Literature and the World* by Alamgir Hashmi (Islamabad: Gulmohar Press, 1988).

7. Notwithstanding its current *fin de siècle* phase, the city has been an important centre for a long time and has attracted such visitors over time as Daniel Jones, Oliver Elton, Ian Jack, Angus Wilson, A.D. Hope, Judith Wright, Elizabeth Sewell, Anthony Thwaite, William Stafford, and A.R. Humphreys. J.R. Firth also worked here for some time.

8. The major shift from earlier contrary opinion has been indicated by a sizable volume of recent critical writing. Even the late Eric Cyprian, a staunch believer in the mother-tongue and the regional languages, came round to the view, by the late 1980s, that both excellence and cultural authenticity/viability were attainable in a second, third, or fourth language – and even in a language with an imperial past – now that he had the necessary evidence. See Eric Syprian, 'A New Vision for Commonwealth Literature', *The Nation* (Lahore and Islamabad), 23 November 1990, 5.

9. The tendency has been popularised and institutionalised as a phoney-nationalist alternative in order to refurbish the neocolonialist structure and to thwart post-colonial development.

The How and the Wherefore

A. Norman Jeffares

Having been asked to write about how I became interested in Commonwealth literature and followed up that interest, I sat down with a blank sheet of paper in front of me and began to wonder first of all how I came to enjoy literature in general. In part I think it happened when my mother began to move me on from Grimm's *Fairy Tales* through Kenneth Grahame and A.A. Milne to more powerful writing. She read me *Gulliver's Travels* before I went to school at seven. That book enthralled me (Willy Pogany's illustrations to it were superb) and through it began my later, developing interest in Irish writing. Swift was a part of the Dublin I knew, not only because of his being buried in St. Patrick's Cathedral and his having founded Swift's Hospital, but because the grandfather of contemporaries, Dr. Leeper, had a portrait of Stella and had collected Swift memorabilia (a snuff box, I think, among other things). When I began reading for myself there were other Irish writers on my parents' shelves. I graduated from Dorothea Conyers to the wonderful humour of Somerville and Ross, from the slapstick of Lover to the turmoil of Carleton. He was a surprising author to find in our house, and after I gave a spirited rendering of one of his stories at some meal, my father suggested I might give him a miss as his language was not to be encouraged. In our Protestant household his exuberant taking in vain not only the names of the Trinity (and various saints) but his use of violent oaths was strongly deprecated, and I was steered towards Donn Byrne and Maurice Walsh.

With all these Irish writers, I quickly established a rapport because they wrote of known and loved places. Then at school my horizons were extended. I took classics as my special subject, and my imagination created its new world, exchanging Liffey and Dodder for Simoïs and Scamander Kippure for Cithaeron, the hardened earth and gravel of the High School playground in Harcourt Street for the gymnasts' garden in Athens, Dublin's Two Rock and Three Rock mountains for the Seven Hills of Rome. John Bennett, an enthusiastic, most civilized headmaster, encouraged wide reading, so Lucian's invention followed upon Swift's. Bennett's was a literary interest rather than a grammatical one, and so I left school with a voracious desire to go on exploring classical literature and spent the next four years as an honours student of classics at Trinity College, Dublin. I had also a good awareness of the richness and variety of English literature and of its development, for at school we were taught English literary history brilliantly by Jack Storey for a period a week in the sixth form, and learned by heart each week examples of the major poets' work from Chaucer up to the Victorians. I followed up this interest in Trinity, managing to fit in lectures (and term examinations which meant useful money for books) during my first three years.

In addition to soaking myself in Greek and Latin literature, I had an interesting awareness of differences between Irish writers and the others whose achievements were described in the literary history used at school and those who featured in the English honours course in Trinity. This nascent awareness of the existence of Irish writing as an entity did not, however, lead me to any precise, panoptic view of it, nor to any analysis of the particular qualities which distinguished it from the rest of English literature. It was an instinctive feeling at this stage.

When I escaped from classics – I found the concentration upon the philosophical-linguistic-grammatical remote from my own interest in the literary aspects of the subject, for the Trinity course was a gruelling one, and English studies seemed to offer more scope, I began to write a Ph.D. thesis upon Yeats's middle and late poetry, a pioneering survey of their sources and symbolism. I began to see into the complex history of Irish literature. The reason was Yeats's early interest in Gaelic literature. Himself a nationalist, but not knowing any Irish, he read translations eagerly, wanting to give his readers, particularly his Irish readers, a sense of Ireland's rich cultural inheritance. When he made his own versions of the Irish epic tales (which dated from the eighth century) and of local legends, he imposed his own romantic pre-Raphaelite, mystic and occult sensibilities upon them. He read the Irish nineteenth-century novelists – Carleton, Griffin and Kickham, for instance – making selections of their work for English publishers. He also read the patriotic poetry which, under the influence of Thomas Davis and *The Nation*, had been so popular in Ireland in the nineteenth century. He sought, however, to establish more rigorous literary standards through his criticism and the example of his own work. He created a new awareness of Ireland's past literary achievements through the Irish literary Renaissance (which was also known from the title of one of his books as the Celtic Twilight movement) which was largely of his making. But he did not find his own true cultural inheritance until he began to investigate the eighteenth-century Anglo-Irish tradition in the nineteen-twenties. Earlier his nationalism had precluded his discovering Swift, Goldsmith, Berkeley and Burke and realising his kinship with their attitudes, their outspokenness.

When I lectured in English in the University of Groningen I explored this tradition myself, my own early interest in Swift deepened and complemented by an early liking for Goldsmith and Maria Edgeworth and by the stimulus of having been Auditor of the College Historical Society (its weekly debates, its committee work and social life probably had more influence on me than anything else in my undergraduate days), for was this not originally Mr Burke's Debating Club, which traces itself back 250 years to him and to the fine tradition of thoughtful argument he established in it – something well described in Conor Cruise O'Brien's enlightening biography of this statesman who did so much to create gradualism in conservative thought, whose wisdom was not always fully appreciated in England.

The liberal system of teaching in Groningen allowed me time to lecture extensively to the Dutch students on Irish and Anglo-Irish literary traditions. In my lectures, for instance, I followed up Irish drama written in the seventeenth and eighteenth centuries, shaped by the classicism most of the authors had learned in Trinity College, their comedies of manners based upon the examples of Greek New Comedy and the plays of Plautus and Terence. It was a line established by Congreve, Southerne, Farquhar, Susannah Centlivre, Richard Steele and Charles Macklin, continued through the work of Goldsmith and Sheridan to Oscar Wilde and George Bernard Shaw, its audience largely in London. Afterwards, through Yeats, came the Abbey Theatre with its blend of contrasting heroic verse dramas and realistic cottage comedies, and the tragi-comedies of Synge and O'Casey. This was an Irish theatre dealing with Irish themes aimed at Irish audiences.

Here was something I knew, the plays set in the wild scenery of Glencree or of Glenmalure that I had experienced on picnics, blended with my knowledge of people who lived in remote glens and valleys in County Wicklow, and then again plays about the slums of Dublin through which, like Synge, I had walked as a child, those overcrowded slums with all their disease and drunkenness, their terrible poverty and gallant cohesiveness, their wild imaginative language.

So it became clear to me in Holland that Swift was the first great Irish writer in English – and the first anti-colonial writer too.

A few years' lecturing in Edinburgh then ensued and taught me a great deal about English literature; one was, naturally enough, expected to teach any part of the undergraduate course – often at very short notice as the Professor, W. L. Renwick, was often ill, and it was good training to take his potentially rowdy First Ordinary Course on a day's notice. It was large and its attention had to be firmly held, with a suitable admixture of joke and anecdote during the imparting of ideas and information: he could cut through fashionable critical nonsense (though, luckily, there wasn't so much of it about in those days) and could seize upon significant idiosyncrasies or facts in the lives of writers with great originality and discernment.

At the insistence of the supervisor of my Oxford doctorate (this one being a life of Yeats), Professor David Nichol Smith, I then went to Australia. (Those of us who were supervised by that great and understanding man thought that anyone who did not go where he suggested would have the flag with their name on it plucked from the globe in his Oxford study in Merton Street and that would be the end of them, academically and indeed in every other way!)

My knowledge of Australian literature was virtually zero. My cousin Robert (who had moved from office to farm to running the Astors' stud at Blackhall in

County Kildare and knew the stud book by heart) had introduced me to what seemed at first the strange, somewhat horsey world of Adam Lindsay Gordon, and I had read Henry Handel Richardson's *The Fortunes of Richard Mahony*, largely because my sister, on hearing that I was going to Adelaide, had advised me not to open it, on the grounds that I would be deeply depressed by reading it. And for some unknown reason I had read Leonard Mann's *The Fool and the Tractor*. (I had, however, *nearly* read some Australian literature at Edinburgh. A Ph.D. candidate had blithely proposed that he would write a History of South African, Australian and New Zealand Literature. The Professor handed him on to me to supervise with the dry comment that he had eliminated South African literature from the thesis and what would I do? I eliminated Australian and as a result began to read New Zealand literature, which came in useful to me later in life.)

I realised that this ignorance of Australian literature would simply not do for a thirty year old holder of an Australian chair of English literature, and, with relatively youthful energy, decided I would read my way through it, an aim reinforced by the editor of *Etudes Anglaises* who asked me for an article on the subject. So I made my own history of it and, with considerable difficulty, condensed it to the required length. Again, there was the pleasure of matching literature to place and person – and that gave rise to inevitable ideas of comparison. There were some parallels with New Zealand literature, and I began to wonder whether Canadian literature had developed in any similar way – from the original letters-home syndrome.

A chance arose to send a member of the English Department to Canada for six months to study Canadian literature. It was an idea supported by Steve Stackpole of the Carnegie Corporation, an enlightened foundation man who deployed his organisation's funds in a most creative way. Brian Elliott was the obvious choice. He had just finished a life of Marcus Clarke by which I was most impressed: his deep knowledge of Australian literature, his enthusiasm and his skilled guidance had greatly helped my forays into it. (Later I was to learn a great deal from Geoffrey Dutton who, all too briefly, lectured in the Department of English. His recent autobiography shows something of the help he gave to other writers while himself being a man of letters in the best sense of the word, equally ready to write poems, novels and excellent biographies, to edit journals and become a most creative publisher.) Brian got an immense stimulus out of his visit to Canada and on his return to Adelaide gave excellent seminars on Canadian literature followed by those of Claude Bissell, later President of the University of Toronto, who came to Australia on a return visit. So on to my childhood reading of Robert Service's *Songs of a Sourdough* and Stephen Leacock's *Literary Lapses* were grafted such modern writers as Hugh McLellan, Earle Birney and P.K. Page. P.K. Page I met in Canberra and I enjoyed her company enormously. Earle became a close friend in later years, greatly appreciated for his warmth of feeling and inventive wit.

When I left Australia for Leeds, arriving there in 1957, I had, then, a reasonable knowledge of Australian and Canadian and a smattering of New Zealand literature. A three-month British Council lecture tour in India enabled me to meet many Indian writers, among them Nirad Chaudhuri and Khushwant Singh. As a child I had been introduced to India by Flora Annie Steele's impressive novel *On the Face of the Waters*, by *Kim* and other fiction by Kipling and by a lot of trashy romantic novels by such writers as Maud Diver and I.A.R. Wylie where the heroes, with eyes surrounded by wrinkles gained by gazing into far distances through the brilliant sunshine, capable of blending (with suitable staining) into the bazaars, enmeshed in intrigues with Eurasian girls, protected the North-West Frontier. There's a lot to be said for realising how good the classics are by reading less successful work.

Shortly after arriving in Leeds I decided to establish reading in Commonwealth literature (I remember with some amusement the Little-Englander horror this engendered in the poet Geoffrey Hill – he was a lecturer who had come to Leeds straight after a First at Oxford and had not then, I think, been outside his native Blackburn, Oxford and Leeds). I got the help of the British Council in financing an annual visiting Fellowship at Leeds to be held by a writer or academic from a Commonwealth country: during the tenure of the post the Fellow would give a course of lectures to students, mainly postgraduates, in the literature of his or her commonwealth literature. We had two postgraduates in 1957 (both subsequently distinguished as authors and academics, Michael Millgate in Faulker and Hardy Studies, Bruce King in Commonwealth and 17th Century English Literature) but the number increased rapidly, the whole School of English having 250 when I left in 1974. The postgraduate school attracted students from many countries: they gained a great deal from meeting and getting to know each other, and the courses in Commonwealth literature opened the eyes of many (not least the British) to the scope of literature written in English outside the UK, and to the role in various Commonwealth countries of literature in defining cultural identity (the effect of, say, Chinua Achebe's five novels upon Nigerian schoolchildren's awareness of their country's emergence from colonial status is obvious – just as Joyce Cary earlier illustrated aspects of colonial rule in relation to tribal traditions).

Douglas Grant, who became a friend when we were at Oxford, came to Leeds after a spell in Toronto (where he learned to appreciate the role of the Canada Council and its stimulating effect upon Canadian writing and publishing) to be the first professor of American Literature in Britain, and approved mightily of the concept of a School of English with an international outlook. The Bruern Fellowship, set up shortly after his arrival, brought a succession of distinguished American scholars to Leeds to teach American literature in a way parallel to that of the Fellows in Commonwealth literature. Though Douglas was primarily interested in English and American literature as I was in English and Anglo-Irish, we shared an enthusiasm for Commonwealth writing; indeed we inducted the then

Professor of Education, Will Walsh, into an awareness of the subject so effectively that he wrote several critical studies in this field. When Lord Boyle became Vice-Chancellor of the University, he so appreciated the pioneering achievement of the School of English in developing the study of Commonwealth literature that he persuaded the University to approve the English School's request for the establishment of a chair in it – and Walsh was appointed the first holder of it (the present professor is Shirley Chew).

A complex Commonwealth-wide nexus soon developed and spread surprisingly rapidly. In my own case, for instance, I went to Canada as a guest of the Canada Council in 1962, visiting a large number of universities and meeting authors and publishers. This visit led to many others (some engineered by Murdo McKinnon); many Canadians came to Leeds and a number of Leeds graduates took up positions in Canada. I also began to visit West Africa, often several times a year, and went to East and Southern Africa also. I developed a policy of appointing lecturers and fellows (both permanent and temporary) who had teaching experience overseas to the expanding staff at Leeds. So over the years, in addition to colleagues who had taught in the US and Europe, we covered Africa (Cameroon, Loreto Todd; Ghana, Alistair Niven, M. Bryn Davies; Nigeria, John Spencer; Sierra Leone, Eldred Jones, Tom Creighton; Sudan, Alistair Thomson; South Africa and Zimbabwe, Arthur Ravenscroft); Australia (Gustav Cross, M. Bryn Davies, Geoffrey Dutton, Tony Gibbs, Randolph Stow); Canada (Carl Klinck, Frank Watt, Claude Bissell); Hong Kong (Alec Hardie); India (Nissim Ezekiel, Srinivasa Iyengar); New Zealand (Andrew Gurr, Kendrick Smithyman, Eric McCormick); Singapore (D.J. Enright); the West Indies (Wilson Harris, John Hearne).

There was an outward movement also: we encouraged members of staff to hold positions overseas on secondment, largely in Africa (at one time the School of English had a lecturer temporarily living in Ulan Bator!) and we encouraged members of staff to undertake British Council lecture tours while there was also a good deal of external examining abroad. The School of English took a particular interest in the University of Cameroon, training many of its staff and assisting in examining and establishing curricula. The head of the Department at Yaounde, Professor Mbassi-Manga, obtained his M.A. and Ph.D. at Leeds.

We began to build up impressive library holdings, the Sahitya Academy and the Indian Government leading the way with generous gifts of books, an example followed by New Zealand. Through the generosity of the Arts Council of Great Britain we built up a collection of tapes and records of writers reading their own work, the Council's Literature Director, Eric White, being an enthusiastic supporter of this scheme. Leeds was a suitable place for this, for it had the enlightened fellowships in the arts financed by Peter Gregory, one of which was for poetry. There were many other poets about as well, among them undergraduates such as Wole Soyinka, a future Nigerian Nobel Prize winner and Tony Harrison, the poet and translator, who later taught for a time in Ahmadu Bello.

My own main contribution was, I suppose, to set up ACLALS, the Association of Commonwealth Literature and Language Studies which held its first conference at Leeds. That was in part prompted by the intensive work I had undertaken in writing the section on Commonwealth Literature for a German encyclopaedia, Kindler's *Der Literaturen der Welt* (1964). The history of ACLALS – the continuation and expansion of its very successful series of triennial conferences held in rotation in Commonwealth countries and the local associations (such as EACLALS, the European organisation) and conferences that have evolved from it – will probably be known to most who read this.[1] Here I should like to pay tribute to three people who aided me and my colleagues in Leeds in this work. The first was Jack Hughes of the Commonwealth Relations Office, whom I first met in India. His advice and unobtrusive help were invaluable and opened many doors – and purse strings. The second was John Chadwick, whose skilled guidance as Director of the Commonwealth Foundation did so much to encourage and support Commonwealth non-governmental organisations. He instantly saw the point of ACLALS and the Foundation supported its work in a most generous way. The third person was Arthur King of the British Council, especially valuable for his aid in establishing the *Journal of Commonwealth Literature*, so effectively edited by Arthur Ravenscroft (a South African academic who came from Salisbury to Leeds) and so well supported by Keith Sambrook of Heinemann Educational Books, the first publishers of the *Journal*. Keith had encouraged many Commonwealth writers, particularly in the Heinemann African series, with its impressive list of titles.

Some of this organisational activity spilled over, naturally enough, into book publishing. At the time I was advising several publishers and reading manuscripts for them and so was able to see to it, in a small way, that Commonwealth literature was not ignored. When editing the quarterly *A Review of English Literature* (from 1960-1968) I had included from time to time articles on various aspects of Commonwealth literature, and, when I agreed to set up a new quarterly and edit it for its first three years for the University of Calgary, the scope was extended to cover writing in English throughout the world – as the title of this still flourishing journal, *ARIEL: A Review of International English Literature* indicates.

All this strenuous work, (which was, of course, undertaken in addition to carrying a fairly heavy programme of undergraduate teaching and graduate supervision in English literature as well as administering the Department of English Literature and, later, for its first three years, the School of English) was enormously enjoyable. It led to such a wide range of reading (travel by trains and aeroplanes has some advantages) and, much more important, it created so many friendships, through ACLALS, and among the graduate students who came to Leeds. I share Yeats's wish: 'Always we'd have the new friend meet the old'.

After I left Leeds and came to Stirling in 1974 my interest in Commonwealth Literature continued. Tommy Dunn, head of the Department at Stirling (and an old pupil of mine from Edinburgh days) had been a professor in Ghana, in Lagos and in London, Ontario; the Reader, Robin Mayhead, had been in Ghana, Alasdair Macrae in Khartoum, Felicity Riddy from New Zealand in Nigeria, Alison Gent had come from Australia, Rory Watson had been in Canada, Alastair Niven in Ghana, while others had experience of universities in the United States and Europe. There was, then, a strong interest in Commonwealth writing in Stirling, and several of my colleagues wrote volumes in the York Notes Series I was editing which contained many Commonwealth writers. Volumes on Australian, Canadian, American and Anglo Irish literature were included in the Macmillan Histories of Literature of which I was general editor. Then when I was Chairman of the Literature Panel of the Scottish Arts Council with Trevor Royle as an enthusiastic Director, we made reciprocal arrangements with the Canada Council and the Australia Council to exchange writers with Scotland (we also ran annual exchange visits of Irish and Scottish poets, and had an exchange of Scottish and Danish writers).

Over the years time sometimes seems to stand still. But visits from former students who now have retired can jolt one's awareness of its very real progress. It seems, however, but yesterday that one met for the first time and recognised the intellectual ability and personal qualities of such students, to select but a few, as Lloyd Fernando of Kuala Lumpur (Professor turned barrister and novelist); Margaret Clayton of Canada (now married to Professor Peter Lewis and the brilliant biographer of Ngaio Marsh), Terence Sturm (from Australia, Professor and author), Saros Cowasjee (from India, Professor and novelist in Canada), Bill New (from Canada, author of *A History of Canadian Literature*), Brendan Kennelly (from Kerry, Professor, poet, translator and critic) and Anna Rutherford (from Australia, who has shared her deep knowledge of Commonwealth literature with generations of Danish students, author, intrepid traveller and distinguished publisher). But there are so many more friends arising out of the Commonwealth connection: John Bray, Dan Davin, Fernando Henriques and Rosemary Wighton, now all dead; John Pepper Clark, Jeanne Delbaere, Ken Goodwin, Doug Killam, Alex Kwapong, Hena Maes-Jelinek, and Edwin Thumboo all blessedly very much alive: all, dead and alive, most generous and friendly people.

Co-editing the recently published and large *Collins Dictionary of Quotations* with Martin Gray (now head of the Department at Luton, who knows his Africa and edited the UK *Australian Studies* with brio) has led to the presence of many entries from Commonwealth countries as well as those from the UK, US and Europe. In the five years of extensive reading and re-reading involved in compiling this Dictionary (like Dr Johnson ensuring that the Whig dogs did not get the best of the argument, I took care that my primary interest, in Irish writing and writers, was not unrepresented!) I experienced an immense pleasure, accentuated by working with Martin, whose sense of humour and literary taste chime with mine.

In addition to reading or re-reading my way through such highly condensed writers as, say, Donne or Gray or Sassoon or Judith Wright or A.D. Hope, I adventured through those writers the sheer size and variety of whose output remains so impressive: Chaucer, Spenser, Milton, Wordsworth, Tennyson, Browning, Whitman and, of course, Shakespeare. So now you may well ask what has over fifty years spent in teaching literature, writing about it, editing and publishing the work of others left me to say about Commonwealth literature in particular? My hopes are that the long tradition out of which such lively, creative, formative current writing in English springs will not be neglected, by either undue (and boring) specialization or by any narrow (politically correct) nationalism. Naturally readers enjoy literature about places, people, situations, and traditions that they know or are close to them. But let us be aware as readers of what else exists, of the vast richness and complexity of past writing in English which has shaped the present. There is so much to compare, so much to appraise and appreciate, so much to enjoy.

Note

1. See 'To Set the Record Right', in Hena Maes-Jelinek, Kirsten Holst Petersen and Anna Rutherford (eds.), *A Shaping of Connections: Commonwealth Literature Studies – Then and Now* (Aarhus: Dangaroo Press, 1989), 253-58. See 'IASAIL: The achievement and the future', in Bruce Stewart (ed.), *IASAIL Newsletter* 2/1 (March 1996), 12-16 for an account of the establishment of the International Association for the Study of Anglo-Irish Literature at a splendid conference in Dublin in 1970. The Association (now IASIL: the International Association for the Study of Irish Literatures) flourishes, with triennial conferences at Irish Universities and at universities throughout the world in intervening years. It was planned at Leeds by Brendan Kennelly, John Kelly and myself, for similar reasons to those which led to the foundation of ACLALS.

The Role of Literature from the English-speaking World in the EFL Classroom: Short Prose Fiction from the New English Literatures

Heidi Ganner

1. Literatures in English and the European book market

English Literature from all over the world has successfully penetrated the European book market. Publishers' interests in originals and translations, the book market for the young reader, and the growth industry of ELT (English Language Teaching) annotated, abridged and simplified texts have all increasingly shifted towards the new English literatures, whose relevance for the European academic and the interested reader is most obviously reflected in recent reference works of English literature. Their pages have been opened for these rival literatures, even if editors and publishers have not gone all the way to change the titles of their companions and guides into Guides to Literature in English – as some have done. A standard work such as *The Oxford Companion to English Literature* (New edition by Margaret Drabble, 1985) would be the poorer for not including Nadine Gordimer, Ngugi Wa Thiong'o, Wole Soyinka, Salman Rushdie, Ruth Prawer Jhabvala, Anita Desai, George Lamming, Margaret Atwood and many others whose origins clearly lie outside the traditional realms, at least geographically, of English Literature.

English Literature has indeed been redefined on the basis of the common denominator of all these writers' language, of which Anita Desai says that it is 'the most flexible, the most rich in nuances and subtleties'[1], making it the natural vehicle of communication and artistic expression, even for writers for whom English is not the mother tongue, or whose rejection of colonialism may make them very hostile towards European culture. It is the instrument of expression particularly for all those who seek to find solidarity outside their own worlds in their struggle for human rights, for freedom or for the liberation of women in countries culturally as diverse as Nigeria, New Zealand, the Fijis, South Africa or the Caribbean.

2. The short story and ELT

The short story is an extremely popular form in the new English literatures, and indeed anthologies of New English Literatures are a new growth industry in themselves. Short story collections by individual authors abound. The brevity of the texts lends itself to ELT teaching purposes more readily than longer fiction and the more demanding forms of poetry.

The stories referred to in this paper, with the exception of one, are from lesser known editions: Patricia Grace's story 'Hills' from her collection *Electric City,* Jean Rhys's story 'Let Them Call It Jazz' from her short story collection *Tigers are Better Looking,* probably the most widely known story, Shashi Deshpande's 'The Death of a Child' from *The Legacy,* and Kamala Das's story with the slightly misleading, ambiguous title 'Running away from Home' from *Panorama. An Anthology of Modern Indian Short Stories.*[2]

Incidentally, all stories are by women writers, which in a way is also representative of the situation in the new English literatures.

2.1 Literature and language
Literature teaching at school level should not and need not take place at the cost of language teaching. Accepting this dogma, I will begin by demonstrating the contribution short stories from the new English literatures can make in this direction.

The new English literatures offer a wide variety of themes – personal, socio-cultural and political, and very often in the mode of a social-realist style of writing; consequently, they serve as fascinating points of departure for practising English in discussions, written and oral, on almost any topic of daily life.

Patricia Grace's initiation story 'Hills' covers not more than five pages. Yet it deals with adolescence and the discovery of sexuality, with growing up as a member of an ethnic minority, with family relationships and parental attitudes, and with police practices, alcohol and drugs as social problems. It offers ample opportunity for students to describe, analyse and criticize situations, feelings and attitudes. Moreover, the story, written in deceptively simple English, gives insight into the language of a culture shaped by the present and by its history. Although in standard English, the story contains elements of the language of an age-group, the slang of youngsters, and subtleties of language which may escape the superficial reader and which can be brought to the surface by a short exercise in translation. The reader, our student of EFL, will suddenly discover that what he seems to understand so easily during the reading process contains difficulties when he is asked to make the transfer into his own language and culture:

> I like it when I get to the top of the road and look out and see the mist down over the hills. It's like a wrapped parcel and you know there's something good inside.
>   And I like being funny. When someone says something I like to have something funny to say back, because I like people to laugh, and I like laughing too. A funny man, that's me. 'Man' may not be quite the right word – but 'boy' isn't either. 'Boy' means little kid, 'boy' means dirty with a filthy mind. It means 'smart-arse'. A 'boy' is a servant and a slave. (65)

Translating these lines into his own language, the student will immediately have to make decisions such as how to translate 'funny' . Does he want a word which maintains the connotation of 'strange', or does he want to opt for a neutral term simply to describe someone who likes to laugh a lot? A decision like this forces on the student the realization of how literary language works by association. 'Smart-arse' requires a careful assessment of slang words which belong to the jargon of youth and their degree of coarseness, which in turn will require an assessment of the tone of the story, which is in key with the characterization of the protagonist. Full insight into a dimension of the English language shaped by the fact that Britain was once an empire dominating the world will be provided by the translation problem inherent in the word 'boy'. Students cannot fail to realize the full dimension of this word in English, ranging from 'kid', 'boy', 'smart-arse', 'servant' and 'slave' in the text itself, and to realize that within the context of Patricia Grace's story it is untranslatable. For the ambitious teacher this could serve as a starting-point for a closer look at the historical development of language and the changing meanings of words. The inauspicious word 'boy' will prove to be a most rewarding example for the functioning of a word in different cultural contexts. It will be a natural step to work from the untranslatability of a specific literary sentence or text towards problems of literary translation in general, towards a discovery of the power of literary language and the potential loss of the wealth of associations in a translation. Valuable insight into the functioning of language can be gained through analysis of a text which is both simple and short as well as interesting enough to hold a young reader's attention.

With Jean Rhys's short story 'Let Them Call It Jazz', a rare example among her fictional works in which she seeks to render West Indian English, we are confronted with a different aspect. For teachers of English the legitimate question arises as to whether learners of English as a foreign language should be exposed to a text which deviates from standard language in such an essential element as the third person singular 's', to name but one of several deviations from the norm in non-standard varieties of English in general, and in Jean Rhys's rendering of West Indian English in particular:

I have trouble with my Notting Hill landlord because he ask for a month's rent in advance. He tell me this after I live there since winter, settling up every week without fail. I have no job at the time, and if I give the money he want there's not much left. So I refuse. The man drunk already at that early hour, and he abuse me – all talk, he can't frighten me. (47)

Teachers may think it unwise to expose their students to what they are likely to regard as 'serious mistakes' in their students' work. Yet the confrontation with such a text may provide new insight into what is right and wrong in a language. For advanced students the text could be used for comparison with other non-standard texts which are more daring in their use of the whole range of English, for example from Creole to West Indian standard English. Rhys's attempt to identify a coloured protagonist through isolated deviations from the norm may seem unsatisfactory and may serve as an explanation for her controversial position in West Indian Literature, where as a white writer, despite her sympathetic rendering of West Indians, white or coloured, she is not accepted. The story 'Let Them Call It Jazz' invites a comparison with Joan Riley's description of a young West Indian immigrant in England, who after her return to the Caribbean finally has to discover that she does not belong anywhere anymore. The fate of Joan Riley's heroine in *The Unbelonging* (1985) is that of the author Jean Rhys. Jean Rhys comes from the other side and her fate also was not to belong, an unbelonging which has found its artistic expression in some of her stories and in the novel *Wide Sargasso Sea* (1966), in which the characters experience the cultural heterogeneity of their environment and their own displacement. It may be worth mentioning that the Black British writer Joan Riley is equally hesitant to use West Indian English in anything more than a moderate attempt to characterize her protagonist linguistically and thereby distinguish her from British English speakers. She, too, hesitates to go full length, most likely in order not to reduce her readership unnecessarily to West Indian speakers of English only. Jean Rhys's story 'Let them Call It Jazz', however, is not typical of her work, which generally conforms to standard English. Her careful handling of language in stories such as 'Pioneers, Oh, Pioneers'[3] or 'The Day They Burned the Books' makes her attractive for literature teaching in a language class. Unlike the younger generation of West Indian writers, most of whom come from an ethnically different background, Jean Rhys provides the link with Europe, which makes her works about the Caribbean more readily accessible for learners in the European context of foreign language teaching. Her story 'Let Them Call It Jazz' linguistically raises not only questions of authenticity of language as far as her mild attempts at rendering the West Indian variant is concerned, but also questions of translation, if not of untranslatability in the case of non-standard varieties of English. Within the framework of foreign language teaching, it is a text like this which can both reveal the problems inherent in the translation of non-standard varieties and yet not push this beyond a student's accessibility, as might be the case with works like

Sozaboy: in Rotten English by Ken Saro-Wiwa (1985), in which the language is too far from British/American and even Nigerian standard Englishes for a learner of English to follow.

2.2 Literature in a socio-cultural framework

Apart from linguistic interest, Patricia Grace's story 'Hills' holds another surprise for the reader. Due to her use of language it goes almost unnoticed that the protagonist in the story is Maori. It is small details that attract the sophisticated reader's attention first. The reader familiar with New Zealand might take small signals in the description of family life as a hint. The obvious ethnic placing of the protagonist, however, only occurs towards the end of the story when he is told to 'shut his black face' (68) and when he refrains from contradicting: 'If I pointed out that I was brown it was like denying blackness, like saying you're halfway to white' (68), which takes the reader right into the midst of a discussion of race, minority, and identity – psychological areas of discussion in which students might feel the need to draw parallels to situations in their own country with more or less integrated minorities. A story so far removed from the student's own world might offer a basis for a more honest discussion of discrimination and abuse, as its New Zealand setting provides the necessary emotional distance. This of course is a primarily pedagogical aspect of literature teaching: to aim at a better understanding of oneself and the world through interpreting fiction. This also applies to Jean Rhys's short story. What she has to say about colour prejudice in 'Let Them Call It Jazz', however, is a more drastic and embittered statement about racial prejudice than Patricia Grace's criticism of attitudes in 'Hills'. It amounts to a statement about the treatment of outsiders in general, a recurrent theme in her work.

The study of texts set in a different socio-cultural context to that of the student reader not only opens up insights into different worlds. Its value also lies in the fact that it may help to see problems of one's own life and culture in a different light. Shashi Deshpande's story 'Death of a Child' is a story on the issue of abortion. Within an entirely different social and cultural framework, in which the woman makes her decision against the child, the author works out what this does to a woman who has all rational arguments on her side, who makes a free decision under no pressure from a male coaxing her into it, who is not restricted by the moral code of the Christian belief nor by law. The story reveals areas of discussion which in the Euro-Catholic context usually become blurred by dogmatic issues in this matter.

2.3 Literature as art form

Last but not least, literature in the classroom has its place in the curriculum to develop the student's understanding of an art form. What Alistair Niven deplores as a 'misplaced emphasis'[5] on recent authors is actually the strongest argument for taking up literature from the wider context of the English-speaking world at large. It is the new English literatures in their artistic diversity that can boast of writers whose modes of narration, choice of themes and styles retrace 19th- and 20th-century British and American literary paths in the literature of our time. And there are many writers who take part in recent developments in literature. Many authors write from the most basic impulses to give their experiences shape, to record rapidly vanishing worlds, to shake up their fellow men to fight against injustice, oppression and discrimination, or to draw the world's attention to it. There are those others whose academic and creative careers within the intellectual and artistic set-ups of British and American universities make them reject literary conventions in favour of experimentalism. V. S. Naipaul's road from a Sherwood-Anderson-style *Miguel Street* (1959) to *The Enigma of Arrival* (1987) in the Great Tradition of English novels is as interesting as Salman Rushdie's success, which is unthinkable without Laurence Sterne, James Joyce or Günther Grass. Keri Hulme in her very specific innovativeness also belongs to the second group. These writers will surely play a limited role, if one at all, at school level. However, a story like Kamala Das's 'Running Away from Home' may serve its purpose and suffice to include even this aspect in one's teaching of trends and developments. In a simple form Kamala Das makes use of a stream-of-consciousness technique, conveying the desperate protagonist's futile flight from a humiliating marriage. The text is marked by a total absence of punctuation, reflecting the author's attempt to render the turmoil of feelings, thoughts and fears of the young Indian mother who escapes from her husband only to fall into the hands of a friend of her husband's who seeks to take advantage of her situation and finally, in male solidarity, returns her to him.

3. Widening horizons

When authors go beyond the minimum of a standard variety of English in the form of heavy social or regional dialect or when parts of an English-language text are rendered in another language, the readership of these texts is greatly narrowed. This is also the case with writers as diverse as the early 20th-century Australian writer Barbara Baynton, whose consistent use of the Australian dialect in her novel *Human Toll* (1907) has barred it from general recognition, whereas her short stories in standard English have become minor Australian classics; or Keri Hulme, whose Maori title and lines (without any helpful glossary or translation) leave the European reader uncomprehending or missing certain aspects of the text. Anita Desai's use of German in her novel *Baumgartner's Bombay* (1989) limits accessibility to her work. These authors reduce their readerships to people with an identical background or at least a command of language(s) not to be taken for granted among readers in general. But even in this respect they are in good company. James Joyce is equally unsuitable for classroom teaching when it comes to those works that created his world fame.

Moreover, authors from different cultural backgrounds will inevitably also create works in languages other than English, so that only part of their literary output will reach European readers, unless they are – like many Indian works – translated or transcreated into English. Even without the barrier of a non-European language many of those works will be difficult to approach. The more they are removed from the Western tradition, the more they are likely to find their readers elsewhere.

Teaching the new English literatures, particularly at school-level, inevitably demands selection. Short stories from all over the world offer a vast field for selection for the teaching of English and of literature on all levels. The establishment of the new English literatures as a rival discipline within existent English and American Studies, in both their literary and linguistic dimensions, is an urgently required step to provide future teachers with information, to keep pace with developments on the book market and to acknowledge that other parts of the English-speaking world may have to offer more than many a European scholar is prepared to admit. This is not just what the Caribbean writer Louise Bennett has ironically called 'Colonizin' in reverse'[6] in one of her poems. It is also the reflection of a world drastically becoming smaller, and at the same time of horizons widening, not least in literature.

Notes

1. Corinne Bliss, 'Against the Current: A Conversation with Anita Desai', *Massachusetts Review* (Fall 1988), 521-37; 533.
2. Short stories referred to: Patricia Grace. 'Hills' in *Electric City* (Auckland: Penguin, 1989). Shashi Deshpande. 'The Death of a Child' in *The Legacy and Other Short Stories*. A Writers Workshop Greenbird Book I (Calcutta: P. Lal, 1978). Kamala Das. 'Running away from Home' in *Panorama. An Anthology of Modern Indian Short Stories,* ed. Mulk Raj Anand (New Delhi: Sterling Publishers, 1986). Jean Rhys. 'Let Them Call It Jazz' from her short story collection *Tigers Are Better Looking* (London: André Deutsch, 1968). Page references in the text.
3. In *Sleep It Off, Lady* (London: André Deutsch, 1976).
4. In *Tigers are Better Looking*.
5. 'Shaping the language to the landscape', *Times Literary Supplement* (14-20 Sept. 1990), 991.
6. 'Colonization in Reverse', in *An Anthology of African and Caribbean Writing in English,* ed. John Figueroa (London: Heinemann/Open University, 1982), 255.

Teaching Canadian Literature outside Canada

Coral Ann Howells

Teaching a literature outside its country of origin always involves us in a complex act of literary and cultural translation, and although the main topic of this essay is a description of the Canadian literature course I teach at the University of Reading, England (and which I have taught in changing forms over the past twelve years) I think it is worth reflecting briefly on the challenges and wider implications of such an enterprise – in its practical and theoretical dimensions.

Where does an undergraduate course on 'Contemporary Canadian Women's Fiction in English' fit into a fairly traditional English Literature syllabus which has compulsory units like Shakespeare, Milton, and nineteenth century British literature? As Rudy Wiebe remarked, 'The problem is to make the story'.[1] I would add, 'The problem is to make the story interesting to readers out of another culture'. How do I tell the story of Canada's literary and cultural identity, indeed its changing identities over two hundred years, to British students in the 1990s who may or may not be familiar with the Canadian or North American context? My emphasis will be on cultural difference, though the course (like most courses in English Departments) occludes a significant element, for it omits francophone literature and Quebec's cultural and linguistic differences within officially bilingual Canada.

Then there is the question of the ideological and academic frameworks within which we are teaching Canadian literature, and in Britain these vary considerably. It may be taught within a frame of post-colonial literatures, or within a North American studies context, or more broadly within a period frame of twentieth century writing (as it is in Reading); more subversively, Canadian women's texts are often introduced on women's writing courses or contemporary literature courses. At Reading my unit description for this final year undergraduate option has a double emphasis on national and gender issues. 'What makes Canadian literature Canadian?' directs attention to the distinctiveness of Canadian writing as a national literature which is different from British or American literature (a useful traditional distinction which Atwood made in *Survival* back in 1972.) My aim is to lead students beyond perspectives derived from their study of British literature while still using these familiar reference points to read new texts. (Of course if I were working within an established post-colonial frame of reference as I did when teaching Canadian literature on the new M.A. in Post-Colonial Literatures at the University of Barcelona, I would trace Canadian distinctiveness and points of relationship with a different set of comparators in other post-colonial literatures. However, one works within existing frameworks, at least to begin with.) The element of cultural difference functions as a continuous subtext on the course so that there is always a double perspective, where texts are read both for their individual interest and also as representative of a national literature. The best essay I know for theorising these matters of the representation of Canadian literature is Barbara Godard's 1992 essay 'Canadian? Literary? Theory?' (see Reading Lists for publication details). The interrogatives draw our attention to some of the complexities in this area. There are two sentences which strike me as particularly pertinent: 'Meanings [in texts] are made through the theoretical frames brought to bear on them' and 'The terms "Canadian literature" or "theory" are not embodied in the texts or authors themselves but are invested by institutionalised practices and their narratives of legitimation' (8). Canadian literature is a heterogeneous collection of texts which are being interpreted as an organic body through the theoretical frames we choose to impose. The interesting challenge in studying a contemporary literature is that these frames are being continually modified in response to shifts in cultural politics.

Course description, teaching and assessment methods

The advertised description for my Canadian Women's Writing course reads as follows:

> This unit aims to introduce and explore varieties of anglophone Canadian women's narrative in relation to wider issues of Canadian identity, feminism and post-colonialism. Attention is given to fiction which reflects the shifts over the past twenty years from a white European-centred concept of national identity towards a more decentred multicultural perspective which includes ethnic, immigrant and Native writing. The texts selected for study may vary, but are likely to include work by the following authors: Margaret Laurence, Margaret Atwood, Alice Munro, Aritha van Herk, Carol Shields, Janette Turner Hospital, Kate Pullinger, and Jeanette Armstrong.

The emphasis is on mapping new territory and helping students to understand what is distinctive about women's writing in the contemporary Canadian context. My aim is to direct attention to the political and cultural implications within these texts, working primarily from the texts and using theory more as a critical tool. 'How might women's stories of their struggles for visibility and voice provide parallels with Canada's search for a distinctive identity in resistance to European and American definitions of their nation?' 'How do you position yourself as a British reader of Canadian fiction?' and 'Are there any features which make these novels and short stories different from the fictions you are used to reading?' These are simple questions designed to encourage active student learning in this new area. Teaching for the course is exclusively through seminar discussion, student presentations and essay tutorials, with no formal lectures. There are no final exams; assessment is by essay work which allows students to pursue individually chosen topics and to develop independent research skills. There is also provision to include several sessions with visiting Canadian writers and critics, to which students respond very positively.

But how do students start to engage with Canadian literature? Initially they need some knowledge of Canada's geography, history and cultural traditions as represented in a literature which goes back two hundred years and where women's writing has always been significant in shaping the forms of literary production. I usually begin by giving out a map of Canada and outlining the major signifiers of Canadian difference, focussing on geography and climate and its New World history of European exploration and settlement, myth-making about the wilderness, the prairie and the Arctic North. That colonial history stands in marked contrast to ideological shifts in the contemporary period which they are studying, where the emphasis falls on Canada's policies of multiculturalism and its implications for writing in particular. Most crucially, the newest group to be heard are the voices of Native peoples, although they are the First Nations of Canada. I think it is worth trying to demonstrate that questions of cultural difference are not only broadly national but may also be racial, ethnic, gendered and regional, and that these are the kinds of differences which are increasingly written into the Canadian texts of the 1980s and 90s.

Course content

Though I have sometimes begun this course with a prelude like Susanna Moodie's *Roughing It in the Bush* (1852) or Elizabeth Smart's *By Grand Central Station I Sat Down and Wept* (1945) to underline the significance of pioneer narratives or women's autobiographical fiction, I usually begin with texts by the three major women writers Laurence, Atwood and Munro. These set the parameters for (one version of) the story of contemporary Canadian women's writing. The 1960s saw the development of a new spirit of Canadian cultural nationalism and in the same period the rise of North American 'second wave' feminism. In many ways women's stories parallel the evolving story of Canadian national identity, insisting on the need to decentre national narrative to make room for 'other' voices which have been ignored or treated as exceptional. How do women write in a Canadian space? As Aritha van Herk explained, she writes 'from the region of the West' and

111

'the region of woman',[2] and this metaphorical positioning provides a useful perspective for this course. We are investigating several sites for the speaking/writing female subject: a geographical location, a social location, a gender location, and with some of the writers an explicitly racial location as well. Women write about the same topics as men, e.g. landscape, wilderness, small towns and cities, emotional relationships – but they write from such different perspectives that we could describe women's fiction as offering 'alternative maps' of Canada. Maps have become a favourite metaphor of post-colonial and feminist writing, and in the Canadian context this image is a powerfully persuasive one relating directly to Canada's history of exploration and settlement and the European appropriation of Native lands. 'What matters is mappable' (to quote Aritha van Herk again) and if something is not on a map it does not count as significant. Women's resistance is marked by their 'alternative mappings' – of landscape, history, interior domestic spaces, of things hidden under surfaces waiting to be uncovered (like fragments of the past, secrets and unspeakable items of gossip) and of course women's bodies and emotions which have been wrapped up in clothes and conventional images of femininity. The fictions of Laurence, Atwood and Munro also serve to highlight the fictive representation of women as writers and creative artists, and to introduce topics related to gender and genre.

As the course progresses, the changing range of newer writing offers continual variations on these major thematic lines as well as illustrating the wide variety of narrative forms in contemporary Canadian women's writing, e.g. quest narratives (*Surfacing*, *No Fixed Address*); fictive autobiography (*The Stone Diaries*); history and its revisions (*The Diviners*, *Ana Historic*, *The Last Time I Saw Jane*, *Fall on Your Knees*, Armstrong's story about Coyote 'This Is a Story'); detective thrillers (*Borderline*); Gothic romance and fairytale (*Fall on Your Knees*) (see Reading Lists for publication details). Taken individually and as a group, these texts also show up that peculiar blend of realism and fantasy which characterises so much Canadian postmodern fiction. Female experience in Canada as elsewhere is revealed to be inescapably plural: 'As for Woman, capital W, we got stuck with that for centuries. Eternal woman. But really, "Woman" is the sum total of women. It doesn't exist apart from that, except as an abstracted idea'.[3]

Perhaps the most challenging part of the course are the Native stories, for in order to understand anything about Native writing we need to know something about First Nations history, anthropology, traditions of orality, and contemporary land claims. The subject balloons out as the focus shifts between cultural studies and literature, and there are real difficulties of 'translation' from the conceptual and narrative frameworks of one culture to another. We hear a heteroglossia of Native voices from different regions and Nations. Up till now Native writing has been a kind of supplement at the end of this course, but next time round I think I shall reverse it all and begin with the anthologies by King and Kamboureli. That way students will see first the striking differences within Canadian literature rather than seeking for similarities between that and the things they already know.

Over twelve years the selection of texts for the course has changed remarkably, both in response to the implications of multiculturalism for the story of Canadian identity and to shifts in post-colonial and feminist theory. On a very practical level, the course has also responded to the increasing diversity of Canadian women's fictions being published in Britain, with dozens of new texts advertised every year. (Sadly of course, they do not all stay in print!) The wider the selection of texts the more patterns of interrelatedness students manage to construct, tracing their own maps through a new literary territory so that it becomes familiar to them. To see students responding in very individual ways is one of the delights of teaching a contemporary course like this. Much of the literary canon feels like already well-tilled ground, whereas this topic generates real excitement of exploration and discovery.

Reading lists

Primary Texts
Atwood, Margaret. 1972. *Surfacing*. London: Virago.
Atwood, Margaret. 1993. *The Robber Bride*. London: Virago.
Laurence, Margaret. 1974. *The Diviners*. London: Virago.
Hospital, Janette Turner. 1985. *Borderline*. London: Virago.
Kamboureli, Smaro (ed.). 1996. *Making a Difference: Canadian Multicultural Literature*. Toronto and Oxford: OUP.
King, Thomas (ed.). 1990. *All My Relations: An Anthology of Contemporary Native Prose*. Toronto: McClelland and Stewart.
MacDonald, Ann-Marie. 1996. *Fall on Your Knees*. London: Jonathan Cape.
Marlatt, Daphne. 1981. *Ana Historic*. Toronto: Coach House Press.
Munro, Alice. 1971. *Lives of Girls and Women*. London: King Penguin.
Pullinger, Kate. 1996. *The Last Time I Saw Jane*. London: Phoenix House.
Shields, Carol. 1993. *The Stone Diaries*. London: Fourth Estate.

Background Reading
Canadian Context
Atwood, Margaret and Robert Weaver (eds.). 1986. *The Oxford Book of Canadian Short Stories in English*. Toronto: OUP.
Atwood, Margaret and Robert Weaver (eds.). 1995. *The New Oxford Book of Canadian Short Stories in English*. Toronto and Oxford: OUP.
Atwood, Margaret. 1992. *Conversations*, ed. R. Ingersoll. London: Virago.
Atwood, Margaret. 1972. *Survival*. Toronto: Anansi.
Atwood, Margaret. 1995. *Strange Things: The Malevolent North in Canadian Literature*. Oxford: Clarendon.
Godard, Barbara. 1992. 'Canadian? Literary? Theory?', *Open Letter*, Eighth Series, 3 (Spring 1992), 5-27.
Hancock, Geoff. 1987. *Canadian Writers at Work*. OUP.

Howells, Coral Ann. 1987. *Private and Fictional Words: Canadian Women Novelists of the 1970s and 80s*. London: Methuen.

Huggan, Graham. 1994. *Territorial Disputes: Maps and Mapping Strategies in Contemporary Canadian and Australian Fiction*. Toronto and London: University of Toronto Press.

Hutcheon, Linda. 1988. *The Canadian Postmodern: A Study of Contemporary English Canadian Fiction*. Toronto: OUP.

Keith, W.J. 1985. *Canadian Literature in English*. London: Longman.

LeBihan, Jill. 1996. 'Canadian Literature', in Richard Bradford (ed.), *Introducing Literary Studies*. London, New York, Toronto, Sydney: Prentice Hall/Harvester Wheatsheaf.

Moodie, Susanna. 1986. *Roughing It in the Bush* (1852). London: Virago.

Moses, Daniel David and Terry Goldie (eds.). 1992. *An Anthology of Canadian Native Literature in English*. Toronto: OUP.

Thieme, John (ed.). 1996. *The Arnold Anthology of Post-Colonial Literatures in English*. London, New York, Sydney: Arnold.

Selected Criticism

Cameron, Elspeth. 1991. 'Janette Turner Hospital', in *Profiles in Canadian Literature*, vol. 8. Toronto: Dundurn.

de Papp Carrington, Ildiko. 1989. *Controlling the Uncontrollable: The Fiction of Alice Munro*. De Kalb, Illinois: Northern Illinois University Press.

Chew, Shirley and Lynette Hunter (eds.) 1996. *Borderblur: Poetry and Poetics in Contemporary Canadian Literature*. Edinburgh: Quadriga.

Howells, Coral Ann. 1996. *Margaret Atwood*. London: Macmillan.

New, W.H. (ed.). 1990. *Native Writers and Canadian Writing*. Vancouver: UBC. Note Barbara Godard's essay on Native women's writing, 'The Politics of Representation'.

Nicholson, Colin (ed.). 1990. *Critical Approaches to the Fiction of Margaret Laurence*. London: Macmillan.

Nicholson, Colin (ed.). 1994. *Margaret Atwood: Writing and Subjectivity*. London: Macmillan.

Ross, Catherine Sheldrick. 1992. *Alice Munro: A Double Life*. Toronto: ECW.

York, Lorraine M. (ed.). 1995. *Various Atwoods: Essays on the later Poems, Short Fiction, and Novels*. Toronto: Anansi.

Notes

1. Rudy Wiebe, 'Where Is the Voice Coming From?' (1974). Reprinted in *The Arnold Anthology of Post-Colonial Literatures in English*, ed. J. Thieme (London: Arnold, 1996), 400-406.
2. Aritha van Herk, 'Interview with Dorothy Jones', *Span* 25 (October 1987), 1-15.
3. M. Atwood, *Conversations*, 201.

'Avowels': Notes on Ambivalence and a Post-colonial Pedagogy

Gary Boire

I'm an aversion to the King James Version

– Steel Pulse

This talk is based on a paper given at the ACLALS conference in Kingston, Jamaica.

1. Introduction

I would like to begin by considering some of the more pragmatic antagonists facing us as post-colonial teachers: the problem of gaining access for our courses inside of entrenched programmes (like some of mine) that are addicted to the idea of a sacralized canon; the problem of intellectually fossilized colleagues who feel that not teaching Old Norse is tantamount to moral brain death; and indeed even the tedious and material problems of procuring affordable texts for the post-colonial classroom within the post-Thatcherite university economy.

Is it possible to evolve a post-colonial pedagogy for oneself that works with other post-colonial pedagogics in solidarity? In a revolutionary solidarity within and against the authoritarian reinscriptions of existing academia? After all, this white, bearded, ex-catholic-canadian-newzealander comes at it all from a vastly different space than many of my colleagues in the field of post-colonial studies.

Is it, then, even possible (or desirable) that we might *collectively* evolve a socially effective, polymorphous pedagogy that would negotiate its changes by teaching, not *past* the posts, but through the spaces in between? By teaching *ourselves* and our students, through a critical dialectical enquiry into the questions of agency, how to *post* our various pasts?

Then I wonder: is this idealization of a 'politics' of 'in-betweenedness', simply another liberal notion, another displacement of postmodern ivory-towerism? After all, sitting on postmodern fence-posts is notoriously ineffective politically.

115

What follows is an attempt to address some of these questions. I want to consider the nature of the inseminating canonized pedagogical beast, as well as some possible ways to 'fix' it (in the veterinarian sense of course). My discussion deals in varying ways with the interrelated triad of 'theory', 'pedagogy', and 'politics'. It is divided into three parts: an historical archaeology, a shovel, and a concluding parable.

2. An Archaeology

What interests me most in the first instance is the archaeology of the problems we face as post-colonial pedagogues – the unconscious territory that not only forms the conditions of their possibility, but which unites various antagonisms into a monolithic, hegemonic, and ambivalently monological antagonist. Whatever variety – whatever so-called multiculturalism – my university might boast, it remains, like most essential cultural institutions, a state apparatus which continually re-enacts that original, ambivalent colonial encounter in the production of a constantly renewable workforce.

I'm not talking at this point about the invidious entrenched racism and sexism that contaminates the academy, masquerading behind the bland smile of so-called employment equity. What I am talking about here is the university as a new arena for material colonization of both students and professoriate.

For the professoriate, the university was historically, and is now, a place where people are forced to consume our goods and services, thereby providing us with jobs and money. But, more complexly, as a 'field' of capitalist production, one based on principles of competition, commodification of knowledge, hierarchy, historical periodicity, and the purity of disciplinary categories, my own institution is, by definition, conflictually ambivalent – premised on an archaeology of disavowal. Let me try to clarify this accusation.

Any cultural field, as Pierre Bourdieu reminds us, constitutes a discursive 'space of forces in constant tension and systemic interdependence ... an arena of permanent struggles and conflicts which, ultimately, involve the structure of the field itself'.[1]

In the case of the University, the various personal investments, the multiple cultural, social, patriarchal, governmental, institutional, and departmental configurations that coalesce to form it, also compete amongst themselves within and against it. In a word, these antagonistic, yet symbiotic, discursive forces coalesce to form an ambivalent, inwardly riven, yet outwardly united field, which, in turn, disavows its own ambivalence and political complicities. Inside the multiple folds of this disavowal, it seeks endlessly to reproduce itself while endlessly avoiding a constant potential implosion.

116

The point is that this disavowal of one's own and other's overlapping complicities within an oppressive system leads to what Bourdieu then calls a *habitus* – 'a system of lasting and transposable dispositions to perceive, ratiocinate, evaluate and act which is the incorporated product of socialisation ... of one's integrated social experiences'. 'Each class of social conditions', Bourdieu continues, 'engenders a type of habitus which tends to perpetuate these conditions by functioning as the principle of the generation and structuration of practices and representations' (Bourdieu, glossed in Wacquant *op. cit.* 72).

Within this system, the Pedagogue-as-Magistrate places his or her students (and him or herself) within a syntax of mis-recognized regulated desires: a controlled linearity in which the pedagogue operates within not so much a middle-passage between an author or information and student but rather what Neil Hertz calls 'a dramatic occupation, more or less earned, of the position of authority itself'.[2]

Now what interests me is that the method of perpetuation (and perpetration), of generation and structuration of pedagogical practices and representations, is essentially a semiotic of mis-recognized power relations. As I wandered in each week at Auckland to lecture to a classroom of over 150 students (where teaching became essentially a theatrics of shouting), and as I wander in each week now at Laurier to 'lectorialize' my smaller groups (who keep asking me what I want in their essays), I was (and am still) haunted by one of Michel Foucault's famous vignettes.

This is his famous example of penmanship lessons in the late eighteenth-century. Quoting from la Salle's *Conduite des écoles chrétiennes*, significantly in *Discipline and Punish!*, Foucault describes *how* one was meant to teach students to write (and I quote at length):

> The pupils must always 'hold their bodies erect, somewhat turned and free on the left side, slightly inclined, so that, with the elbow placed on the table, the chin can be rested upon the hand, *unless this were to interfere with the view*. A distance of two fingers must be left between the body and the table. ... The teacher will place the pupils in the posture they should maintain when writing, and will correct it either by sign or otherwise, when they change this position'.[3]

As Foucault quips with uncharacteristic humour, 'Good handwriting ... presupposes a gymnastics – a whole routine whose rigorous code invests the body in its entirety' (152-53).

The student body, as it were, was to be approached as, not only a blank and malleable surface, a body whose productivity was to be increased while its potential for subversive resistance was to be minimalized, but as an automatic mechanism, an object meant to mesh with the objects it manipulates – shades of Marcuse's double alienation! This dynamic, in turn, more interestingly, was to be executed through, on the part of the pedagogue, a conscious erasure of knowledge in the formation of knowledge itself, a kind of imposed 'splitting' to use the language of abuse therapy.

As Foucault theorizes,

> from the master of discipline to him [sic] who is subjected to it the relation is one of signalization: it is a question not of understanding the injunction but of perceiving the signal and reacting to it immediately according to a more or less artificial, prearranged code (166).

Penmanship, in other words, as a type of scribal gymnastics, here functions for me metonymically: disciplinary pedagogy transforms the student-other into the clone recipient of seminal discipline and inseminating minimalism. The student as colony; the student whose name is always Marcel Marceau.

Picked up with relish and serendipitously incorporated into modernist principles of a unified, subject, progressivist ideals, totality, and mastery, this ancient but still persistent pedagogy winds its reptilian way along the smooth contours of an historical *telos*, while it paradoxically inculcates an ahistorical sense of oneself. The mystifying signalizations which Foucault pinpoints not only remove students from a sense of their own historical and cultural particularity (and by extension, their own relativity), it also delusively suggests the trans-historical position of the authoritarian pedagogue. It also then paradoxically inculcates the belief in the possibility of historical mastery: there is one past which one can master if only by becoming a pedagogue.

Within this juridical sense of pedagogical sentencing there is, needless to say, little room for the bad grammar of post-colonial writing. And even less room for the flourishing of a post-colonial 'avowel' – the disruptive de-sentencing of a post-colonial, resistant pedagogy. How, then, can we rearrange, to pilfer from Elean Thomas, this 'last room' of the educational empire?

3. A Shovel

Given the pervasive magnitude of this kind of archaeology, the mere introduction of a few courses in post-colonial writing in today's Canadian universities does little. Given the hegemonic and chameleon-like capabilities of the western university, in fact, a few post-colonial courses, like underfunded programmes in Women's Studies, Gay Studies, Pacific or Maori Studies, or even Cultural Studies, are often merely necessary tokens for the continuation of that university's own mystified liberalism. They form, as it were, the otherness which permits the existence of the official academic self.

How do we, as post-colonialists struggling ourselves with the divisions of gender, class, race, ethnicity, caste, and sexual orientation, avoid a cruel replication of the disciplinary colonial educational encounter, without falling into the bland alternative of merely hip facilitators with a liberal agenda? How can we resolve the problematic of authority within an anti-authoritarian project?

118

One beginning answer was provided by a lapel button popular in Germany during the late eighties; it read: Don't Worry, Be Happy, Smash the State. And in my more oblivious moments I think I would embrace a university that is declassed, dehierarchized, deinstitutionalized, decanonized, derequisiteized, socially and politically autonomized. But then, in my more oblivious moments, I also believe I will go to Heaven, stop worrying, and be happy.

A more realistic answer, I think, is provided in the writings of postmodernist educational theorists like Stanley Aronowitz, Henry A. Giroux, Nelida Pinon, Mas'ud Zavarzadeh, R. Radhakrishnan, and Heather Murray – all of whom draw, in varying degrees, on the empowering theories of Paolo Freire. We must teach our students to read and write. But more importantly, we must teach them why and how we do and why and how *they* should learn to.

Nelida Pinon, especially, provides me, at least, with an initial stepping stone. She argues in inimitable fashion, that

> You must know who is the object and who is the subject of a sentence in order to know if you are the object or subject of history. If you can't control a sentence you don't know how to put yourself into history, to trace your own origin in the country, to vocalize, to use your voice'.[4]

Syntax. History. Traces. Vocalizations. These four terms begin to suggest for me how we might begin to evolve an educationally fruitful, politically active, and theoretically rigorous post-colonial pedagogy.

I think we must address, in the first instance, the delusive dream of Roland Barthes that the seminar in particular – perhaps the most dominant pedagogical form in Canada – is somehow a utopian free space, 'withined' and 'withdrawn', from the real. It is now a cliché to say that the classroom is a classed-room, a space of interstitial struggles and collisions; more important is to acknowledge and address, to avow, that it is also an interstitial *symbolic field* in which, as Pierre Bourdieu and Jean-Claude Passeron have argued, 'both teacher and teaching are already 'receivable' by the students precisely because of the legitimation I already conferred on every pedagogic transmitter by the traditionally and institutionally guaranteed position he occupies in a relation of pedagogic communication' (cited in Murray, *op. cit.,* 195). The classroom as field, as site of symbolic violence.

As Heather Murray has so persuasively argued, we need to deconstruct this violent institutionalized charisma, to evolve an historized pedagogy which avows its own forming configurations. 'A 'conditional' analysis', Murray argues,

> conditional in both senses, as self-reflexive and cognizant of determinants, and as provisional undertaken by both teachers and students, using the classroom, its situation, and its work as one example of the production of literary discourse is ... a first step in teaching and learning theory theoretically. Which is to say, to teach and learn politically (*op. cit.*, 198).

The result of such a self-reflexive 'locating' could be, not a new and unidirectional, reactive monolithic discourse, but a hybridized critical pedagogy which incorporates a meta-critical plurality of (1) theoretical positions; (2) pedagogical methods (the work group, the directed studies course, and, in English at least, the interactions of the seminar); and (3) most crucially, a range of interdisciplinary topics culled from the entire prism of cultural production: the interstitial spaces, not only amongst privates and publics, but amongst film studies, television, journalism, local histories, local arts, music, and political theory, to name but a few.

I'm aware that hybridization can easily transform into an ineffective plurality: as Terry Eagleton has opined, in our postmodernist celebration of multiplicity, we run the powerful risk of simply reduplicating the dividing, commodifying, and regionalizing tactics of capitalism itself. I'm aware that if we risk a postmodernist strategy, as Arun Mukherjee has warned, we also take the risk to rehomogenize and retotalize the multiplicities that are the post-colonial worlds.[5]

But I'm also aware that we currently run the more invidious liberal gauntlet of a self-imposed liberal silence: as a friend in Jamaica remarked, we run the risk of not saying anything about anything at all. How then do we tread between such fine lines of nationalism and internationalism, postmodernism and post-colonialism, appropriation and silence? Consider, if you will, four 'avowels', four operational convictions.

1. To operate with the conviction that a post-colonial theory and practice is not limited to the so-called post-colonial literatures. What this allows is a radical unreading of, in my own case, the entrenched Anglo-American canon within a canonized structure; it allows a pedagogical positionality that recognizes that 'resistance' can be, not solely a univocal oppositionality, a setting up of an alternative canon, but also a guerilla-like series of internal repositionings – repositionings aimed against and within that myth of Canonicity (and its ideological supplements) which sustains authoritarian and institutionalized pedagogical power.

For as R. Radhakrishnan so eloquently puts it,

> not negotiating with the canon can have the disastrous consequence of dehistoricizing the entire revolutionary-pedagogical undertaking. Reading the canon subversively is an effective way to retrieve the past in all its determinate indeterminacy .... the target should be canonicity as algorithm, not just a particular canon as symptom'.[6]

2. To operate with the conviction that to think is to act within a theoretical field. The accusations made against some theorists that theory is an excluding jargon misses the point completely. The counter-argument that such an accusation is itself a theoretical position is obvious. What is not so obvious is that that accusation is proof of the power of an ideology that still divides and educates by insisting on

binarist separations and by occluding or naturalizing the lines of power within the university.

What I operate toward is the conviction that through the embrace of theoretical specificity and theoretical self-reflexivity, we can facilitate ourselves and our students to recognize the interstitiality of, not only so-called 'theoretical discourses', but, more crucially, of all areas of cultural and political production.

3. To operate with the conviction, one shared with Terry Eagleton and Frederic Jameson, that the academy is anything but an ivory tower, but certainly a site of particularized class struggle. The aim of my post-colonializations of the canon and of theory thus involve, not so much an overthrow of established disciplines, genres and pedagogical techniques, but the politicized awareness of their historical configuring power.

4. To operate with the conviction that a post-colonial pedagogy must involve, not *only* the crucial ongoing struggles to introduce new courses, to rewriting curricula, but the evolution of an endlessly evolving pedagogy that increases pleasure as it increases engagement. This would involve both the form and content of our courses.

In terms of the latter, we might still entice our students to read post-colonial works by emphasising their 'distant mirror' qualities, but by a politicized and self-reflexive dialectic with both our own and the texts, discursive archaeologies, we can avoid what Victor Ramraj has so succinctly described as a type of literary tourism. We can avoid the liberal paralysis of exoticization of the different.

In terms of pedagogical 'form', we need not experiment simply with higher percentages for class participation, preannounced examination questions, or a type of pedagogical acrobatics (show and tell). We need to experiment rather with a form of classroom dynamic that involves both professor and student alike as active producers of political/literary knowledge. I think, lest we abnegate our own political responsibility, that we must still contend with the vexed problematic of *marking*, but that mark might well be the result of yet a further dialectical negotiation, rather than an externally imposed *fait accompli*, a tablet delivered from Mt. Sinai.

4. A Concluding Parable

In her brilliant story, 'A young girl-typist ran to Smolny: Notes for a film', the Vancouver writer, Cynthia Flood, describes a poignant moment. A retired and mutilated labourer – he has lost the ends of his fingers in an industrial accident – signs a subscription to a revolutionary magazine. His signature is described as being in 'a clear spiky hand which owes nothing to H.B. McLean'.[7] At this point Flood inserts an explanatory footnote to the name, 'McLean', which reads:

> System of handwriting instruction favoured for many years in Canadian public schools, and designed to pulverize any individuality in students' methods of moving pens across paper. Each lesson begins with [and here Flood quotes from McLean] 'Ready for printing – Desks cleared – printing materials ready (practice paper, pencils, and compendiums on desk). Pupils adopt attitude of attention. ... All pupils should sit in a comfortable, hygienic position'. (74)

For my purposes this text is quintessentially serendipitous. In its mixture of syntaxes, histories, traces, and vocalizations, the scene spells out an instructive parable, a possible new sentence which we might learn to read, write, and teach.

As a type of borderland pedagogue (the term is borrowed from Henry Giroux), this post-colonial professor tries to initiate a type of syntactical disruption, a process of teaching students by teaching myself how to address the questions of agency in a heterodoxical, polyglot, multi-media postmodern world. And in that process I teach/learn the methods by which my students (and I) might create a syntactical rupture: a realization that subjectivity (student and/or professorial) is not the beginning of writing but the consequence of it.

As Henry Giroux and Stanley Aronowitz remark,

> we need to combine the modernist emphasis on the capacity of individuals to use critical reason in addressing public life with a critical postmodernist concern with how we might experience agency in a world constituted in differences unsupported by transcendent phenomena or metaphysical guarantees. (*op. cit.* 117)

Such a new whirled disorder won't change the world. But I do believe, lest I go insane like Gulliver or silent like a good liberal, that it is through such a plan and such 'avoweling' that I can begin, however tentatively and however limitedly, to politicize both myself and my own student body.

Notes

1. Bourdieu, glossed in Loic J. D. Wacquant, 'Symbolic violence and the making of the French agriculturalist: An enquiry into Pierre Bourdieu's sociology', *Australian and New Zealand Journal of Sociology* 23/1 (March 1987), 65-88, 72.
2. Cited in Heather Murray, 'Charisma and authority in literary study and theory study', in Donald Morton and Mas'ud Zavarzadeh (eds.), *Theory/Pedagogy/Politics: Texts for Change* (Urbana and Chicago: University of Illinois Press, 1991), 187-201, 193.
3. La Salle, quoted in Michel Foucault, *Discipline and Punish: The Birth of the Prison*, trans. Alan Sheridan (New York: Random, 1977), 152; my emphasis.
4. Pinon, cited in Stanley Aronowitz and Henry A. Giroux, *Postmodern Education: Politics, Culture, and Social Criticism* (Minneapolis: University of Minnesota Press, 1991), 114.

5. Terry Eagleton, *Ideology: An Introduction* (London: Verso, 1991). Arun Mukherjee, *Towards An Aesthetic of Opposition: Essays on Literature, Criticism, and Cultural Imperialism* (Toronto: Tsar, 1988).
6. R. Radhakrishnan, 'Canonicity and theory: Toward a post-structuralist pedagogy', in Donald Morton and Mas'ud Zavarzadeh (eds.) (*op. cit.*), 112-36, 132.
7. Cynthia Flood, 'A young girl typist ran to Smolny: Notes for a film', in *The Animals in Their Elements* (Vancouver: Talonbooks, 1987), 74.

Strategies for not Teaching Post-colonial Literature: The Better Part of Valor

Norman Simms

He who fights and runs away
Lives to fight another day.

1. Introduction

This is an essay written on the other side of the world. I am in Israel, and why I write it here is part of the story of why I do not teach post-colonial literature. Although I have written many books and articles on the new literatures of the South Pacific, not just the smaller island states but also on Australian Aborigines and New Zealand Maori. I have never taught a course in these literatures, nor do I intend to. A paradox? An expedient? Yes, both, and a complicated issue.

I have not only written scholarly books and articles, book reviews, and reports in this area of literature, I have also spent many years editing journals (*Cave, Outrigger, Pacific Moana Quarterly, Rimu, Matrix,*) and anthologies, working closely with the writers and the would-be writers from countries such as Fiji, Solomon Islands, and Samoa. Yet I choose not to teach courses in this field. Instead, I lecture in medieval and eighteenth-century English Literature, and I have done so in Canada and the United States, in New Zealand and France, and now in Israel. I am neither an anthropologist, sociologist, archaeologist nor any kind of 'ologist'. On occasion I have given scholarly papers and guest lectures on topics related to the colonial and post-colonial literatures of the South Pacific. When I did so I tried to use the skills and knowledge gained from the study of other cultures, ancient or medieval or modern, because I did not think the new literatures required special pleading. But I have not done so for the last several years.

This does not mean I believe these literatures should not be taught in the universities – indeed, they should! But I no longer think I am the one to do it. I didn't always think like this, of course, and to explain the strategies behind my decision, which is a complex one – on the one hand to walk away from the task, and yet to back those who have the qualifications and the energy to do so –requires two kinds of background. For that reason, this little essay will be a personal statement of 'where I stand' by recounting how I got here. I will later explain why I think the task is worthy, and therefore worth doing well or not at all.

It is necessary to explain why I am writing this essay in Israel because the fact that I am sitting here in 1996 is very much to the point – the point being a highly emotive and political one, as anyone may guess, who comes to the task of dealing with an emergent set of literatures and who is not an intimate product of the specific historical and psychological conditions which give rise to that literature. This is, then, my 'positional statement', my reflexive perspective as an outsider, Jew and Israeli, as well as long-time resident of New Zealand.

2. An Israeli Perspective

If I were to say, as I have often had to in my writing, that I cannot see colonialism as an unmitigated disaster, it surely brands me as a reactionary, and now even further taints me, with a position here in Israel. But I cannot see that colonialism is merely something done by one people (the self-proclaimed superior and civilized people) to another (the stigmatized inferiors, primitives, savages, and downtrodden). Colonialism has always been a complicated set of events that happens to all the peoples involved, changing them, and transforming the worlds they live in – the real worlds of physical, economic and military events, as well as the existential or mental world of feelings, learning, and social relations. There is no doubt that conquest, disease, exploitation and even annihilation are brought down unjustly on one side more than on another, but if we take only the model of the worst occurrences then, we unfairly overlook, not just the gallant resistance – sometimes for three or four hundred years – of indigenous peoples, but also their positive, substantial, creative and lasting influence on the course of all subsequent history. For example, Maori culture today is not a simple consequence of the defeat of a helpless people; it has to be seen as a creation out of their own dynamic adaptations and creative spirit in the face of surprising and complex new circumstances which came upon them in the last years of the eighteenth century. These were, furthermore, not events in which an active force entered a static 'classic' situation, but one in which two active and complex societies began to engage one another. For many years, the presence of the alien force was small, haphazard and incoherent, and when it did begin to gain a strategic advantage over the 'other' in the 1860s, it was as much because new technologies, brought into being by the general history of colonialism created European wealth, power, and science, as because the indigenous Maori people were changing themselves, responding in diverse ways to the experiences of half a century of colonialism. To understand what happens would require more than the study of a few specific encounters – often based on violence and trickery, to be sure – on all sides! It would require an understanding of the state of Europe at this time, as well as a scrutiny of the changing and seething flux of ideas as the Age of Enlightenment (no matter how ironic we might eventually want to understand the label) gave way to the French Revolution and the period of Romanticism and organicist science.

I say all this as part of a defense against my being viewed as a latter-day stooge of western imperialism, and before I explain why I have to speak like this when I am in Israel – indeed why I have to be in the Land of Israel to write this essay. Being here makes me more acutely aware of the terms *colonialism, imperialism, conquest, exploitation* than I ever was in twenty-six years in New Zealand. I am able to think of these issues, not dispassionately in some ivory tower, but full of feelings – anxiety and fear, along with hope and pride. I am aware that there are many peoples who claim to be indigenous, victims of colonialism, racism, capitalism, nationalist fanaticism, religious bigotry. There are more than one people, however, who feel dispossessed, alienated, oppressed. I am aware too of double standards and of foreign instigation of anti-social violence.

For me, to see from inside Israel, to take this epistemological position, is to be alert to the conjunction of many languages, ethnic groups, and religions, to be a part of a new old land (as Theodor Herzl said) coming into being, with people from the Third World and from the technologically advanced countries, people who are part of English, Spanish, German, Russian, North African, Asian cultures – all of them pushing and jostling, living and working together, noisily, often rudely, but all part of one enterprise. Yet there are, on the one side, individuals and groups who are militant, religious, nationalistic, and self-righteous; and on the other, people who are humanistic, secular, modern, and intellectual, not to mention a great number who are in-between. All of us, with all our differences, in this babble of tongues and this hodge-podge of backgrounds, can at any moment be blown to smithereens just by riding on a bus, may be stabbed by teenagers in the market, have had our heads cracked open by a mob of stone-throwers, or be shot at by a fanatic driving past in his car. From this perspective, the existential pains concocted by Maori activists sound very hollow. It becomes easier here to come to grips with the concept of assimilation and education and to see that the problems in New Zealand are most amenable to resolution. The radicals who adapt the slogans of alien struggles and who yearn to be part of the dispossessed of the earth cannot create a literature that is anything but shallow and false, while it becomes easier, from this distance, to attend to the nuances of social difference, individual alienation, and ritualized creativity. It is also to appreciate, and put into context, the real struggles of those who wish to generate a literature that expresses new kinds of voices and new kinds of personal and social experiences.

The new literatures of the Pacific Island states are wonderful experiments in nation-building, and each Island state has its own special history of encounter, reception and resistance to the coming of European powers – traders, missionaries, government agents. They cannot be diluted into a single mush and stirred up with ladles carved in other environments. The dynamic, creative richness of prior culture, with its range of diverse custom and tradition, has not all disappeared, and may often be found transformed in ecclesiastical hymns, civic oratory, political discourse, nostalgic yearnings for lost times and places by those who have left, actually or metaphorically. No one should gloss over the pains, the sufferings and the crimes committed, but I see no point in studying the literatures of the post-colonial period without first understanding the rich and complex heritage of the indigenous cultures and the dialectical complexities of colonialism itself. To promote such a literature only as a self-hating rebellion against one's fathers and mothers, a stick with which to break the heads of mythical monsters in far-away lands, a surrogate utopian vision for one's own desiccated sense of family continuity – none of this seemed wise or worthy of my attention, much as I enjoyed, respected and learned from the Pacific Island stories and poems I studied and wrote about.

3. The Old Kiwi Arguments

For a certain period of time the argument against teaching Pacific Island literature in New Zealand was similar to that used to avoid teaching not only Maori literature, but also New Zealand literature in general. This was a great shock to me when I arrived in the country from Canada in 1970, and it seemed to be an attitude that prevailed right into the early 1980s. The argument ran short and sweet: there just isn't enough good New Zealand writing to warrant a full-year course. While there seemed to my colleagues justification for introducing courses in American Literature, even for setting up a program in American Studies, backed by special grants from the US State Department, if New Zealand literature was going to be taught, I was told, it would just be a sampling of novels and poems in the first year introductory course. As in the standard Penguin anthology, the very concept of New Zealand Literature was suspect. The collection began with a few exotic examples of Maori chants and *waiata*, preliminaries to the 'real' writing that would follow with European settlement. Yet an academic compromise was suggested: New Zealand literature could be taught in combination with Australian writers, perhaps in a distribution of three-quarters 'Oz' to one quarter 'Kiwi'. When this course was set up I went in, as an outsider, to teach two or three lectures about Maori literature in English. Both I and the subject were exotic. Efforts to invite the Maori Studies or Maori Language lecturers to participate came to nothing, a result of lethargy, procrastination, and lack of seriousness.

At this time, from about 1970 to 1985, I was busy writing reviews, essays, and books about the new literatures of the Pacific, from New Zealand Maori through the Pacific Islands to Australian Aborigines, and diligently editing journals and compiling anthologies, working with the authors themselves or with collectors in the field. There thus seemed to be a radical disjunction between my academic labors – the teaching of core courses in English Literature – and my active concern with living, creative and human writing and my scholarly interests. My involvement with the new literatures seemed to me part and parcel of theoretical and methodological interests, and the context in which I viewed the new literatures was both a product of my interest in medieval and classical cultures and, more significantly for me, those other literary cultures became clearer and more alive for me because of my intimate work with the Pacific Island writers and literatures. Whether I taught specific courses or not seemed irrelevant and I was not prepared, both for personal and professional reasons, to take on my colleagues over this issue. There was certainly no clamor from the students or the community for new courses.

Yet there came one moment when I attempted to bring matters to a head. This was long before the politically correct and the culturally safe versions of New Zealand society were set forth; near the end of the 1970s there was a vague stirring, and a Winter Series of lectures was set up at Waikato University to explore New Zealand issues. For some reason, I was chosen to speak on literature. What I did seems a bit crazy to me now, but at the time, working so closely with Maori writers, Island editors, and non-establishment kiwi poets, it came out naturally. I stood in front of the audience of colleagues from the university and good citizens of the town and declared that *pakeha* (European) New Zealand writing was a provincial sub-literature or folklore, while Maori literature – written and oral genres (songs, oratory, chants, proverbs, riddles, etc.) – constituted a national literature. Though the situation has changed markedly in the past ten to fifteen years, at the time I spoke I think my argument was at least partly valid, and its terms of reference may still be useful today.

Pakeha novelists, playwrights, poets and essayists, when successful – and they were and still are remarkably, disproportionately so, given the small population base – succeeded as individuals. Their writings did not, however, constitute a coherent body of work with a recognizable set of characteristics, because they were self-conceived as part of British Literature in general, took their points of allusion and reference basically from English writing of the past century and a half, and produced no sense of growth and development. Children in schools were not taught New Zealand authors; no local children's books were available in those seemingly far-off days. Kiwis grew up seeking literary 'touchstones' in a set of writings alien to their immediate social, emotional and geographical environments. There were only a few random bits of what could be called scholarly studies in local authors, and certainly no one was attempting to 'translate' or 'introduce' New Zealand literature to the outside world. In particular, Maori texts – whether written or oral, and again in those days you could count the number of published novelists and poets virtually on the fingers of one hand – were either relegated to textbooks on anthropology or tourist collections.

There were many internationally-known New Zealand writers – Katheryn Mansfield, Janet Frame, Ngaio Marsh, Sylvia Ashton-Warner – but they were not known internationally as New Zealanders. If you check the standard bibliographical listings, as well as the publishers' blurbs, you will see that they were (and often still are) presented as 'English' or in some vague way part of the Commonwealth. That the names that immediately spring to mind now, as then, are women, also says something about the nature of the writings as a whole. The big masculine names in poetry and fiction today were known then, of course, but only in New Zealand. The women, however, being driven literally or metaphorically out of New Zealand (or out of their own names into male *noms de plume* or out of their minds) by its macho pioneering culture, succeeded well in England or America and were anthologized as non-descript modern authors. Success in writing, both in terms of achievement and popularity, did not translate into being part of a consistent literature, and even the small circles of writers who helped each other in hard times, such as John A. Lee or other 1930s authors, was not construed as a creative literary movement.

For these reasons, I said somewhat arrogantly and provocatively to the Waikato audience, the *pakeha* writers were provincial and their writings at best made up a folklore. Provincial writers are not bad writers, but they live and work at a distance from the metropolitan centers where their books are received, evaluated, and given a seal of approval. A folklore is a set of texts which works as a subordinate, disadvantaged collection of cultural statements, subordinate to a prestige body of literature from the metropolitan centers, and disadvantaged by not being propped up by the institutions of official culture – libraries, schools, government subsidies, critical journals, and lively publishing houses.

On the other hand, the second part of my argument was that Maori texts collectively constituted a national literature. Small as were the number of writers and minuscule the amount of published work they produced, nevertheless, these authors were continuous with the living oral tradition of oration, chanting, and storytelling, so that whatever the few Maori novelists or poets said were viewed by the community out of which they emerged as speaking on their behalf – and hence often enough publicly condemned and chastised; while local and overseas readers, small in numbers as they were also, viewed the productions not so much as the individual statements of particular authors as the 'voice' of the Maori people. Each Maori story or song was thus deemed to be in some way or other a 'picture' of the Maori mind, community, or soul. True or not, fair or unfair, this perceived status of Maori writing gave to it a different quality as a body of literature than the works of the successful and not so successful *pakeha* or European authors. No one would ever have said that Janet Frame speaks for the average New Zealander or that Katheryn Mansfield reveals the kiwi spirit!

Needless to say, the audience responded with less than wild enthusiasm. Colleagues in the audience stood up and shouted: 'Fool!' 'Idiot!' and 'Ignorant American!' Later, when the texts of the First Waikato Winter Lecture Series were collected for publication, my contribution was not included.

4. Theoretical Matrix

Behind this talk and in the books I still was to write, there was a belief that the literatures of the Pacific should be seen in a set of theoretical and methodological paradigms that were being developed in the so-called post-modernist movement, a movement which I understood (wrongly, I now concede) as meaning a return to the unanswered questions and unresolved tensions when modernism began in the post-Romantic period of the nineteenth century and which could now be resumed and recast with all the insights of modern anthropology, psychoanalysis, social theory and textual analysis, and that it would be a freeing up of the old positivist boundaries. My books each progressed further and deeper into the disciplines of psychohistory and history of mentalities, and each of them used as points of reference the cultures of the Pacific, using them to test supposedly global theories from Europe or America, and refining and refocusing the insights being generated by deconstructionists, post-structuralists, and new historians. But it became evident, at precisely the same time, when the sparks of interest in New Zealand, Maori and Pacific Literature started to glow, that this was not how the writers or the public or my colleagues at the university wanted to deal with the new literatures. What came as the biggest blow was indeed the realization as I prepared, first *New Writers of the South Pacific*, which was published, and the supplement – twice as long when I last worked on it – which couldn't be published for lack of interest. What was inspiring the new young writers, as well as the older ones, was something quite different from the political agendas my colleagues talked about and which the strident nationalists were proclaiming. The disjunction between what I could see in the literatures and what was being publicly said about them became intolerable. I backed off yet again.

This is the last story I have to tell. In the next few years (1980-1995) there began to emerge a series of new Maori writers, poets and novelists, and even many polemicists, some of them using the cover of anthropology to serve up arguments for Maori sovereignty and pushing towards a delegitimization of European courses and institutions. Alan Duff stands out as one of the most vociferous of these stridently anti-academic authors. However, the rise of Maori consciousness, along with its liberal and then politically correct cohort of followers, has also led to an emergence of Pacific Island writing in New Zealand, and this in turn triggers the publication – though not necessarily the better writing of – Pacific Island novelists, short story writers, playwrights and poets. Once the publication moves from fugitive and shoddy local productions, whether in the islands themselves or in backyard presses in New Zealand, to slick printing jobs, the response of the public is to grant recognition and respect, or at least as much can ever happen in New Zealand. More importantly, the new books begin to be taught in the schools, and eventually in the universities, and there follows from that step an industry of journalistic, critical and scholarly writings, all of which gathers momentum into the appearance of specific courses – and as has been recently set up at the University of Waikato – a School of Maori and Pacific Island Development.

As this process occurred, some kiwi authors, like Michael King, made a public withdrawal, apologizing for their temerity in speaking for the Maori in their previous historical and biographical books. Others, like James Ritchie, proclaim themselves 'bi-cultural', and put all their efforts into serving the Maori cause. Keri Hulme, for many years a television personality, asserts a Maori identity in *the bone people* and takes the necessary anti-intellectual stance, whilst enjoying the fellowships and grants that universities dispense. Significantly, young people – Maori and Pacific Island – begin to grow up in a new atmosphere of ambiguous pluralism called 'bi-culturalism' (them *versus* us), tinted strongly by a guilt-driven pro-Maori culture (or perhaps it is better to say, anti-*pakeha*, anti-colonialist and anti-imperialist version of cultural safety), and feel free to write and publish. These young people then come to the university and demand courses in their own culture, and also ask for teaching in the style that they can understand and which flatters their new nationalist aspirations. Rather than set up courses in the way in which I have suggested earlier, my younger colleagues do their 'thing', a thing which it seems is to teach any courses the students want in the way they want it: the customer is always right. Old fuddy-duddies who believe in academic standards and archaic notions of learning learn to move aside. And Norman Simms makes a strategic move to Israel ... at least for the time being.

Poetic Language and the Construction of Post-coloniality: A New Zealand Example

W.H. New

In the notes that follow, I wish to demonstrate some of the ways in which language in literary practice – I refer to *word choice*, *structural form*, and sometimes *subject* – constructs the political positions of colonial and post-colonial writers. Four New Zealand poems serve as my examples:

1. William Pember Reeves' 'A Colonist in His Garden' (1906),
2. Allen Curnow's 'House and Land' (1941),
3. Hone Tuwhare's 'Not by Wind Ravaged' (1964),
4. Fleur Adcock's 'For a Five-Year-Old' (1967).[1]

All are available in standard New Zealand anthologies. I do not propose to undertake an extended exegesis of the four texts, nor to argue the question of direct 'influence'.[2] Instead, by treating these four poems as a group and observing the variant use they make of images involving landscape, dwelling-place, and gender relationships, I hope to indicate how some particular language choices established the colonial context that post-colonial writers later rejected, and how other choices carry political nuances of a post-colonial kind.

1. Reeves

The overt subject alluded to in Reeves's title, 'A Colonist in His Garden', clearly sets up a colonial paradigm – one that would be easy, though I think misleading, to accept as representational and nothing more. Far from simple, the language in the title already articulates an attitude, an expectation as well as a subject; it is a language of power, functioning to affect gender, possession, and hierarchy. All three of these subtexts become relevant as the poem proceeds.

Structurally, the poem (made up of twenty regular six-line stanzas) divides into two unequal sections: a six-stanza 'letter' which the colonist in New Zealand ostensibly 'reads', and a fourteen-stanza 'spoken' reply to the letter-writer. The letter-writer, still in England, deliberately tries to draw the colonist back to 'England, life and art' – a trio of assumed (rather than argued or articulated) equations between political validity, individual activity, and aesthetic respectability. The letter-writer, an 'Old Friend', does so in part rhetorically, by denigrating New Zealand through false simile and a hyperbole born of a controlled reversal ('Isles nigh as empty as [the] deep,/ Where men but talk of gold and sheep/ And think of sheep and gold'). He does so also by exaggerating the character of political egalitarianism – equating an ostensible absence of 'gulf' or 'height' with a refusal of *artistic* discrimination – and by appealing to nostalgia through a set of conventional tropes. He mentions the flash of a swallow, a 'gust of April', the 'Scents of the garden', a mossy sundial, the colours of an 'orchard wall', the skylark, the yew-tree, golden turf: all of which draw on nature in order to validate history. New Zealand is cast as the world of the 'bold aggressive New'; England, by *preference* to the letter-writer, is depicted as a world where 'age hath virtue' and where 'beauty weds grey Time'. The past in turn is made to validate discrimination; and the letter-writer, in consequence, is heard to dismiss the colony by rejecting it as 'A land without a past', calling it the home of 'a race/ Set in the rut of commonplace'. In this first section of the poem, Reeves seemingly establishes a set of hierarchical assumptions that ask to be questioned, or perhaps even displaced – for in his reply the colonist is going to refuse to return.[3] The refusal, however, does not equate with political resistance. True to its title, the reply instead exemplifies the character of a *colonial* rather than a *post-colonial* reaction.

For when the colonist – 'in his garden' – speaks back to the centre of Empire,[4] he does not question the validity of the letter-writer's tropes, but instead tries to ratify his own position by demonstrating how the terms that express Imperial approval can be re-located in the colony. By such a process the colony becomes 'acceptable' to him – and to the degree that the process reconstructs England, the colony can conceive of itself as sophisticated. Admittedly the colonist does dispute the question of time: time is not uniformly beneficent, he sees, and he argues both that the 'charming' garden of the past is not necessarily the reality of the English present, and that, while age might burnish one's perceptions of customs and buildings, it makes *people* 'wrinkled ... and grey-haired' and does not consequently or concomitantly give them aesthetic value. But when the colonist goes on to deal with the tropes of nature and history, his unquestioned involvement in colonial rhetoric becomes apparent. He claims a history, for example, by referring to *his own experience* in the colony: history is all of 'forty years' long, and it records the *contrast* between the world as it used to be (as his own memory reconstructs it) and the world as it now is after colonists have 'fought' and altered it. Collectively, the colonists have claimed 'vistas', transformed the 'desert' or the 'bare plain' into a garden, introduced 'skylarks' and 'English blackbirds' into the 'mute' skies, planted poplars, birches, oaks, and 'English turf', and turned the 'pastoral miles' to economic purpose.[5]

The subtexts are clear. They tell of military opposition as the assumed 'natural' posture towards the earth; they equate non-European nature with wilderness, to be erased or tamed; they are insensitive to alternatives (the misleading absolute 'mute', for example, tells about a failure to hear more than it confirms a lack of speech or sound); and they ignore the presence of the native peoples (that the place is inhabited by *no-one* – 'Nor man, nor beast, nor tree' – is a presumption more than an observation), *constructing absences* in order to justify occupation.[6] Women, moreover, are essentially absorbed into this construction.[7] Fighting nature is cast as a *manly* activity, as is social planning, for out of his own experience, generalized into that of the entire colony, the colonist designs his actions as those of a 'rough architect of State'. It is 'We men' who 'take root', facing 'the blast'. The metaphor is instructive; from planting the garden, such men become *one with* the garden itself, using their (Adamic) Englishness in other words to establish authority and hierarchy. Beasts and trees are tamed; the Maori are ignored; women, like lands, are made possessions. When the colonist's daughter appears in the final stanza of the poem, she is characterized both as 'The lady of my close' and as a sweet 'English rose'. The rhyme emphasizes the link between gender and private property, and because it is the concluding rhyme of the poem, it also establishes this link as the colonist's most telling declaration of 'natural' order. The diction, too, reiterates the colonial desire to reposition Imperial sensibilities rather than fundamentally change them. 'England' remains the arbiter of order here, and 'English' a category of taste. One generation's 'order', however, is another's problem. While it would be pointless to castigate Reeves's colonist for not being more far-sighted, it is possible to see how the poem's structure and diction encode the social attitudes that 'post-colonial' writings would dispute and attempt to address.

2. Curnow

Insofar as Allen Curnow's 'House and Land' depicts the site of an 'original homestead' – complete with a resident owner, 'old Miss Wilson', who has nominally taken over after the death of her father – it seems to take up directly the issues that Reeves's poem raises. (Numerous students in my classes have suggested that Miss Wilson 'is the colonist's daughter'; their ironic observation does not blindly assume that Curnow is writing directly about Reeves's character, but addresses rather the tenor of the social attitudes that the two poems, read in tandem, reveal.) Old Miss Wilson is completely bound by her father's perspective – with her pictures, her British lineage, her silver teapot, and her imported name ('The Hall') for the place where the family perhaps once lived. She sees not directly but through seeming similarity and relationship; new people remind her of old family members, suggesting that she has no capacity to estimate difference. She is bound by simile, by likeness; she can attribute value only in accordance with the terms of her own training. And when she speaks of the land around her as once being 'all father's',[8] the phrase indicates not only that she accepts his version of possession but also that colonial attitudes persist unquestioned through the next generation. For her, the father remains essentially still alive.[9]

The same holds true, though in more indirect ways, for the other figures in the poem as well: the historian, whose initial enquiry ('Wasn't this the site.../ Of the original homestead') betrays a faith in origins and a desire for empirical confirmation; the cowman, whose laconic and vernacular dissatisfaction reads more as a resistance to the idea of a female employer than as a rejection of colonial hierarchies; the rabbiter, whose marginal appearance is communicated in a single couplet that echoes the diction and rhythms of Robert Louis Stevenson's 'Requiem';[10] and the poet, whose far-from-neutral conclusion (that a 'great gloom/ Stands in a land of settlers/ With never a soul at home') resonates with the dilemmas of colonial discourse. 'Home' (a term pointedly omitted from the poem's title) remains elsewhere, identified still with the Old Country apparently; and 'soul' (left undefined) remains as a consequence perhaps beyond reach.

But it would be misleading to treat 'House and Land' as though it were merely reiterating Reeves's colonial garden. Several differences derive from Curnow's handling of diction. I have argued elsewhere[11] that an interpretation of Curnow's poem has to take *voice* into account, the point being that aural variation in speech sound within the poem at once articulates the social hierarchies that colonial experience designed, and pierces the illusion of egalitarianism that many citizens of the new *nation* of New Zealand, by the middle of the twentieth century, had embraced as a social given, as a factual characteristic of their culture. Miss Wilson's accent is trained to a British standard;[12] the cowman's is geared to local example rather than trained by imported copybook; the historian's is governed by the assumed objectivity of academic generalization (when the cowman bluntly *announces* that he's going to leave the farm because it's 'too bloody quiet', the historian *writes* that 'The spirit of exile ... / Is strong in the people still'). The voice of the poet-within-the-poem makes use of these other three accents[13] – acknowledging the more-than-merely-nominal difference between the verbal *illusion* of Miss Wilson's reference to 'The Hall' and the empirical *fact* of her own farm's 'privy' and 'fowlhouse'. But this poet nevertheless stands apart from all of them, unable to reconcile the multiplicity of voices he knows how to sound. The female voice is clearly marginalized by irony. None of the voices, moreover, appears to be Maori. A society might exist in this land, but if the poet in the poem is to be believed it is a society burdened rather than served by the disparities born of a settler culture. Hierarchies of class, gender, race, and language all intervene between self-conceptualization and community.

Curnow, nonetheless – who must be distinguished from the separate 'poet' voice in the poem – has constructed a single text (i.e., the irregularly stanzaic poem called 'House and Land') out of the voices competing for social (and perhaps literary) primacy within this cultural and temporal frame. In doing so, he has begun to question the authoritativeness of a single register of speech. Where Reeves's poem simply borrowed, or re-placed, the Empire's diction – reinstating and reinforcing the political assumptions that went along with it – Curnow's poem opens diction up to enquiry. Clearly not all the forms of enquiry *within* the poem displace the colonial state of mind, least of all the historian's questions, with their tacit faith in answers, conclusions, evidence, and closure. But the recognition and articulation of disparities in the culture – disparities embedded within the highly-troped configurations of 'house' and 'land' – marks an intellectual departure from the passive occupation of colonial territory, whether this territory is claimed as space or conceptualized as words.

3. Tuwhare

To turn to Hone Tuwhare's 'Not by Wind Ravaged' is to see how a modern poem by a Maori writer deals with the impact of European settler history upon the land and upon Maori culture,[14] and how it also uses the tropes of language, nature, and 'house'. Here, however, the tropes serve not to reiterate settler history but to subvert it. In thirty-one lines, divided irregularly into four sections, the poem takes up traditional Maori poetic forms, specifically the lament. First it laments the 'Deep scarred' landscape – which (as the title says) is 'not by wind ravaged', nor by 'the brawling stream', but (inferentially) scarred instead by the European occupation. The Europeans, or *pakeha*, because they did not respect the land as it was, 'stripped' it 'of all save the brief finery/ of gorse and broom'. Although such an act produced the equivalent of the colonist's garden and Miss Wilson's vista, it attacked in the process not just at an empirical external 'wilderness' but at the basis of the value system of the culture in place. This sense of the loss of culture is intensified when the speaker in Tuwhare's poem, the one who cries the lament, equates the apparent disappearance of his community and a community voice with the ravaged land. He is divided from nature both by his lack of a traditional greenstone ritual 'offering' to give the land and by his 'bitterness', which denies him emotional rest. When the poetic lament goes on to praise nature for its compassionate capacity to forgive – to 'embrace/ those who know no feeling other/ than greed' – the speaker seems to find some satisfaction, but it is

136

short-lived; the satisfaction induces further lamentation because the need to deal with the period of greedy occupation has been a powerfully burdensome intrusion into 'natural' process. The speaker realizes that even the greedy will eventually turn to dust, and that 'the dust of avaricious men' will ultimately 'succour exquisite blooms'. But in the meantime, the ravaging persists and the silenced culture struggles to come to terms with its own loss.

Yet there is a careful paradox drawn here. The silencing exists only to the degree that the European coding of the culture is accepted as the frame or the norm. If that coding can be rejected, then a prior voice can be reclaimed: hence this poem adopts a very particular verbal strategy, combining the transplanted English with a traditional local form. The displaced culture has thus to displace the colonized attitude, to subvert the language of Empire in order to reclaim place and the value system encoded in place. Deliberately, therefore, Tuwhare's poem interrupts 'standard' English with 'standard' Maori; it invokes the land using a Maori vocabulary, restating the value of a 'natural' connection with the world even while lamenting the history of loss. 'O voiceless land, let me echo your desolation', Tuwhare intones; 'The mana of my house has fled,/ the marae is but a paddock of thistle'. If the *marae* – the community with its shared value system – has been overwhelmed, the poem argues, this has happened because the place has been overrun not just by the imported plant (the 'thistle') but also by the imported word ('paddock'), which in this case clears and encloses landscape and at the same time rearranges social relationships and power. If the 'mana of the house' has fled, likewise, its spirit or soul is lost; no-one is any longer at home. The terms of the poem neither deny the effects of history nor argue for a naive recidivism. But to rearticulate the Maori terminology is in part to reclaim a 'natural history' of speech in the land, disputing the hierarchies of *colonial power relations* by disputing the discourse that imposed them.

4. Adcock

Fleur Adcock's 'For a Five-Year-Old' adds an important commentary on this series of poems, for it probes the way attitudes are constructed – constructed in language and in behaviour – and how they are thus communicated from generation to generation. The central speaker is, moreover, a woman, and this recentring of a female voice declares the possibility of a different kind of paradigm or control being communicated to the future. The colonist in Reeves's garden declared his daughter to be both English and a possession; Curnow's Miss Wilson operates inadequately in the present, governed by the past but not in control of the metaphorical estate her father planned; Tuwhare's speaker laments being cut off from the inheritance he deems more natural than the ravaged land he has been offered in its place. In Adcock's brief lyric, the speaker, or meditating voice, is the mother of a young child.

In the child's room one morning, early, after a rain, she quietly encourages the girl or boy (the gender of the child is kept carefully non-specific) to carry a snail outdoors, gently and caringly, so that it might 'eat a daffodil'. The mother realizes that her own gentleness is a mask, and that in other circumstances she has 'trapped mice and shot wild birds,/ ... drowned your kittens, ... betrayed/ Your closest relatives, and ... purveyed/ The harshest kind of truth to many another'. And yet the gentleness in these particular circumstances seems a necessary mask rather than a despicable hypocrisy, a desire in fact for the betterment of the next generation: 'I see ... that a kind of faith prevails:/ Your gentleness is moulded still by words/ From me ...'. That the gentleness is not absolute is important to the woman, but not (or not yet) to the child; the only (momentary) absolute is the fact of the relationship between them: 'that is how things are: I am your mother,/ And we are kind to snails'.

The pronoun shifts that are apparent in these closing lines emphasize the difference between individual fact and communal desire. It is the singular 'I' who explains, sees, traps, betrays, and purveys in the poem, repeatedly asserting self; but she also identifies with her child, and (because she is unable to forget or forgo her role as mother) she takes up the collective identity 'we' in order to encourage greater kindness in another. Not without chagrin, she recognizes the inconsistency of the present state: 'But that is how things are'. The collectivity, however, emphasizes the possibility of something better. Moreover, within this house, accommodating nature even ambivalently, she comes to understand the power that her own words have with her child; using them to mould gentleness, she frees the child potentially into something different from herself, allows the future to be better than historical precedent might suggest is likely. Articulating a female presence in the house, in other words, declares an alternative reality to that which has been previously accepted as normative and unassailable. The ambivalence towards nature might suggest that the alternative is not guaranteed to be effective, though the consciousness about the ambivalence might suggest a greater self-awareness, a more realistic assessment of limitations, than that represented by colonial claims upon exclusive authority. Over the course of time, history showed colonial claims to be mere mimicry; this mother's conscious masking, by contrast, paradoxically leaves mimicry behind.

This arrangement of poems obviously distorts a linear notion of literary history; it also constructs its own form of context by structuring the reading of particular tropes, those of garden (or nature), house (or community), and gender (or 'naturalized' role). This focus, however, can function to demonstrate how the resonances of a particular language – a particular set of tropes – can reveal overt or covert political attitudes. In these New Zealand examples, it is clear that Reeves's image of the garden, ostensibly setting up a more or less Edenic ideal, could not be sustained. Because it had depended on various forms of exclusion (based on race, gender, property control or boundary), it was a controlled version of the perfect, an illusion limited by the fact that, whatever else, *authority* was not being 'perfectly' shared. When, in various ways, later twentieth-century New Zealand poets chose to reject the colonial status that such an illusion constructed for them, they had to find ways to redefine the terms that implicitly had made them marginal. Curnow's balanced experiment with multiple registers of speech, Tuwhare's deliberate placing of high-powered Maori terms, Adcock's re-centring of a female voice: all are strategies of resisting the univocal authority of empire or the mimic authority of the colonist's position. Within each poem, the margins are separately defined: class being the social marker in Curnow's work, race and gender being the respective markers in the works by Tuwhare and Adcock. Clearly these definitions *do not construct uniform versions of 'colony'* – or of 'post-colonial'. All three of these later poems do, however, question the kind of society that is created, even in the name of the perfect garden, by cultural violence, the kind of society handed on – in the form of rules or roles, through paradigms of acceptable behaviour – from generation to generation. All three use tonal variation as one of the structural features through which language interrogates received authority. And though none of the three modern poems asserts an unqualified faith in change, all demonstrate, by the way they write back against the paradigms of colonial limitation, an uncompromising desire to take apart and reconfigure the empire's house of words.

Notes

1. Reeves's poem was first collected in his selection of previously published verse, *The Passing of the Forest and other poems* (London: printed privately for the author by Allen & Unwin, 1925), but it first appeared in *New Zealand Verse*, an anthology edited by W.F. Alexander and A.E. Currie (London, Felling-on-Tyne, and New York: Walter Scott Publishing Co., 1906; rev. ed., Auckland: Whitcombe & Tombs, 1926); 22-26. Curnow's poem appeared in *Island and Time* (Christchurch: Caxton, 1941); 20-21; Tuwhare's in *No Ordinary Sun* (Auckland: Blackwood & Janet Paul, 1964); 20; Adcock's in *Tigers* (London: Oxford, 1967); 1. The following editions are currently available: William Pember Reeves, 'A Colonist in His Garden', in Allen Curnow, ed., *The Penguin Book of New Zealand Verse* (Harmondsworth: Penguin, 1960), 98-101. Allen Curnow, 'House and Land', in *Collected Poems 1933-1973* (Wellington: Reed, 1974), 91-2. Hone Tuwhare, 'Not by Wind Ravaged', in *Selected Poems* (Dunedin: John McIndoe, 1980), 21. Fleur Adcock,'For a Five-Year-Old', in *Selected Poems* (Oxford & Auckland: Oxford University Press, 1983), 8.
2. As Curnow and Adcock are both anthologists of New Zealand poetry as well as poets in their own right, they are clearly familiar with each other's work. In his *The Penguin Book*

of New Zealand Verse (Harmondsworth: Penguin, 1960), Curnow collected both Reeves's 'A Colonist in His Garden' (98-101) and his own 'House and Land' (201-02), though this version of 'House and Land' is missing the fourth stanza of the original. So is the version printed (153-54) in Robert Chapman and Jonathan Bennett's ed., *An Anthology of New Zealand Verse* (London & Wellington: Oxford, 1956), a collection that also includes 'A Colonist in His Garden' (33-37). Adcock's *The Oxford Book of Contemporary New Zealand Poetry* (Auckland: Oxford, 1982) includes poems by both Curnow and Tuwhare, though neither of the two lyrics I refer to here, and none of her own. Vincent O'Sullivan's *An Anthology of Twentieth-Century New Zealand Poetry*, 3rd ed. (Auckland: Oxford, 1987), includes Curnow's 'House and Land' (complete, 87-8), Tuwhare's 'Not by Wind Ravaged' (179-80), and Adcock's 'For a Five-Year-Old' (294), but not the poem by Reeves.

3. Reeves himself, instructively, returned to England permanently in 1896, two years before publishing *New Zealand, and Other Poems* (London: Grant Richards, 1898) and ten years before publishing 'A Colonist in His Garden'; whether this disparity between the colonist's choice and his own indicates some regret at having returned to the 'ravage Time hath made' in the home country, or a simple sentimentality about a New Zealand seen from afar, is open to interpretation.

4. On theoretical aspects of this question, see Bill Ashcroft, Gareth Griffiths, and Helen Tiffin, *The Empire Writes Back* (London: Routledge, 1989); Homi Bhabha, ed., *Nation and Narration* (London: Routledge, 1990); Ian Adam and Helen Tiffin, eds., *Past the Last Post: Theorizing Post-Colonialism and Post-Modernism* (Calgary: University of Calgary Press, 1990); and the Post-Colonialism and Postmodernism issue of *WLWE*, 30:2 (Autumn 1990).

5. The sentimental but acutely imperial image of the English garden occurs in other colonial literatures as well, as the following passage, set in India, from *The Simple Adventures of a Memsahib* (1893; rpt. Ottawa: Tecumseh, 1986): 165-66, by the Canadian writer Sara Jeannette Duncan, illustrates:

> As to the garden, there was not a tropical seed in it, they were all English flowers, which made the mallie's excellent understanding with them more remarkable, for they spoke a different language. It was not much of a garden, there was absolutely no order or arrangement – it would have worried me – but the Brownes planted a vast amount of interest and affection and expectation in it; and it all grew. There were ... nasturtiums..., phloxes..., pansies too, and pinks, and not a quiet corner but was fragrant with mignonette. A row of sunflowers tilted tall against the side of the house, and they actually had ... balsams and daisies. Violets too – violets in exile, violets in pots.... To some of us, you know, England at last becomes a place where one dies daily of bronchitis...; but this never happens if every cold weather one plants one's self round about with English flowers. They preserve the remnant of grace which is left in the Anglo-Indian soul, and keep it homesick, which is its one chance of salvation. Young Browne seldom said anything cynical in the garden, and as for Helen.... She could always go down and talk of home to her friends in the flower-beds, who were so steadfastly gay, and tell them, as she often did, how brave and true it was of them to come so far from England, forgetting, perhaps, that from a climatic point of view nasturtiums like heathendom.

The ironic voice shows the aging English narrator to be *aware*, here, of the presumptuousness that lies at the heart of the memsahibs' collective attitude to botany, but the passage nevertheless reiterates the colonial trope by which the *transplanting* of 'home' effectively reconstructs behaviour.

6. For further reading on this subject, see, e.g., Eric R. Wolf, *Europe and the People without History* (Berkeley: University of California Press, 1982); Francis Barker *et al.*, eds., *Literature, Politics and Theory* (London and New York: Methuen, 1986); and *Cultural Critique*, 6 (Spring 1987).

7. For related comments on 'territoriality and woman', see Gayatri Chakravorty Spivak, *In Other Worlds: Essays on Cultural Politics* (New York and London: Routledge, 1988), especially 77-92, 103-17, 197-221.

8. This phrase, from stanza four (*Island and Time*, 20), is missing from the Penguin anthology version. The complete poems does, however, reappear in Curnow's *Selected Poems* (Auckland: Penguin, 1982): 39-40.

9. Cf. Katherine Mansfield's 1921 short story, 'The Daughters of the Late Colonel', *The Stories of Katherine Mansfield*, ed. Antony Alpers (Auckland: Oxford, 1984): 386-402.

10. See Robert Louis Stevenson, *Collected Poems*, ed. Janet Adam Smith (1950; 2nd ed. London: Rupert Hart-Davis, 1971): 130. Curnow's rabbiter is 'home from the hill,' just as Stevenson's 'hunter' is, while 'Home is the sailor, home from the sea'. The word 'home' in 'Requiem' – although in this particular instance it alludes primarily to Stevenson's own impending death – also speaks of physical and mental exile.

11. See 'New Language, New World', in C.D. Narasimhaiah, ed., *Awakened Conscience* (New Delhi: Sterling, 1978): 360-77.

12. Cf. the accepted accent of the Christchurch district of Fendalton, approved by Dame Ngaio Marsh, the New Zealand mystery writer, in 'It's Not What We Say ...', *New Zealand Listener* (14 October 1978): 23. MacD. P. Jackson also quotes an apposite comment from Maurice Gee's 1978 novel *Plumb*: "'I walked along by the creek or stream – Edie in the Englishness imposed on her by her mother would have it stream, would have the paddock field, would even have the ti-tree picnic hut Robert built on the lawn a summer-house. She never adjusted to colonial ways.'" See 'Poetry: Beginnings to 1945' in Terry Sturm, ed., *The Oxford History of New Zealand Literature in English* (Auckland: Oxford, 1991), 342; this chapter, and the one following ('Poetry 1945-90' by Elizabeth Caffin), refer in some detail to Curnow and Reeves, in more general terms to Tuwhare, and in passing to Adcock.

13. I.e., those of the historian, the cowman, and Miss Wilson; the rabbiter is silent, or silenced (perhaps Maori?) – parenthetical to the speech acts of the others though contructed in and by the words of the poet.

14. For introductory comments on the Maori cultural influence in New Zealand, and for essays on settler culture, New Zealand speech, women's roles, the egalitarian myth, and other subjects, see *Culture and Identity in New Zealand*, ed. David Novitz and Bill Willmott (Wellington: GP Books, 1989).

Teaching Pacific Literature

Paul Sharrad

1. The field

In the past (and still in some places), Pacific Literature has been taught as the writing of western travellers and sojourners about the islands of Oceania. My argument is that this perpetuates colonialist views of the world and erases indigenous cultures that predated white contact in oral literature and continued as evolving mixtures of tradition and print culture into English (and French) writing, achieving its major output during the decolonising era of the seventies. However, there is a place for brief exposure to colonialist writing (I use Ballantyne's *The Coral Island*), if only to understand what it was that Albert Wendt and others were writing to counter.

Depending on one's focus and the availability or lack of other more specific courses, Aboriginal and Maori writing can be included, though both are concentrated primarily within the cultural politics of their respective nations and the former has not had the Oceanic outlook that links Maori to other Polynesian groups. Less justified, in my opinion, is the occasional discussion of Southeast Asian writing under a Pacific label, although a case could be made for including Philippine literature, since the writing in English at least is a product of some of the same cultural and historical dynamics (missionising, World War Two) as those affecting Micronesia, PNG and Hawai'i.

For various reasons (origins in British-sourced education and publishing systems, and in departments of English Literature), Pacific Literature has been constructed mainly around the anglophone South West of Oceania (predominantly represented by the journal *Mana* and Albert Wendt's two anthologies, *Lali* and *Nuanua*). However, there is significant work in English in Hawai'i (collected in the long-running journal *Bamboo Ridge*, for instance), and a growing output in recent times from Micronesia (*Storyboard* is a relatively new journal from the University of Guam). To be completely comprehensive, however, a course should include some reference to writing in indigenous languages and pidgins, as well as to francophone, Kanak and Maohi works from New Caledonia and French Polynesia. The difference here, resulting from the different political conditions, serves to underline the fact that the whole field has its origins first in colonialism and then in nationalist struggles to break with the political past while retaining ties to cultural tradition.

2. History and issues

It is crucial to give students some idea of both the richness and different communicative mode of oral/performative culture as a basis for discussion of the transition to 'literature' that followed Pacific contact with Europeans. Tapes and videos are useful here. The politics of 'reducing' such traditions to writing (whole cosmologies to 'fairy tales'; solemn rituals of social bonding to tourist entertainments) can be a point for discussion and a basis for understanding of the continuing importance of theatre and the small written literary output from island communities where (vernacular) word-of-mouth remains a viable means of communication. (Early written texts were often letters from the increasingly peripatetic islanders to folk back home, as in the missionary letters of Ta'unga from New Caledonia to his base in the Cook Islands, or in contemporary form, the letters to emigrant workers in New Zealand from a Niue family in John Pule's novel, *The Shark that Ate the Sun*.) Exposure to oral texts like the Hawai'ian *Kumu li po* creation chant-genealogy or to the Maori *waiata* also helps student to appreciate some of the aesthetics of print texts which carry or contrive to preserve the collective immediacy of oral address. The difficulty with teaching traditional material outside of its immediate context is in avoiding exoticising it: works that show the continued resonance of tradition in contemporary life are Epeli Hau'ofa's poem 'Blood in the Kava Bowl', the film of Aibert Wendt's *Flying Fox in a Freedom Tree* and Patricia Grace's novel, *Potiki*.

Pacific literature (as opposed to 'letters') has its beginnings in the spread of the school system after World War Two as part of a general move towards decolonisation. Notably in the educational hubs of Suva and Port Moresby (and Honolulu, though the political impetus was not there), a sixties generation being groomed for national leadership with examples from Africa and the Civil Rights movement began to grapple with the task of expressing cultural identity in modern terms. Creative writing was one vehicle for this process. It bypassed the language of polite mission schooling and colonial bureaucracy, even though it was in the English language used by both and tended to retain their stilted style. A 'Third World' consciousness encompassed radical rage against discrimination and cultural assimilation along with a sense of alienation borrowing the language of French existentialism (John Kasaipwalova, Grace Molisa and Albert Leomala exemplify the former, while Russell Soaba, Subramani and Albert Wendt show signs of the latter tendency; Ruperake Petaia's poem 'Kidnapped' blends both aspects in a fine irony showing the centrality of schooling to all this).

The seventies was the decade in which Pacific Literature achieved international notice and the kind of 'critical mass' that enabled courses to be set up. Major works like Albert Maori Kiki's autobiography *Ten Thousand Years in a Lifetime*, Vincent Eri's novel *The Crocodile,* Subramani's short stories, Albert Wendt's poem sequence *Inside us the Dead* and his novel *Sons for the Return Home*, plus first collections from Witi Ihimaera and Patricia Grace and the founding of local writers' groups in Hawai'i all date from this period. All of these works principally deal with identity – asserting a local viable culture and politics in opposition to colonial impositions, exploring a new combination of tradition and modernity, locating the place of the writer in the emerging national collectivity, finding a style and function for English other than its official government or mission status. After independence (or arrival at some degree of visibility within the state, as with Maori issues or 'local' writing in Hawai'i), the trend was away from anti-colonial protest towards critiques of globalization and continued economic and cultural dependency, while the tensions and crossings between tradition and modernity continued as a key theme. In more recent times work has emerged by and focussing on migrant groups in Pacific metropoles, and by women championing cultural identity while questioning the macho bias of tradition. There has also been a revival of vernacular language in some parts of the Pacific that has resulted in parallel text work (Pesi Fonua in Tonga, Kauraka in the Cook Islands and publishing in New Zealand, for instance). This historical model is a fluid one, since Samoa gained political independence in the sixties before the main period of anti-colonial expression, and Micronesia, only recently attaining political self determination, has been producing 'national pride' poems typical of the seventies elsewhere.

Indeed, one of the challenges of teaching a regional literary course is to attend to the specific differences of each literary production while maintaining a sense of the coherence of the field as a whole. In the context of literary history this can easily lead to the patronising of a 'young' literature by the application of critical standards inappropriate to its stage of production as well as by comparisons that imply an external model of 'maturity'. We can talk of the heteroglossic PNG story that mixes folklore and writerly craft as equivalent to the place and operations of Chaucer within the history of British literature perhaps, but that should not suggest that PNG writing's development follows the same evolutionary process or imply that what we have is some primitive form which will grow to become the same refined product as the nineteenth-century novel of England. This issue arises, of course, once we concentrate on writing in English rather than pidgin/bislama or indigenous languages. Similarly, while noting the shorter and more violent history of black-white contact in Vanuatu and the more fluid social structures, we should beware of reinstating the stereotypic differences between Melanesia and Polynesia featured in much colonialist writing. Part of the growth of literature in Oceania has been a quest for indigenous forms and styles and for local critical values. Again,

144

while it is vital to establish the difference between a new post-colonial field and the European tradition from which it initially works to liberate itself, it is necessary to avoid a reductive model of cultural identity that fixes insider readers into a limited range of expression or makes the material an exercise in anthropology for the outsider.

For various reasons, Pacific literary production has tended to be a series of 'one-offs' – small-press pamphlet publications for classroom use, occasional poems or stories appearing in a journal during someone's university education. Literary output has blossomed in those areas where some kind of community of writers and readers could be maintained in contact with a printing facility. Key figures in building a literary culture have been Ulli Beier at the University of Papua New Guinea, Marjorie Crocombe and Albert Wendt, both at the University of the South Pacific, Darryl Lum and Eric Chock amongst others in Honolulu. New Zealand has supported Pacific publishing within the national commercial network as well as through university-connected journals and presses. Witi Ihimaera and Albert Wendt have been major promoters there. The University of Hawaii Press is another key publisher of Pacific texts. Writers who have persisted sufficiently long to establish a literary reputation have generally been teachers and academics. Konai Helu Thaman, Wendt, Epeli Hau'ofa, Subramani, Russell Soaba, Vilsoni Hereniko and Nora Vagi have all had long associations with univerisities.

Bibliography

Journals:
Mana, the most influential gatherer of creative writing from the South Pacific Creative Arts Society, Suva. Long edited by Marjorie Crocombe and now by Prof Vilsoni Hereniko of the Center for Pacific Islands Studies, University of Hawaii, Honolulu, Hawai'i 96828. Copies available through the Institute of Pacific Studies, University of the South Pacific, PO Box 1168, Suva, Fiji.
Papua New Guinea Writing. A schools journal important as vehicle of early writing and building an audience for texts.
Ondobondo. A more contemporary journal of the Creative Writing group at the University of PNG.
Manoa, English Department, University of Hawaii, Honolulu 96822.
Journal of the Contemporary Pacific, History Department, University of Hawaii
Bamboo Ridge, Bamboo Ridge Press, PO Box 61781, Honolulu, Hawai'i 96839-1781.
Storyboard, University of Guam.

Anthologies:
Wendt, Albert (ed.). 1980. *Lali: A Pacific Anthology,* Auckland: Longman Paul.
Wendt, Albert (ed.). 1995. *Nuanua,* Auckland: Auckland University Press.
Crocombe, Marjorie *et al.* (eds.). 1992. *Te Rau Maire.* Rarotonga: USP Extension Centre.
Westlake, Wayne and Richard Hamasaki (eds.). 1984. *A Pacific Islands Collection,* (*Seaweeds & Constructions* no.7). Honolulu: Elepaio Press.

Beier, Ulli (ed.). 1973. *Black Writing from New Guinea*. St Lucia: University of Queensland Press.

Beier, Ulli (ed.). 1980, *Voices of Independence*. St Lucia: University of Queensland.

Powell, Ganga (ed.). 1987. *Through Melanesian Eyes*. Melbourne: Macmillan.

Ihimaera, Witi and Don Long (eds.). 1980. *Into the World of Light*. Auckland: Heinemann.

Ihimaera, Witi (ed.). 1992 and ensuing volumes. *Te Ao Marama*. Auckland: Heinemann.

Criticism:

CRNLE Reviews Journal (Flinders University of South Australia): occasional reviews plus special issue, number 1, 1989.

Commonwealth (University of Dijon): occasional articles plus special issue, 12/2, 1990.

Meanjin (Melbourne University): occasional articles plus special issue 49/4, 1990.

Pacific Communications Journal (University of the South Pacific) especially 14/1, 1985.

Sharrad, Paul (ed.). 1984. *Readings in Pacific Literature*. Wollongong: New Literatures Research Centre.

Simms, Norman. 1986. *Silence and Invisibility*. Washington: Three Continents Press.

Span (University of Waikato): occasional articles and reviews.

Subramani. 1985. *South Pacific Literature: from Myth to Fabulation*. Suva: University of the South Pacific.

Sumida, Stephen H. 1991. *And the View from the Shore: Literary traditions of Hawai'i*, Seattle: University of Washington Press.

Waddell, Eric *et al.* (eds.). 1993. *A New Oceania: Rediscovering our Sea of Islands*. Suva: University of the South Pacific.

Bibliographies:

Aoiki, Diane. *Moving Images of the Pacific Islands* (films and videos) available on the World Wide Web: http://www2.hawaii.edu/oceanic/film

Chakravarti, Prithvindra and Kaka Kais. 1974. *Bibliography of New Guinea Writing from Papua New Guinea*. Port Moresby: Institute of PNG Studies.

Chakravarti, Prithvindra and Papiya. 1986. *Papua New Guinea Literature in English: A Bibliography 1974-85*. Port Moresby: Owl Books.

Goetzfriedt, Nicholas J. (ed.). 1995. *Indigenous Literatures of Oceania: A Survey of Criticism and Interpretation*. Westport, Connecticut: Greenwood Press.

Miller, Melissa M. (ed.). 1989. *Moving Images of the Pacific Islands: A Catalogue of Films and Videos*. Honolulu: Centre for Pacific Islands Studies, University of Hawaii.

Simms, Norman (ed.). 1991. *Writers from the South Pacific: A Bio-bibliographical Critical Encyclopedia*. Washington: Three Continents Press.

Williams, Esther Wininamaori (ed.). 1984. *Lisitala: a Bibliography of Pacific Writers*. Suva: Pacific Information Centre, University of the South Pacific.

Book sources

Institute of Pacific Studies, P.O. Box 1168, Suva, Fiji.

The Polynesian Book Shop, Karangahape Road, Auckland, New Zealand.

The Cellar Bookshop, 18090 Wyoming, Detroit Michigan 48221, USA.

University of Hawaii Press, 2840 Kolowalu Street, Honolulu, Hawai'i 96822.

Selected texts

Fiction:

Campbell, Alistair. 1989. *The Frigate Bird*. Auckland: Heinemann.
Eri, Vincent. 1970. *The Crocodile*. Brisbane: Jacaranda.
Grace, Patricia. 1978. *Mutuwhenua*, Auckland: Penguin.
Grace, Patricia. 1986. *Potiki*. Auckland: Viking.
Grace, Patricia. 1991. *Selected Stories*. Auckland: 1991.
Hau'ofa, Epeli. 1983. *Tales of the Tikongs*. Auckland: Longman Paul.
Hau'ofa, Epeli. 1987. *Kisses in the Nederends*. Auckland: Penguin.
Hulme, Keri. 1984. *the bone people*. Wellington: Spiral.
Ihimaera, Witi. 1972. *Pounamu, Pounamu*. Auckland: Heinemann.
Ihimaera, Witi. 1974. *Whanau*. Auckland: Heinemann.
Ihimaera, Witi. 1986. *The Matriarch*. Auckland: Heinemann.
Pule, John. 1992. *The Shark that Ate the Sun*. Auckland: Penguin.
Soaba, Russell. 1977. *Wanpis*. Port Moresby: Institute of PNG Studies.
Soaba, Russell. 1985. *Maiba*. Washington, D.C.: Three Continents Press.
Subramani. 1988. *The Fantasy Eaters*. Washington, D.C.: Three Continents Press.
Taylor, Apirana. 1990. *Ki Te Ao: New Stories*. Auckland: Penguin.
Wendt, Albert. 1973. *Sons for the Return Home*. Auckland: Longman Paul.
Wendt, Albert. 1979. *Leaves of the Banyan Tree*. Auckland: Longman Paul.
Wendt, Albert. 1991. *Ola*. Auckland: Longman Paul.
(Some earlier titles are available in reprint through the University of Hawaii Press.)

Poetry:

Campbell, Alistair. 1992. *Stone Rain: The Polynesian Strain*. Christchurch/Melbourne: Hazard Press.
Déwé Gorodé. 1985. *Sous les cendres des conques*. Noumea: Edipop.
Kauraka, Kauraka. 1987. *Dreams of a Rainbow*. Suva: Mana Publications.
Malietoa von Rieche, Momoe. 1988. *Tai: Heart of a Tree*. Auckland: New Women's Press.
Manutahi, Charles Teriiteanuanua. 1984. *Le Don d'aimer: poèmes libres*. Papeete: Polytram.
Mishra, Sudesh. 1987. *Rahu*. Suva: Vision International.
Mishra, Sudesh. 1992. *Tandava*. Melbourne: Meanjin Publications.
Molisa, Grace Mera. 1983. *Black Stone*. Suva: Mana Publications.
Nandan, Satendra. 1985. *Voices in the River*. Suva: Vision International.
Thaman, Konai (Helu). 1987. *Hingano*. Suva: Mana Publications.
Tuwhare, Hone. 1987. *Mihi*. Auckland: Penguin.
Wendt, Albert. 1976. *Inside us the Dead*. Auckland: Longman Paul.

Drama:

Carroll, Dennis (ed.). 1983. *Kumu Kahua Plays*. Honolulu: University of Hawaii Press.
Garrett, Simon (ed.). 1991. *He Reo Hou: Five Maori Plays*. Wellington: Playmarket.
Hereniko, Vilsoni. 1987. *Two Plays*. Suva: Mana Publications.
Vagi Brash, Nora. 1997. *Toromuimui*. Port Moresby: Oxford.
Wan Smolbag Theatre, a community educational group. Plays on video from Wan Smolbag Theatre, PO Box 1024, Port Vila, Vanuatu.

Firing the can(n)on: Teaching Post-colonialism in a Pacific Context

Lars Jensen

In this essay I will explore Australian, New Zealand and Pacific literatures through a regionalised post-colonial perspective. It is thus my intention to examine the Pacific region's literature outside its traditional confines of a nationalistic literary paradigm, which has tended to haunt in particular Australian and New Zealand constructions of national histories. Although the establishment and growth of a vernacular literature constitute a necessary step in the process of liberating national and post-colonial literatures from the shadows of an Anglo-centric canon, the evolving literatures have tended to become inscribed into a new nationalistic canon which, although nationalistic rather than imperialistic, remains exclusivist. According to such a nationalistic perspective, the settler experience in the alien bush is regarded as the formative experience for post-colonial settler societies, disregarding the fact that such nationalistic fabrications are as exclusivist as the canons they seek to replace. This finds its most clear expression in the contradictory role assigned to indigenous literatures which, although central to any contemplation concerning Australian and New Zealand space, continue to occupy a marginal position in relation to constructions of a national space. Because the transformation from colonial space to national place records a transition from an alienated state to one of familiarisation, the indigenous literature are excluded, since they do not map out such a transformation. Rather their universe betrays the European origins of the settler myth, and questions the textual legitimisation of the European presence. Furthermore, the bush legend, with its emphasis on one national formative experience, often blocks alternative ways of contextualising literature which offer less mainstream – and exclusivist – views: e.g. indigenous, migrant and multicultural considerations that are, indeed, more relevant to current cultural discourses in increasingly fragmented post-colonial settler societies.

Nationalistic readings of post-colonial settler societies pose a particular problem for teachers teaching literatures from the Commonwealth to students outside the areas concerned. This is particularly true for the teacher who teaches in an

English-as-a-second-language situation, because here time is often consumed trying to establish defining characteristics for the specific cultures that are then subsequently to be exploded by adopting alternative approaches. The odd situation which results is one where the teacher often finds himself in the dilemma of simultaneously establishing and deconstructing canons. The teaching of post-colonial literature presupposes the knowledge of the history, institutions, texts etc. against which the post-colonial texts operate, a knowledge which is very often not there. Post-colonial literatures here suffer the added disadvantage of not being recognised on the same level as American and British literature. In other words, post-colonial literature has to be argued for, whereas the relevance of British and American literature is taken for granted. The immediate appeal of post-colonial literature (to those who decide university syllabuses) lies not so much in the different perspectives and challenges it poses, but in post-colonial literature's status as odd (quaint) and exotic (colourful). This is a position which marginalises it in relation to the established course structure which engages in the study of 'recognised' literature, and in this way renders post-colonial studies incapable of challenging the foundations on which choices of 'mainstream' texts and readings of texts are made.

Given that this situation is not likely to change, how then is it possible to envisage a new departure, inside the token space set aside for post-colonial studies? Perhaps what is called for is a different way of introducing post-colonial literatures: to move them outside the confines of Western paradigms and nationalistic discourses while relating the reading to what constitutes, for example, Australian, New Zealand and Pacific cultural experiences. Whereas the liberation process from Western hegemonistic paradigms is as old as post-colonialism itself, I wish here to explore the possibilities of moving beyond the limitations of nationalistic agendas. My approach to doing this will be to escape the notion of post-colonial writing as being primarily engaged in formulating national identities. I intend to do this through what might be called a 'by-pass operation'. In the Pacific context this can be implemented through the adoption of a regionalised perspective, thereby avoiding the bush ethos and instead contemplating Australian and New Zealand literature outside the construction of colonial inscription as successful familiarisation. My reading does not dismiss the importance of the settler experience in either country, but aims to explore literary territory from an angle that opens opportunities for new interpretations, new ways of imagining colonial and post-colonial beginnings. For the Pacific the benefit derived from this approach is to add the related Maori literature and the shared concerns of Aboriginal literature, a connection Albert Wendt points out in *Nuanua* (see the course outline at the end of this article for publication details).

There are two approaches I wish to pursue in the following: one that emphasises literary constructions of white-indigenous contact space, and one that explores the Pacific through an interdisciplinary approach. First I will compare the Australian and New Zealand literary experiences by looking at the current trend in post-colonial literatures to reconstruct and reimagine colonial beginnings. These writings represent both an investigation of the frontier history and mythology, and an explication of how late twentieth century writers continue to be preoccupied by the binaries created by the frontier in a colonial space, between order/civilisation/Eurocentrism and chaos/colonial nature/alienation. This recent trend in post-colonial writing to reinvestigate colonial beginnings is intimately related to current cultural concerns of national identity and reconciliation with the indigenous populations. The urge for reconciliation feeds into the discussion on national identity, because it sees as central to Australian and New Zealand identity the bridge that the indigenous populations provide between predominantly European populations and a space which defied European aesthetic definitions of space.

The literary space created by writers engaged in reinterpreting and redefining beginnings is a space in which colonial beginnings are investigated differently from the traditional depictions of first encounters, colonisation and national ascendancy as particular moments in time. Historical rewritings such as David Malouf's *Remembering Babylon*, Liam Davison's *The White Woman*, Maurice Shadbolt's *Monday's Warriors* (see the course outline at the end of this article for publication details of these works) all suggest that the space which first contact, colonial, national and post-colonial writing inhabit is a space that is constantly being renegotiated in a process of defining what constitutes an Australian and a New Zealand experience. Post-colonial writers achieve this deliberately ambiguous position through focusing on the in-between space, or on the transitional figure, who is white but in some way also inhabits an indigenous space. What they expose is the white settlers' inadequate response resulting from the binaries inherent in the frontier model – binaries which later constructions of nationalistic Australian and New Zealand spaces have been built upon.

From the point of view of liberating literary analysis from nationalistic preoccupations, the move beyond the sheer contemplation of settler experience carries with it the added advantage of a more evident, shared experience with other post-colonial societies, e.g. Pacific nations and the Caribbean. It is an approach which exposes the indispensability of the indigene to post-colonial perceptions of Australian and New Zealand literature, though marginality may obviously take many other forms (e.g. migrant writing other than the British/Irish). The indigenous counterparts to these concerns are formulated by Aboriginal and Maori writers, whose aim might not be to construct a historical universe (though some of them do, for example Witi Ihimaera in *The Matriarch* and Philip MacLaren in *Sweet-Water Stolen Land* (see the course outline at the end of this article for publication details)), but where the legacy of colonial oppression is part of the backcloth for their universes – not just because injustices took place to such a degree that they still weigh as a heavy burden, but also because structures of oppression continue to dominate white-indigenous relations in both countries.

150

What white writers and black post-colonial writers share is, however, the desire to transcend these binaries. The main difference between white settler and indigenous narratives lies in the way they construct the space between white and indigenous writing, e.g. the degree to which history intrudes into the narrative. White Australian and New Zealand post-colonial writings have finally shed their history of either ignoring or marginalising indigenous presence, and have only fairly recently begun to investigate the intermediate space; whereas indigenous writing always grew out of a desire to carve out a space inside which an indigenous point of view could be articulated. Here Aboriginal and Maori literatures share many concerns with Pacific literature, which is also of a fairly recent date and is also preoccupied with rectifying stereotypical Western images of indigenous people, while presenting a Pacific universe that has validity in its own right, regardless of Western constructions of what constitutes good literature. This is a process which for all indigenous groups concerned began in the 1960s as a protest-oriented literature and which has later established its own validity.

However, where indigenous writing in Australia and New Zealand is overtly concerned with the legacy of white invasion, and today with threats of appropriation of indigenity in order to satisfy white settler societies' anxiousness to belong and help ease the transformation from an alien cultural background to an 'authentic' Australian and New Zealand identity, the Pacific islanders are generally more concerned with the present economic and cultural onslaught from both sides of the Pacific rim. Though 'protected' by the greatest ocean on earth, they are placed in the centre of the world's most powerful economic association, APEC. Other threats include the American desires to use Pacific islands as atomic waste pits, and legacies of European imperialism such as the current French self-delusions of military grandeur. Melville's observations on French imperialism in *Typee* (see the course outline at the end of this article for publication details) are as relevant as ever.

Pacific literature is more concerned with the current onslaught than with the destructions brought upon the islanders in the past, though they share with Aboriginal and Maori literature the awareness that current problems are a natural continuation of the earlier European imperialism. An example of this is Florence Syme-Buchanan's 'Boat Girl', published in *Nuanua*. Yet Pacific literature also reveals that, in contrast with other indigenous literatures, quite often the first encounter is of a fairly recent date. Hence writings such as Ignatius Kilage's 'My Mother Calls me Yaltep' (in *Nuanua*) is a first person narrative of the first white intrusion into a Papua New Guinean village. The story acutely expresses the idea that first encounters are not always about monumental change, but more about the ways in which cultures at loggerheads both engage in a struggle to undermine each other's positions. Like other stories and indeed the white rewritings of the early contact period, this story shows an adaptability to change which discredits both the theory of the fatal impact and the notion of indigenous societies as essentially static. Alistair Te Ariki Campbell presents an interesting interpretation of Pacific culture in 'The Frigate Bird' (in *Nuanua*), where the protagonist is locked up in a cabin on what seems an endless journey around the Cook Islands. Although the point about the slow, prospectless, lazy life on Pacific Islands is confirmed, it also indirectly lends support to alternative models of time to Western definitions. The Pacific society is here projected as one that deliberately makes its own time, rather than living on what in essence becomes a 'borrowed' Western time which, to stay with the image, has to be 'repaid with interest'.

Simultaneously with this literature of critical investigation into the consequences of the Western onslaught, there also exists a literary strand which deals exclusively with an indigenous universe. In this context Pacific literature lends itself more readily to comparisons with Canadian Inuit literature. Hence a perusal of Penny Petrone's *Northern Voices*[1] is helpful for the way it distinguishes between different types of Inuit texts. The Inuit, like some Pacific nations, were never permanently invaded, because their territory was ill-suited to white settlement. Two indigenous texts will serve as illustrative examples of a more exclusively indigenous universe. The first one is Papua New Guinean writer Thomas Tuman's short story 'Kuim Koimb', which sheds interesting light on the significance of cannibalism in Papua New Guinean society, and elevates it from an unproductive representation as a taboo. It invites juxtaposition with a number of white texts, anthropological readings as well as colonial literature and exploration narratives (suggestions for suitable interdisciplinary texts are provided at the end of this article). The second text, 'Kisses in the Netherends' (in *Nuanua*) by the Tongan writer Epeli Hau'ofa, also explores the significance of the 'post-colonial body': through the eyes of the character Seru, who in a kava-inspired moment envisages Tonga as a body, where each island population represents a part of that body. Hence:

> In his vision, Seru saw the human body as a world in itself, a world inhabited by human-like creatures, the tuktuks, who organised themselves into tribes occupying territories located only in those parts of the body that contained organs and members, the most populous being lands in the lower erogenous regions. The arms and the legs were completely uninhabited, and were visited only occasionally by a few intrepid hunters.

It is hardly surprising to discover in the biographical material on Hau'ofa that he is an anthropologist. This kind of writing, which is a search for an indigenous perspective outside the dichotomy of a white-indigenous literary space, is also emerging in Maori and Aboriginal literature; though here the frontier legacy still forms part of the backdrop, as the white presence is indeed hard to ignore. Examples of this writing would be Keri Hulme's *The Bone People*[2] and James Bardon's *Revolution by Night*[3].

I would like to finish this search for new angles from which to understand Australian/New Zealand/Pacific writing with two specific corpora of texts, one which attempts to explode conventional representations of an Australian and a

New Zealand experience and in particular nationalistic oriented definitions of colonial and post-colonial space; and another which explores Pacific literature outside the traditionally established context of white and indigenous literatures. Hence I suggest here an interdisciplinary approach that I recently made use of in a course at Roskilde University.

Course 1. Literary representations of white-indigenous contact space in Pacific literatures

David Malouf, *Remembering Babylon* (London: Chatto and Windus, 1993)
Rodney Hall, *The Second Bridegroom* (London: Faber and Faber, 1991)
Philip MacLaren, *Sweet Water-Stolen Land* (St Lucia: University of Queensland Press, 1993)
Sam Watson, *The Kadaitcha Sung* (Ringwood: Penguin 1990)
Liam Davison, *The White Woman* (St Lucia: University of Queensland Press, 1994)
Witi Ihimaera, *The Matriarch* (London: Heinemann, 1986)
Maurice Shadbolt, *Monday's Warriors* (London: Bloomsbury, 1991)
Robert Louis Stevenson, 'The Beach of Falesa' in *South Sea Tales* (Oxford: World's Classics Oxford University Press, 1996)
Herman Melville, *Typee* (Oxford: World's Classics, Oxford University Press, 1996)
Albert Wendt, *Inside Us the Dead: Poems 1961 to 1974* (Auckland: Longman Paul repr., 1980)
Albert Wendt, *Sons for the Return of Home* (Auckland: Penguin, 1987)

Course 2. Interdisciplinary course on Polynesia: *Being Specific About the Pacific*.

I give the full texts here, although in the actual course, due to the workload students can be expected to cope with at the university here, I used only extracts.

1. Introduction to the interdisciplinary approaches; the literary (and in particular the post-colonial), the anthropological, the historical. The course aims through the juxtaposing of white and Polynesian views to present different points of view, which will hopefully create a space where we can think about the goals and limitations to our project: how to grasp the nature of the contact space between white and indigenous perspectives. Suggested reading: Albert Wendt's introduction to *Nuanua: Pacific Writing Since 1980* (Honolulu: University of Hawaii Press, 1995)

2 + 3. The white man and the Pacific in colonial literature.
Herman Melville, *Typee* (Oxford: World's Classics, Oxford University Press, 1996); Robert Louis Stevenson, 'The Beach of Falesa' in *South Sea Tales* (Oxford: World's Classics, Oxford University Press, 1996).

4 + 5. The go-betweens: anthropologists and the Pacific.
a) American anthropologist Margaret Mead and the discourse on the Samoans.
Derek Freeman, *Margaret Mead and the Samoans: The Making and Unmaking of an Anthropological Myth* (Cambridge, Mass.: Harvard, 1983); *The Samoa Reader: Anthropologists Take Stock*, ed. Hiram Caton (Lanham: University Press of America, 1990).

b) Cook's bones of contention – Obeyesekere and Sahlins on Cook's death in Hawaii.
G. Obeyesekere, *The Apotheosis of Captain Cook: European Mythmaking in the Pacific* (Princeton N.J.: Princeton University Press, 1992); Marshall Sahlins, *How 'Natives' Think: About Captain Cook for Example* (Chicago: Chicago University Press, 1995).

6. Travel-writing: White nostalgia revisits the Pacific. Retracing the steps of Stevenson.
Gavin Bell, *In Search of Tusitala* (London: Picador, 1995).

7 + 8. The indigenous response and the evolution of an independent Pacific voice. Short stories from *Nuanua* and poems by Albert Wendt.

What this course does not sufficiently interrogate is the question of how to apply Polynesian mythology, and how traditional Polynesian society functions and how this is being explored and problematised in the Polynesian literary universe. Yet given the limitations imposed by the realistic amount of course-work, integrating this perspective more fully would mean the sacrifice of one of the other approaches.

Notes

1.   London: University of Toronto Press, 1988.
2.   London: Picador, 1986.
3.   Sydney: Local Consumption Publications, 1991.

The Politics of Post-colonial Reading Practices as they Relate to the Work of Aboriginal Writers

Kathryn Trees

I am currently teaching 'post-colonial writing' at Murdoch University. I have a very strong political commitment to improving relationships between Aboriginal and non-Aboriginal people. This concern is not merely academic or theoretical, but is largely the result of my own history. In my Ph.D. I have focused primarily on the relationships of non-Aboriginal Australians to texts written by Aboriginal writers such as Alice Nannup (author of *When The Pelican Laughed*[1]), Glenyse Ward (*Wandering Girl* and *Unna You Fellas*[2]), and Mudrooroo.[3] I also work with the Australian Judiciary, designing cross-cultural awareness programmes so that magistrates and judges are better informed about Aboriginal people and their cultures before making decisions about them.

Although it is not always possible to work simultaneously in the field of literature and in overtly political arenas, I believe that teaching in courses framed by the term 'post-colonialism' requires a commitment to bring these two sometimes disparate entities together. Otherwise there is a danger that post-colonialism, whilst embracing a politics of emancipatory self and social empowerment, serves to maintain the tradition of liberalism, the tenets of which already include an ethics of care, solidarity and liberation. This occurs through the separation of theoretical/academic knowledges from practical strategies which can allow for an easy transition between first reading texts written by indigenous writers within a post-colonial context or course, then empathising with the experiences, recognising the injustices and social inequities, and finally believing that this process, in itself, contributes to change. What I am suggesting is that it is absolutely necessary to teach politically, as opposed to merely teaching politicised texts.

How does anyone, student or teacher, construct an identity as a post-colonial critic? Is it possible to become this critic without having access to the appropriate socio-economic histories of the writers, subjects or texts that are being read or taught? The question is one of praxis and identity.

Is reading, critiquing and engaging with texts written by Aboriginal people different for white Australian readers, assuming a position of post-colonialism, than for the same readers engaging with a text written by a South American writer for instance? For me there is a significant difference in teaching texts written by or about the indigenous peoples of a country in which one lives, and teaching other post-colonial texts or about other post-colonial countries. This is not because of some belief that it is possible for a member of a dominant culture to fully understand how indigenous people experience living in subordination to systems of government whose primary concern is not in their best interests. I take Trinh T. Minh-Ha's point that 'the injunction to see things from the natives' point of view speaks for a definite ideology of truth and authenticity; it lies at the centre of every polemical discussion on "reality" in its relation to truth'.[4] Rather, it is because by virtue of being white in Australia, one is implicated in a colonial or settler system that privileges non-indigenous people.

It is necessary to engage with key questions (what are the differences? what are my responsibilities?) in teaching texts written by Aboriginal writers. Unless these questions are seriously engaged with, the ethical critique and decolonising process that is promised by post-colonialism becomes unattainable. Instead, the post-colonial position becomes merely an aesthetic, textual, theoretical experience.

One of the first steps in this process is to teach students to interrogate their own cultural/historical positions so that they learn to approach literature with more of a sense of their own subjectivity and how this subjectivity is formulated, so that they are able to appreciate how this affects their understanding of post-colonialism, especially when post-colonialism from an Aboriginal viewpoint may be seen to be non-existent. This is an important point if consideration is given to critiques of post-colonialism made by various Aboriginal writers and activists. In December 1992, Alice Nannup said 'my work is not fiction but perhaps post-colonialism is'. Mudrooroo describes post-colonialism as a 'predatory beast, on the prowl, ready to eat up the writings of Aboriginal people and shit them out as turds of colonial bullshit'. And Bobby Sykes, activist and writer, said of post-colonialism 'what, have I missed something? Have they gone?' Although this last comment need not be taken literally, it clearly foregrounds some of the tensions the term generates in relation to Aboriginal people. Most obviously it suggests that this is an inappropriate description of both the writings and the lived experiences of Aboriginal peoples. Obviously the categorisation of texts is an institutional practice that can at times be quite different from the writer's experience (the agendas for each can be quite separate), and this difference needs to be foregrounded.

Part of the method for teaching students to become post-colonial critics is to encourage them to deconstruct their 'given' identities, then reconstruct them. Hopefully this allows them to identify their own political positions and their relationship to the work with which they are engaging.

This interrogation of identity must necessarily be extended to considering the impact of historical and contemporary socio-political conditions and legislations on the identities and lives of Aboriginal peoples. Past legislation, such as that legitimising the taking of children from their families (most often those fathered by white men), the removal of people from their homelands, and the denial of access to language and culture, education and employment, still has serious ramifications. Australia is a country where Aboriginal peoples' sovereignty is not recognised, where the majority of Australians know little (and perhaps care even less) about Aboriginal cultures or the actual socio-economic conditions that Aboriginal people live in, and where land rights are strongly opposed by most state governments. What does this mean for post-colonialism? An understanding of these issues needs to inform the reading of texts to avoid generating complacency among students and teachers.

One example of the repercussions of the abduction of Aboriginal children is Stella's story. Stella is a 29-year-old woman I met in Wickham, a mining town in the north of Western Australia, in 1991.

It was approximately 9:30 p.m. one Friday in October 1990. At the home of Kaylene, a Yamagi woman and a teacher with the State Education Department, there came a sharp rap on the door. A woman holding a baby with a young girl standing beside her asked to come in to escape from the drunken man she lived with, who had been beating her and her 9-year-old daughter.

Kaylene recognised the woman – Stella – and asked her how it was she was living in Wickham. Stella had been a member of a six hundred strong community at Onslow, in the late seventies, when a salt mining company came into the area to determine the best location for a new salt mining and processing plant. Kaylene had been sent to Onslow at that time to work in the newly established primary school. Part of her brief was to inform the community members about the possible mining and the effects this would have. She was never instructed to warn about rape or cultural dislocation. At this time Stella was eleven years old. She, like many other young children and women, was raped by newly arrived white miners. Within a year many fair-skinned children were born. And salt mining did not even take place at Onslow but at Dampier.

Stella then told of her move from Onslow to Wickham and the fear that she now lived in. She lived with the father of her baby, a Wajella, white man, working for Hamersley Iron. He would often beat her, and this night he had begun beating her nine year old daughter, not his child, as well. Stella left and did not want to go back until she was sure he would be asleep.

Kaylene asked why she did not go back to Onslow. Stella's response was that he had threatened to take the baby if she ever tried to leave. She knew many people who had been taken from their parents or had children taken from them. Stella was not being merely threatened, she was being told of his power as a white man, with all its colonial implications. Here is just one continued ramification of past government policy.

What effective rights does Stella or any other Aboriginal woman in a similar situation have? She has no effective access to legal protection for herself or her children because she has no knowledge of her rights as a mother under Australian law. What she has is a knowledge of colonialism – the taking of babies. Thus in the 1990s to talk of post-colonialism as a social fact is simply not true, especially when the Stellas of this world are the continuing victims of white paternalism – a dominant feature of colonialism.

This experience is of course not literature, therefore it may be excluded from a post-colonial writing course and thus not challenge its paradigms. However, how can one be a post-colonial critic and not take account of current colonialism or neo-colonialism? To suggest that this is possible is to once again set theory and praxis apart from each other.

On the 'post-colonial writing course' on which I teach, students read Alice Nannup's *When The Pelican Laughed*, which spans the period from 1905-1992. This is the life story of Alice Nannup, a Yindjibarndi woman born in 1911, on the Abydos station in the Pilbara. Alice's mother was a member of the Yindjibarndi group and her father was 'white'. At the age of twelve Alice was removed from her family by the Department of Aboriginal Affairs. It was promised she would be educated and then returned home when she was eighteen. Alice, in fact, received little education. She spent some time at the infamous Moore River Settlement, where thousands of Aboriginal people were incarcerated, often having been taken from families because they were 'part' white. This was followed by many years in domestic service. The repercussions of this were innumerable – loss of parents, siblings, extended family, community, language, effective parenting models, learning to live with injustice and pain. She eventually married and raised ten children. Finally, sixty-four years after her removal, Alice returned to her home country.

It is my contention that when *When The Pelican Laughed* is taught in isolation from contemporary socio-economic conditions it is more easily objectifed and commodified. The reader is more readily able to identify with the writer, in this case Alice Nannup, and to distance her/himself (assuming a non-Aboriginal reader) from the perpetrators of violent, inhumane acts – in this instance, the Australian government. The perceived distance between past government polices and the reader allows for the belief that conditions are now markedly different, as evidenced by Alice Nannup's ability to have her story published, and circulated in the public sphere through universities and conferences. And of course there have been positive changes for some Aboriginal people. However, as I have already shown, there are very real continued effects of past oppressive government policies that students need to consider if they wish to perform a deconstructive post-colonial reading of texts written by Aboriginal people.

Decolonisation, a vital element of post-colonialism, may be seen as a form of social deconstruction. It is often understood as unrealistic, unobtainable and very often undesirable, or it is simply dismissed as ridiculous. However, if there is to be any semblance of an equitable, just Australian society (overcoming class, gender inequities etc.), it must be possible to imagine a process of decolonisation.

For many students, their participation in this process may begin within post-colonial writing courses. So that while it is necessary to highlight the objections Aboriginal people may have to the suggestion that we live in a post-colonial period, it is also necessary not to undermine the usefulness of post-colonial theory as a potential political strategy. And post-colonialism is, by definition, political.

In conclusion I come back to the work of Trinh T. Minh-Ha. Her definition of a responsible work is, I suggest, crucial to post-colonial criticism and pedagogy. 'A responsible work today seems to me above all to be one that shows, on the one hand, a political commitment and an ideological lucidity, and is, on the other hand interrogative by nature, instead of being merely prescriptive' (*op. cit.* 149). In other words, effective practice of post-colonial pedagogy in Australia is work that brings together both Aboriginal histories and white Australian histories, 'work that acknowledges the difference between lived experience and representation; work that is careful not to turn a struggle into an object of consumption' (*ibid.*), and requires that responsibility be assumed by the writers, the teachers and the students, 'without whose participation no solution emerges, for no solution exists as a given' (*ibid.*).

Notes

1. Alice Nannup, *When the Pelican Laughed* (South Fremantle: Fremantle Arts Press, 1992).
2. Glenys Ward, *Wandering Girl* (Broome: Magabala Books, 1987); *Unna You Fellas* (Broome: Magabala Books, 1991).
3. Novels by Mudrooroo include *Wild Cat Falling* (1965), *Doctor Wooreddy's Prescription for the Ending of the World* (1983), *Master of the Ghost Dreaming* (1991) and *Wild Cat Screaming* (1992).
4. Trinh T. Minh-Ha, *When the Moon Waxes Red* (London: Routledge, 1991), 149.

Pedagogy and Resistance in the Context of Commonwealth/ Post-colonial Literatures

Susan Gingell

There is no such thing as a *neutral* educational process. Education either functions as an instrument which is used to facilitate the integration of the younger generation into the logic of the present system and bring about conformity to it, *or* it becomes 'the practice of freedom', the means by which men and women deal critically and creatively with reality and discover how to participate in the transformation of their world. (Richard Shaull[1])

While Shaull's rhetoric recognizes no shades of grey between education as indoctrination and education as liberation, the underlying truth of his perception prompts me to use a pedagogical strategy that primarily passes on the information it needs to convey embedded in questions that require students to be active learners. I have chosen two poems and formulated questions on them to exemplify this pedagogy at work.

Imperial Adam

Imperial Adam, naked in the dew,
Felt his brown flanks and found the rib was gone.
Puzzled he turned and saw where, two and two,
The mighty spoor of Jahweh marked the lawn.

Then he remembered through mysterious sleep
The surgeon fingers probing at the bone,
The voice so far away, so rich and deep:
'It is not good for him to live alone.'

Turning once more he found Man's counterpart
In tender parody breathing at his side.
He knew her at first sight, he knew by heart
Her allegory of sense unsatisfied.

The pawpaw drooped its golden breasts above
Less generous than the honey of her flesh;
The innocent sunlight showed the place of love;
The dew on its dark hairs winked crisp and fresh.

This plump gourd severed from his virile root,
She promised on the turf of Paradise
Delicious pulp of the forbidden fruit;
Sly as the snake she loosed her sinuous thighs,

And waking, smiled up at him from the grass;
Her breasts rose softly and he heard her sigh -
From all the breasts whose pleasant task it was
In Eden to increase and multiply

Adam had learned the jolly deed of kind:
He took her in his arms and there and then,
Like the clean breasts, embracing from behind,
Began in joy to found the breed of men.

Then from the spurt of seed within her broke
Her terrible and triumphant female cry,
Split upward by the sexual lightning stroke.
It was the breasts now who stood watching by:

The gravid elephant, the calving hind,
The breeding bitch, the she-ape big with young
Were the first gentle midwives of mankind;
The teeming lioness rasped her with her tongue;

The proud vicuna nuzzled her as she slept
Lax on the grass; and Adam watching too
Saw her dumb breasts at their ripening wept,
The great pot of her belly swelled and grew,

And saw its water break, and saw, in fear,
Its quaking muscles in the act of birth,
Between her legs a pigmy face appear,
And the first murderer lay upon the earth.[2]

Before reading the poem aloud, I would invite students to consider how their oral readings might differ from mine, and why. After reading the poem and considering their responses to this question, I would move on to ask the following:

1. To what extent does the poem contest or replicate the power relations represented in the following passage from Book IV of Milton's *Paradise Lost*:

For contemplation he and valour formed;
For softness she and sweet attractive grace,
He for God only, she for God in him:
His fair large front and eye sublime declared
Absolute rule[3]?

2. a) With whom are animal images in the poem primarily associated?
   b) With whom are plant images primarily associated?
   c) What significance do these associations have for hierarchical structuring of power relations?

3. a) How does Hope represent Eve?
   b) What does Hope mean by Eve's 'terrible and triumphant female cry' in stanza 8?
   c) How, if at all, would your reading of this phrase be affected by knowledge of analogous wording in Hope's poem 'Pasiphae' published the same year as 'Imperial Adam' (i.e. 1952)?

      Pasiphae retells the myth of the wife of King Minos of Crete, who secreted herself in a black box shaped like a 'mimic cow' in order to seduce a bull, and Hope renders the sexual union that resulted in the birth of the minotaur this way:

      > When straight her fierce, frail body crouched inside
      > Felt the wet pizzle pierce and plunge, she wept.
      >
      > She wept for terror, for triumph; she wept to know
      > Her love unable to embrace its bliss
      > So long imagined, waking and asleep.
      > But when within she felt the pulse, the blow,
      > The burst of copious seed, the burning kiss
      > Fill her with monstrous life, she did not weep.[4]

4. The title of Hope's poem designates Adam as 'imperial'.
   a) What justification does the poem offer for seeing him as a kind of emperor?
   b) What are the implications of the title designation of Adam as 'imperial'?
   c) What is the poem's attitude to imperialism and how do you know?

5. How do the poem's intertextual relations with the Bible and *Paradise Lost* work in interpellating or calling the reader into the same ideological position as the poem occupies?

6. How do the poem's technical and formal elements contribute to the inter-pellative process in relation to imperialism and patriarchy? I particularly invite you to consider capitalization practice, verse form, rhyme, and sound patterns.

7. Are there any features or dimensions of this poem that interest you which have been left unopened by my questions?

I have chosen the Brand poem 'October 25th, 1983' as an example of resistance literature. It was written out of the experience Brand had in Grenada working as an Information Officer in the Agency for Rural Transformation of the socialist New Jewel movement. The book from which the poem is drawn, *Chronicles of the Hostile Sun* (1984), records and constitutes resistance to the recolonization of the Caribbean by American-led capitalist forces.

October 25th, 1983

The planes are circling,
the american paratroopers dropping,
later Radio Free Grenada stops for the last time
In the end they sang –
'ain't giving up no way,
no i ain't giving up no way'

The OECS riding like birds on a cow
led america to the green hills of St[.] George's
and waited at Point Salines
while it fed on the young of the land,
eating their flesh with bombs,
breaking their bellies with grenade launchers

america came to restore democracy,
what was restored was faith
in the fact that you cannot fight bombers
battleships, aircraft carriers, helicopter gunships,
surveillance planes, five thousand american soldiers
six caribbean stooges and the big american war machine,
you cannot fight this with a machete
you cannot fight it with a handful of dirt
you cannot fight it with a hectacre of land free from bosses
you cannot fight it with farmers
you cannot fight it with 30 miles of feeder roads
you cannot fight it with free health care
you cannot fight it with free education
you cannot fight it with women's cooperatives
you cannot fight it with a pound of bananas or a handful of fish which belongs to you

certainly you cannot fight it with dignity.

because you must run into the street
you must crawl into a ditch
and you must wait there and watch
your family,
your mother, your sister, your little brother,
your husband, your wife,
you must watch them
because they will become hungry,
and they will give you in to the americans,
and they will say that you belong to the militia,
or the health brigade,
or the civil service,
or the people's revolutionary army,
or the community work brigade,
or the New Jewel Movement –
they will say that you lived in the country,
they will say that you are Cuban,
they will say that you served cakes
at the Point Salines airport fundraising,
they will say that you are human,
they will say
that one day last month
you said that for four and a half years
you have been happy.
they will say all this because they want to eat.

And finally you can only fight it with the silence of your dead body.[5]

Again, I would invite students to identify variant oral readings and consider what differences of meaning they produce.

1.   What are the implications of this being a diary entry in the longer work 'Diary – The Grenada Crisis'?

2.   a)   What expectations about genre are created by the title?
     b)   To what extent are these expectations met or frustrated by the poem as a whole?

3.   a)   How does Brand use images and capitalization practice in the first two stanzas to co-opt the reader into her way of seeing?
     b)   How does her use of pronouns in the remainder of the poem continue the interpellation?

4.   a)   Why does she break the first three lines of stanza three where she does?
     b)   What disjunction is being replicated here?

5. When I presented this poem to a research seminar at my university, a colleague in Veterinary Medicine, Meg Smart, heard in the anaphoric lines 'you cannot fight ...', an echo of Winston Churchill's famous speech of 4 June 1940, meant to strengthen resistance to the imperialistic designs of Nazi Germany:

> We shall go on to the end. We shall fight in France, we shall fight in the seas and oceans, we shall fight with growing confidence and growing strength in the air; we shall defend our island, whatever the cost may be. We shall fight on the beaches, we shall fight on the landing-grounds, we shall fight in the fields and in the streets, we shall fight in the hills; we shall never surrender.[6]

To what extent does Brand's poem reproduce or resist the values inherent in this earlier text of resistance orature?

6. How does the poem's closure reinforce the point made in the previous stanza about the relationship between words (specifically here, speech) and social control?

7. Are there any features or dimensions of the poem that interest you that have been left untouched by my questions?

Notes

1. Richard Shaull, Foreword to Paulo Freire, *Pedagogy of the Oppressed*, 15.
2. A.D. Hope, *Collected Poems 1930-1965* (Sydney: Angus and Robertson, 1966), 83-84.
3. Milton, *Paradise Lost*, Book IV, lines 297-301.
4. *Collected Poems*, 85.
5. Dionne Brand, *Chronicles of the Hostile Sun*, 1984, 42-43.
6. Winston S. Churchill, *Memoirs of the Second World War* (New York: Bonanza Books, 1978), 284-85.

From Periphery to Centre – Teaching Caribbean Literature within a Post-colonial/ Commonwealth Context

Velma Pollard

1. Background

Glyne Griffith, in the introduction to his exposition on the West Indian novel, identifies the 'tradition of critical practice which differentiates the formal aspect of literature from literature's cultural realm' as a hindrance to the location of literature's sociopolitical intent and argues for 'real engagement with the question of cultural concerns'.[1] And while Griffith's comments are made within the context of a discussion which is highly intellectual and perhaps far removed from the classroom which is the focus of this paper, the dichotomy he introduces may be extended to include not only the method of critical practice but the selection of content for such practice. The distinction can then be made between literature whose content is culturally remote from the reader and is therefore less meaningful and literature which is culturally accessible and therefore more meaningful.

The view of all literature as formal and outside of the reality of life was easy to maintain in colonial times when 'children of the Empire' came to the study of literature through writing that had little to do with their environments. The content of Literature taught in Colonial Caribbean schools in the first half of the century told, in Olive Senior's words, 'nothing about us at all'.[2] It was written by a mass of people described today as 'dead white men' whether they were Dutch, Spanish, French or (as in the case of the anglophone Caribbean, which is the interest of this paper), English. And while one might find this description of proven literary lights distasteful, it must be recognized as a metaphor for distance in time and space and most significantly in culture.

That the distance was not the exclusive preserve of Literature is as much a cliché in the writing on the colonial condition as is the fact that it was not reserved for

Caribbean classrooms. The colonial affliction pervaded both the serious and the frivolous aspects of school life far from the imperial centres and was at odds with the reality of home life. Shashi Deshpande's testimony of her schooldays in India illustrates this:

[I]n the English school we went to [where] we did sums that went 'John has ten apples and Tom has five' learnt poems about strange things like tuffets and muffins, daffodils and daisies ...

[T]here were school concerts during which we sang 'Simple Simon met a pieman (pieman?) and danced a vaguely Greek kind of dance, wearing flowing white dresses with coronets of paper flowers on our heads. We learnt to sing songs like 'The owl and the pussy cat' ...

[A]t the end of the narrow dusty road ... we kicked off our socks and shoes ... there were neither apples nor daisies here; instead we ate mangoes and guavas and plucked Jasmine buds off fragrant bushes to plait into our hair ...[3]

One might compare those descriptions with a selection from Merle Hodge's ironic *Crick Crack Monkey,* which treats school days in Trinidad:

Books transported you always into the familiar solidity of chimneys and apple trees, the enviable normality of real Girls and Boys who went a-sleighing and built snowmen, ate potatoes not rice, went about in socks and shoes from morning until night and called things by their proper names, never saying 'washicong' for 'plimsoll' or 'crapaud' when they meant 'frog'.[4]

But with time the situation changed. By 1960 George Lamming, Caribbean fiction writer and essayist, was able to make his much-quoted comment on the Caribbean novel:

For the first time the West Indian peasant became other than a cheap source of labour. He became, through the novelist's eye, a living existence, living in silence and joy and fear, involved in riot and carnival.[5]

A similar remark could have been made about Caribbean poetry. And the curriculum changed. Caribbean children were able to read about characters whose nearness they could feel in the landscape of the poetry and the prose.

Anne Walmsley (1992) looking at the process of the creation of a Caribbean canon, traces the history of Caribbean school anthologies and their establishment within the curricula of Caribbean schools. [6]Considering that description of 'passage' it is not at all surprising that twenty-three years after the publication of *Crick Crack Monkey,* Merle Hodge is able to comment through the child narrator in her second novel, *For the Life of Laetetia:*

In literature class Mr. Joseph was reading a book to us, a chapter at a time. It was called *The Year in San Fernando* and it was the only thing that could make Marlon Peters and his gang pay attention ...

The whole class was captivated. It was a story about *us,* and *our* world! We were surprised, and thrilled, that the ordinary, everyday things we took part in could find their way into a story! It meant that we were *real,* and had weight, like the people in stories. (My emphasis)[7]

The significance of the term 'real' applied to foreign boys and girls in the earlier quotation from Hodge, and the same term used to apply to local children in the later, should not be lost. It marks a shift in perception that has taken place in two decades. And if the change is filtered through Walcott's remark: 'Every question, eventually, even with literature, is a question of power ...', then the shift of perception is the result of a shift of power or at least of the understanding of how one relates to power. Indeed the political move from colony to independent Commonwealth country might have been the catalyst for such a shift.

Carew sees the political change as the impulse for the surge of writing that the sixties produced:

It was when an ineluctable tide swept the peoples of the colonial world towards national independence that art and literature began to sprout like wild flowers after the rains...[8]

And Griffith states firmly that 'it cannot be taken as mere accident that the rise of the West Indian novel coincided with the political movement for West Indian self-government'.[9]

These are comments about confidence and identity and a new sense of personhood, and are related to Lamming's remark about the novel (quoted earlier) as well as to all the questions of identity so frequently discussed and so clearly resolved in the diagnosis of reality which Hodge put in the mouth of Laetetia (quoted above).

2. Literature and the Classroom Today

The shift in focus from foreign to local allows the classroom practitioner a certain freedom to be creative about the teaching of literature. Those who train teachers must lead them to use that freedom and that creativity. The challenge of the early post-independence Caribbean classroom was to introduce Caribbean literature to the students. Attitudes to language for example allowed some writing to enter before others.

The challenge of the Caribbean classroom today is to lead students to relate the writing to the culture which engendered it. It would be ironic if the alienation which prevailed when the literature was foreign, continues to prevail when the literature is local. But for some reason this is the threat today.

2.1 One Unit

What follows is a description of part of one attempt to counteract the threat mentioned above. It is an introductory unit of an undergraduate course 'The Teaching of Literature'. The idea is to exploit the literariness of the Caribbean environment in an effort to unite the literature of the books and the culture of the society in such a way that students identify equally with both. Some background information on the subscribers to the course is in order.

Students come to this course with different levels of preparation. Some are registered in the postgraduate Diploma in Education programme. They have a first degree which includes at least four courses in Literature and may or may not have taught before entering the programme. Others are graduates from High Schools and Community Colleges (with A-Level passes in English) who will go out to be teachers of English at the end of the three year degree programme. By far the largest number are teachers who have graduated from Teacher Training Colleges and in most cases have taught for several years in elementary schools and in the lower grades of secondary schools. This last group is likely to have had less exposure to a wide range of literature than the others.

Students are encouraged to regard the presentation as a kind of master performance from which they may gain pointers for their own future teaching, and the unit as an unbound notebook to which they may add their own selections and from which they may reject given pieces if/when they use it in their own classes.

The classes this group will face when they go into the field are as varied as the group itself in terms of their experience of Literature.

Interviews conducted by students as part of undergraduate and postgraduate mini research projects suggest that high school students in general are not enthusiastic about literature; not even about Caribbean literature. And they are not always exposed to a great deal of it. Teachers are sometimes afraid of literature especially poetry and so avoid it.

There is a constituency of young people out there in the schools waiting to be interested in the literature of their environment. The teacher should be in a position to capitalise on that interest and enthuse them to such an extent that they move from an appreciation of Caribbean literature to an appreciation of all literature.

The unit is centred around a religious ceremony – a baptism by water. Religion is a popular theme in a country which is famous for the large number of churches in relation to the population. The first selection is an excerpt from Olive Senior's 'Confirmation Day'. A young girl is being 'confirmed' into the Anglican Community of which her father's family is a part. During that ceremony she is remembering the contrasting 'baptism' which she had experienced some time before in her mother's church, a Pentecostal community. A point is being made here about social class where the induction into the middle-class established church is contrasted with the induction into the lower class Pentecostal community. It is a distinction slightly less real today than it was forty years ago. But class is not the focus of the unit though reference to it is inevitable. What is to be noted and appreciated is the careful detail with which Senior paints the scene and draws the reader in. The point of view is that of the young girl. Her reverie guides the reader. The following is her present:

[N]ow we are in another time another church and the smell of incense mingles with the smell of the church and the smell is the smell of the aged ...

And I think as the Bishop stands there in robes trimmed with gold chanting words that sound as if he speaks in a foreign language that the Confirmation will transform me too, utterly. And the smell of the church will be transformed into the smell of the bats in the nave of the church, into a world of fonts and gravestones.[10]

It is counterpoised to the related experience of her past:

I in my white shift not gipuire but cotton my knees trembling with the early morning cold went down and fought with all my might not to go a second or a third time for in the bottom of the river I had seen the mud and the reeds and the terrible reality of His existence and knew that if I went down three times I would be obliterated by His greatness. And the day became a day of the brothers and sisters who were not my brothers and sisters singing and praying praying and singing for me and my mother crying crying for me Oh-Oh-Ohhhhhhh[11]

A scene similar to that described in the second extract is the background to the next selection, which is a music video 'Revival Time' by a popular singing group – Chalice. The chords on the keyboard support the lively initial chorus:

Aaaamen Aaaamen
  Aahamen Aamen
  Aamen

The lead singer is dressed like a Revival preacher with his white robes and turbaned head. A crowd of similarly robed believers stand on the riverbank passionately involved. The pastor figure is a young man with a sweet clear voice which soon takes over with:

children children
  come to the river
  you want to born again
  you want to feel brand new

He takes one of the faithful and plunges her backwards into the river water.

The discussion afterwards compares the rendering of the same event in two different modes. Questions of 'point of view' and of artistry loom large.

A point needs to be made here about the relaxation and enjoyment obvious in the usually sombre adult students each time I have taught this unit. The introduction of the audio-visual element changes the tone of the presentation.

The next selection is a short poem 'Detail from "Ritual of the River"' by Edward Baugh. Baugh's preacherman is an almost exact representation of the handsome young singer in the Chalice video:

Strapping young preacherman dipping
them, cool morning water, hands sure as faith,
the faithful rejoicing, singing them over[12]

And to be passed around the class is a newspaper clipping, a photograph of two bishops performing a real baptism in the Rio Cobre.

The movement from prose to song (video) to poetry is meant to be smooth, without a hitch, which means that the audiovisual preparation has to be done beforehand.

It is worth mentioning that there will be students in the group who have never seen this baptismal event, never been participant or observer of something that is an integral part of Jamaican and indeed of Caribbean culture. A unit such as this has the added advantage of inducting those into a part of the culture they need to be aware of.

Students are reminded that the contents of a unit depends on what is available to them. Nothing is cast in stone here. The present selection is one person's choice and does not for example include dub-poetry only because a dub poem written on this theme is not immediately to hand. The intention is to make literature real by relating it to other realities in the experience of the students they will eventually teach.

Students' reaction to this unit is invariably rewarding. And this is due as much to the heightened appreciation of the written word that the visual representation encourages as it is the sense of ownership of the material which allows for relaxation and uninhibited discussion afterwards.

3. Conclusion

That the students have studied Caribbean History and Geography makes for a significant difference between the teaching of Caribbean Literature and the teaching of other literatures in a Caribbean classroom. There are fewer explanations to be given fewer 'notes' to be consulted. The psychological impact of all of this, the identification with and pride in the material, have already been noted in the words of the young girl, Hodge's Laetitia (quoted earlier).

Teachers understand that there is great art, great literature in the environment around them. What is written is related to what is part of day to day living. The teacher is as involved in the process of selecting material as any anthologist might be. The literature 'book' is a book without binding.

As Walmsley's article (quoted earlier) indicates, including in the product for the classroom, literature other than the written, is not a new idea. *The Penguin Book of Caribbean Verse*,[13] whose categories have come under some criticism, and *Voiceprint*[14] whose name indicates its focus, both include Traditional songs, written versions of Dub poems, Calypsos and Reggae songs. While the use of audiotapes and music videos improves the delivery, if these are not available texts such as those offer the teacher a more than adequate choice certainly of verse. She/he can select appropriate prose.

There is no dearth of 'good' Caribbean material to present to students. In the last half century or so the output of literature from the Caribbean has been prodigious.

New writers have climbed on the shoulders of the old, refining their art. Olive Senior, poet and fiction writer, addressing Jean Rhys in 'Meditation on Red'[15] makes a comment which while it salutes Rhys as one of the mothers of Caribbean Literature easily applies to Caribbean artists and their writing now, and the confidence with which they demonstrate their excellence:

> [T]hat craft
> you launched
> is so seaworthy
> tighter
> than you'd ever been
> dark voyagers
> like me
> can feel free
> to sail

The classrooms where tomorrow's Caribbean men and women sit today, benefit from that freedom.

Notes

1.   Glyne Griffith, *Deconstruction, Imperialism and the West Indian Novel* (Mona: The Press, University of the West Indies, 1996), xvi.
2.   Olive Senior, *Talking of Trees* (Kingston: Calabash Press, 1985), 26.
3.   Shashi Deshpande,'Them and Us', *Unbecoming Daughters of the Empire,* eds. S. Chew and A. Rutherford (Mundelstrup: Dangaroo Press, 1993), 103-4.
4.   Merle Hodge, *Crick Crack Monkey* (Oxford: repr. Heinemann, 1981), 61.
5.   Quoted in Griffith, 32.
6.   See Anne Walmsley, 'From Nature to Roots', in *From Commonwealth to Post-Colonial* (Mundelstrup: Dangaroo Press, 1992), 365-72.
7.   Merle Hodge, *For the Life of Laetitia* (New York: Farrar Straus Giroux, 1993), 75-76.
8.   Griffith, xx.
9.   Griffith, 2.

10. Olive Senior, 'Confirmation Day', in *Summer Lightning* (Harlow: Longman Group, 1986), 82.
11. 'Confirmation Day', 83.
12. Edward Baugh, 'Detail from "Ritual of the River"', *Malahat Review* 107, 142.
13. *The Penguin Book of Caribbean Verse,* ed. Paula Burnett (London: Penguin).
14. Voiceprint, ed. Stewart Brown (Longman: Harlow, 1989).
15. Olive Senior, *Gardening the Tropics* (Toronto: McClelland and Stewart, 1994), 51-52.

The Trials, Tribulations and Ironies of Teaching Post-colonialism as 'English I' in an Australian University

Russell McDougall,
with an Epilogue by Sue Hosking

Dialogue: that is what we always tell students we want: discussion. And if they sit quietly in tutorials or seminars, expecting repeat performances of our lectures, we feel vaguely, or specifically, miffed. I begin with 'us' and 'them' because, despite our saying we want dialogue, we so rarely act out that desire, or demonstrate it, let alone structure our courses around its possibilities, that the effect for students is so often to confirm our 'otherness' by silence – or by its written equivalent, the essay (they think/we think) we have to have.

There is still a fear of fragmentation in Australia in many of the places where literature and/or literary criticism is taught – traditionally, in universities – fear, that is, that the mainstream of English literature will be diluted and diverted into smaller creeks, backwaters and quagmires. It comes in various forms: fear of lack of coverage (of being uncovered, unhoused, unclothed); fear of new clothes, that may turn out, despite all evidence, to be the Emperor's; professional fears, territorial and otherwise; fear of divorce, and of starting over, of the work involved. But fear is not to be trivialised, for that is a response that plays into its hands – by confirming its own effect – which is denial of dialogue.

I want to focus on one course that I designed, coordinated, tutored and lectured from 1988 to 1990 – 'English I' – in order to foreground here the inevitable problematic of teaching post-colonialism. My sense of it is that teaching post-colonialism is not like teaching other kinds of literature and criticism, that it brings with it side-effects that, in my experience, other kinds of English Department courses do not, and that it raises certain kinds of question inevitably, even against the will sometimes of its teachers. Teaching post-colonialism, then, cannot be legislated. So, if I focus on my own admittedly limited experience in curricula development and course coordination it is not because I believe the course of my own design to provide the only or even necessarily the best model, but because this is what I know, and because it does have the (some would say, 'dubious') virtue of raising some of the larger questions about the teaching of post-colonial literature, and about its relation to the discipline in which most of us do that teaching – that is, 'English'.

When I first began teaching first-year English at the University of Adelaide the year-long course was divided into a number of blocks, introductions to the novel, to drama and poetry (mostly English, though with notable exceptions – James, Chekov, Ibsen, Beckett, Eliot), to language study, and to Australian literature. Not many people liked this course – neither students, lecturers nor tutors – though some had liked it once, before patches here and there had, over several years, sought to repair what others had seen as its defects. The major objections were:

1. that it was, or had become, too fragmented; and that the absence of an introductory and a concluding lecture, as well as any bridging lectures to signpost the course as a whole, intensified this problem;
2. that it was tired, and that it was tiring – not only for its bored students but also for its lecturers, who necessarily were locked into one of its blocks and, furthermore, were identified by students as being correspondingly limited;
3. that it relied upon false assumptions about the kind of literacy that had already been achieved by students before enrolment;
4. that the reading load – with all the poetry taught in one block, all the drama in another, and so on – was unevenly distributed over the year, so that there was a particular problem in having students read all of the novels;
5. that the role of the language component of the course was unclear, indeed unexamined;
6. that there was no particular motivation for students to familiarise themselves with basic critical vocabulary.

One alternative, it was thought, would be to return to something like the course that had previously been abandoned in favour of this one – a chronological survey of English Literature, with a glance here and there at American Literature – an option still favoured at first-year level by many Departments of English in Australia. Yet there was some suspicion of this, the return of the repressed, as the Australian Literature block of the replacement course had clearly been the most successful part of the innovation – not simply the most popular with students – but the most engaged, for 'us' and 'them' (and a number of 'us' were non-specialists).

What evolved is a course with the following aims, as set out for students in the English I Handbook:

At its broadest, English I aims to provide students with an introduction to the study of the English language and to something of the wide variety of literary texts written with it.

The texts selected are not intended to represent some canon, or to illustrate the historical development of English Literature (i.e. the literature of England). In fact, the course is designed to avoid a narrow concentration on the literature of Great Britain, important though that undoubtedly is. Since the time of the first American colonies, the English language, through the processes of colonization, adaptation and – later – independence, has become the vehicle of many different cultures and literatures. This course aims to look at some of the consequences of this, and to study some British texts and some from these 'newer' anglophone literatures in the light of each other. It is hoped that in this way a notion of a central core of 'essential' or canonical texts ('English Literature') will be replaced by the notion of a conversation which has historical and political dimensions in addition to the more narrowly literary.

... Following from the nature of the texts set, a further aim is that students should develop a questioning awareness of the bases of literary/critical judgement and evaluation, and be encouraged to investigate their social and political implications.

This course sought to make a virtue of fragmentation, setting texts side by side in flexible relations that might be grounded generically, thematically, ideologically – in terms of race, politics or gender – or all of these (see Figure 1).

It might be argued that this is not really a post-colonial course, as quite a number of its texts – and some even of its apparent intertextual relationships – are English. But that would be wrong, I think. To begin, as so many English Departments do, with a survey of English (with perhaps some American) literature, and then to move in second year to a course defined as 'post-colonial' (or 'Commonwealth' or 'New Literatures', though these are each different) as one among many options, structurally encodes in the discipline's offerings the reductive notion of post-European literatures 'as marginal continuations or extensions of, say, a central British tradition (a view frequently expressed in the reductive metaphors of trunk and branches, parent and child)'.[1] Instead, the structure implied by the present course is of discourse and counter-discourse. Of course, this characterisation of the intertextuality of the course holds most immediately for the juxtapositions of post-colonial texts with their English opposites. Nevertheless, while this kind of relationship was not privileged among others (thematic, generic, etc.), it was so crucial in the design as to have an unpredictable side-effect: that is, post-colonial revision introduced into the course not only a certain kind of writing strategy but also a different kind of reading strategy, so overturning the 'usual' assumptions about literature (about theme, and genre, for instance) that students began to read the 'other' texts in 'unusual' ways – in more questioning, even subversive ways. (At least, a substantial number of students did – I'll come to the others later.) The course had, from its inception, included lectures on critical terminology, extending notions of allegory, metaphor, other modes and tropes of writing in the context of recent theoretical developments, including those of post-colonialism. When, in the second year of operation, I realised the reading effect of the course's post-colonial

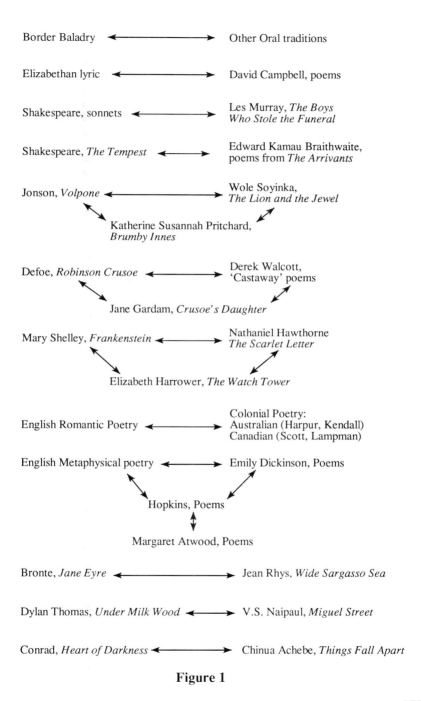

Figure 1

element, I introduced a lecture on discourse and ideology, demonstrating key concepts and methods of analysis with reference not only to a number of the set texts, but also in relation to the official pronouncements of the University and the Department – the language of tertiary administration and policy.

So – post-colonialism became in a sense the impetus for the course, if not a literal description. It added some urgency to reading as a learned process; it precipitated student interest in reading as institutionalised practice, an interest in the institutional structures of which they realised themselves a part (so that they looked much more critically, for example, at the course itself and at the Department's other offerings) – that is, they became at least mildly interested in the idea of education as decolonisation; and it gave extra purpose to the language component of the course (not a block of lectures, but spread over the whole year's programme), which had from the beginning been based on a principle of multiplicity and difference, with lectures on both synchronic and diachronic concepts of language, on semantic change, and on Other Englishes.

When at the end of the third year Andrew Taylor and I edited the volume of essays called *(Un)Common Ground*, which contains revised versions of some of twelve of the lectures given in the course, we introduced our subject in this way:

> Post-colonial studies ... have advanced very fast in the last few years, forcing a re-thinking of the place, role and status of English literature. The variety of texts addressed by the present course at the University of Adelaide, and discussed in these essays, is a direct result of this relocation of English literature within a widely defined Literature in English.
>
> ... In all these countries [i.e. those of the English-speaking world] versions of the English language have assumed a cultural and political force, confronting, subverting or abrogating the orders of conventional (i.e. imperial, colonising) English, and thus providing escape from its imperial constraints, as well as from its failures to articulate and construct adequate representations of their social realities. In a way which parallels the protean developments of the language, the various literatures in English have also developed, responding to a diversity of challenges and answering multiple cultural and political needs, depending upon place and circumstance. The result has been more than simply to destroy the hegemony of a single, colonialist, discourse (that of 'Eng. Lit'.) and to permit the emergence of other discourses. These can be characterised, it must be stressed, not only by nationality, but also by gender, race and class. It has also led to a questioning and undermining of the claims of unity and coherence propagated by traditional colonialist discourse (which maintained its power by marginalising or rendering inaudible other discourse) since any post-colonial discourse, by its very nature, is constituted by difference, heterogeneity, and multiplicity.[2]

The deliberate fragmentation in the narrative design of the course was essential to the realisation of reading as process, as 'appreciation' grounded upon interrogation, for it provided an echo of the openness of that process. The appropriateness of fragmentation as a structural principle derives from several sources, among them the Louis Hartz thesis of historical fragmentation, and the narrative strategies of fragmentation developed in much post-colonial writing precisely in service to counter-discourse to unsettle false clarities of universality, centrality and the exclusive identity-formations of imperialism and colonialism.

Another structural principle of design which helped inspire an openness in students, realising for the first time that reading is strategy and does involve choices which have a social and political as well as a literary dimension, was that the course should provide a performance framework for an 'infinite rehearsal' of possibilities. The concept derives from the post-colonial writer and theorist, Wilson Harris, who, in an essay entitled 'Comedy and Modern Allegory', writes:

> There is no final play, all is rehearsal....
>
> The impact of rehearsal implies that embryonic masks of reality sustaining insights into eclipsed potential for genuine change need to be re-sensed again and again until a quantum change occurs.[3]

Multiple masks, interconnected personae, perform this service through one after another of Harris's fictions, each sliding intertextually toward both the next and the last and reaching out to many, many other texts as well. Most explicitly, the narrator of *The Infinite Rehearsal*, begins 'this fictional autobiography' with a confession:

> I know that in unraveling the illusory capture of creation I may still apprehend the obsessional ground of conquest, rehearse its proportions, excavate its consequences, within a play of shadow and light threaded into value; a play that is infinite rehearsal, a play that approaches again and again a sensation of ultimate meaning residing within a deposit of ghosts relating to the conquistadorial body – as well as the victimized body – of new worlds and old worlds, new forests and old forests, new stars and old constellations within the workshop of the gods.[4]

This might have stood as an epigraph to the course as a whole, for its relevance is not simply narratological; it may also describe the act of reading. Having one text jostle with others more or less interrogatively (so that one lecturer after another found him/herself similarly and unavoidably unsettled from the 'natural' authority of his/her position) provided a powerful reading model: a 'final' reading is never possible, as a final performance privileges one performance, or reading, beyond rehearsal.

There were, of course, objections, both in the planning stages and later, during the running of the course, by some students as well as some staff – which are instructive enough in themselves to warrant mention here.

In the developmental phase, when a new course is planned and proposed, there is no active student representation at the University of Adelaide. Staff objections at this stage were as follows.

First, this course would not be some other 'ideal' course: mainly, it would not be a chronological survey of English Literature. But, then, if one looks down the left-hand column of texts (listed previously), there is a rough chronology of English Literature.

Second, this course would apparently not emphasise the so-called 'best that has been written' in English. But, with very few exceptions (which had then to be argued for individually – Shelley, Thomas, Prichard, Harrower, Gardam), the set texts would probably be among most people's 'Greatest Hits of the Commonwealth'.

Third, the dialogic relationships suggested by the arrangement of lectures, juxtaposing one text with another, would tend to lead the students and so straitjacket each text so that it could not be considered flexibly enough in terms of its full literary potential. This was not so easy to counter, because by 'literary' was meant non-political, whereas the emphasis of the course as a whole is that writing is always, unavoidably, political. The objection was, if not withdrawn, at least dampened by a consensus of principle: that, of course, there would be no onus on any lecturer to teach a text from a prescribed point of view, nor even to acknowledge its placing in relation to other set texts, and that anyone who wished to teach 'literature as literature' and not say anything about his or her ideological commitment or theoretical approach to a given text was perfectly at liberty to do so. The enshrinement of this principle of academic freedom in the end turned out to be a major advantage. We had already agreed that, although it would obviously be necessary to have one or two people (preferably the coordinators) lecture often enough to give the students a sense of direction, dialogue would best be demonstrated by having as many lecturers as possible involved in the teaching of the course. In the very first lecture, I delivered a deconstructive monologue to try to foreground for students the contradiction that lecturing in this course necessarily would involve. Then, throughout the year, 'infinite rehearsal' acquired its own momentum. Perhaps the best moment in the first year of the course's running, when suddenly it all seemed to 'click' for most of the students and I knew it was working, occurred when one lecturer decided to spend half of his first lecture on Robinson Crusoe voicing his disagreement with the general principles and rationale of the course.

At the end of the first year of the course's being offered, anonymous student evaluation was sought by questionnaire. A total of 343 students enrolled for this course. Of these, 196 completed the questionnaire: 156 (78.5%) female, 42 (21.5%) male.

	Female	Male	Total
Under 21 years	119	27	146 (74%)
21-25 years	11	4	15 (7.6%)
25-30 years	12	6	18 (9%)
31-35 years	10	1	11 (5.5%)
Over 40 years	4	3	7 (3.5%)

(No other demographic analysis is available; but the student population of this, like most other English Department courses at the University of Adelaide and elsewhere in Australia at that time, was overwhelmingly White Anglo-Saxon Protestant Female.) The Independent Analyst commissioned by the Department to comment on the results of this survey, summarised the findings of her Report as follows:[5]

> Overall, students' responses are remarkably positive about the course. They did not find it easy: 95% of the students indicated on a five point scale that they found ... the difficulty of the course 'reasonable' to 'difficult'... However, in answer to the question 'How do you feel about the content of the course?' only 14% (28 of the 200 respondents) answered 'negative' or 'very negative'. As well, to the question 'How clear do you consider the logic of the course?' 80% responded 'reasonably clear' or 'very clear'.
>
> I take these responses as showing that the new course proved demanding but satisfying. This conclusion is strengthened by responses to questions about how issues of race and gender were handled. To the question 'How well do you think this course has dealt with the issue of gender in considering literary texts?' 87% answered 'reasonably' to 'very well', and in answers to the parallel question on race, the percentage in these categories was even higher, at 97%.

However, there were undoubtedly what the Report calls 'pockets of disaffection'. Chosen at random, here are some students' (anonymous) objections:

Female students – under twenty-one
1. Lots of works on Africa and the West Indies expected us to know something of the history of the places – which many of us didn't.
2. One personal concern of mine has been the lack of Shakespeare.
3. The 'FEMINIST ISSUE' has been thrashed to death. Not everything ever written by a female was a secret desire for her to burn her bra.
4. I think the aims of this course, while for the most part achieved, tend to be rather indulgent and a little arty-farty intellectualisation ... rather ivory towerish.
5. I feel there should be more Australian literature.
6. School English courses place great emphasis on modern and/or Australian literature and the English I course has avoided the traditional English canon (i.e. the classics). Therefore, WHEN DOES THE MODERN STUDENT OF ENGLISH COME INTO CONTACT WITH 'THE CLASSIC ENGLISH CANON'.

7. There was no cohesion between lectures or lecturers (especially when they use our time to bitch at one another)!
8. Connections between books appear weak and abstract inventions of the English Department! I would prefer a more concrete course.

Male students – under twenty-one
9. The English Department is run by the salvos [Salvation Army], and they feel they must help any struggling writer who comes along to sell at least 500 copies of a book, when his work isn't fit to be used in a Toyota jingle!!
10. The emphasis on the evils of imperialism and how good black people can write in English (no good examples to prove this) really discourages me from doing English next year.
11. I feel that many lecturers have launched into critical analyses without really explaining their foundations. Have we really been exposed to structuralism and deconstruction? If so, I would have liked to have been told at the time.! ... I do feel that the course was rather fragmented, but if there were a firm grounding in some sort of critical theory, such fragmentation could actually have been constructive.
12. The course has aimed to challenge the idea of the canon, yet the number of canonical texts in the course is ridiculously low. Canonical texts were not studied in school, so we are without a basis for comparison.... Lecturers were keen to give 'alternative' readings. We would get much more value out of these if we were given some idea of standard readings.
13. I feel that I have been discriminated against because I am white, male heterosexual ... I feel like a laboratory rat who has been asked his feelings about sick, bizarre experiments.
14. The course is too anti-British ...

Male students – twenty-five to thirty
15. The negative tone used in most of the novels is intolerable. Having to read them one after another is mental torture. I suggest you make it a bit more positive, enjoyable, happy, in the future.

Female students – thirty-one to forty
16. Much to my surprise, there has been a considerable and consistent sex bias in the language used by lecturers ... There are those of us who would welcome the opportunity to attend, for example, a supplementary lecture ... where it becomes apparent that the majority of the class thinks feminism is a dirty word.
17. There seems to be a considerable resistance amongst some of the 'old school' lecturers to this new course ...

Answers to all questions were analysed by sex, and some were analysed according to age. 'Age was not generally found to be a significant factor in the spread of the responses, although students over 21 were marginally more positive ... For most questions, male and female answers averaged out marginally differently, but with stronger differences sometimes emerging' (Report) – particularly in relation to the gender and race issues.

How well do you consider this course dealt with the issue of gender in considering literary texts?

	% Female	% Male	Total Numbers
Very Well	15	7	27
Quite Well	44	38	84
Reasonably	29	35	59
Poorly	10	10	20
Very Poorly	2	10	7

As the analyst noted, the percentages here are interesting: 59% of all females rated the course as handling gender issues either well or very well, and only 12% of females rated this aspect of the course poorly or very poorly; whereas, only 45% of all males rated the course's handling of gender well/very well, and 20% rated this poorly/very poorly. Overall, 13% of all students felt disaffected in regard to the gender issues of the course.

How do you view the emphasis placed on gender in this course?

	% Female	% Male	Total Numbers
Much Too Strong	8	16	19
Too Strong	22	39	50
About Right	63	41	115
Too Weak	6	4	12
Much Too Weak	3	0	1

This means that, overall, 58% thought the emphasis was reasonable, although there was 'a marked male/female difference, which shows up in the fact that 55% of males compared with 30% of females indicated the emphasis was strong/too strong' (Report).

How do you view the emphasis placed on race in this course?

	Total Numbers
Much Too Strong	4
Too Strong	22
About Right	163
Too Weak	8
Much Too Weak	0

'Here 82% found the emphasis reasonable but there was again a marked male/female difference: 11% of all females but 20% of all males said the emphasis was strong/too strong and the 8 who checked ["Too Weak"] were all female'. (Report).

No major structural changes were made to the course as a result of this survey, which after all was remarkably positive in its overall response, though undoubtedly some lecturers did alter the style, and perhaps even the content, of their lectures in order to forestall students' in the following year gaining certain unintended impressions (the 'anti-British' slant, for example). Also, in the normal course of study-leave and teaching-load requirements, some of the texts acquired new lecturers, and this necessarily changed the balance of the course in certain areas. However, even allowing for the sexism or racism (or both) of some of the disaffected, a number of the criticisms are worthy of comment.

First, there is the question of theory. At the University of Adelaide, as at many other Australian universities, this is a still a vexed question: in particular, at which level should it be introduced? Several years ago, when the old English I course was still in operation, a component of literary theory had been built into it, taught by a highly competent metacritic and theorist who was as well a wonderful teacher. There had been lectures on New Criticism, structuralism, semiotics, deconstruction, feminist, Marxist and psychoanalytic theory (nothing on post-colonialism). Most people, including (I think) the lecturer concerned, thought this had not succeeded. Students had either ignored it or absorbed it half-baked. Subsequently, theory became a compulsory subject at the Honours (i.e. fourth-year, or extension) level. There it seems successful; but, of course, many students do not proceed to Honours, and so would not acquire (except by osmosis, by the practical example of certain tutors and lecturers) any theoretical insight into their critical procedure. With the 'new' English I, the aim was to introduce theory 'without pain', or 'through the back door', so that it might become a point of reference for later excursions. Certainly, some theoretical propositions and procedures are articulated more directly: the post-colonial revisionist strategies of fragmentation, polyphony, counter-discourse and infinite rehearsal underpinning

184

concepts of heterogeneous community, multiplicity and difference. These are toward the foreground – or were while I was at the University of Adelaide, as I was until 1991 – along with feminist debate over a number of texts and various notions of 'influence' or structuralist intertextuality. Less audible, though still discussed *en passant* throughout the course, are the ideological differences and procedural intersections of post-colonialism, post-structuralism and feminism. (The absence of a post-modernist text on the course probably contributed to the mere implication of this theoretical debate, which became much more open when Vikram Seth's *The Golden Gate* replaced Les Murray's *The Boys Who Stole the Funeral*.) The prominence of the anti-feminist objection to the course – from what, it should be stressed, was a very small but vocal minority of students – is, however distressing, also particularly interesting. In part it may be accounted for as an objection to theory, as feminism is more up-front in its ideological engagement with literature than many other critical modes and is therefore almost impossible to sneak through the back door as 'theory'. It is also obviously undesirable, politically, to try to do so. Not that we did try, really. But no-one foresaw in the planning stages that, by simply rectifying the gender imbalance in the ratio of female to male writers (and, as much as possible, female to male lecturers) represented on the previous English I course, and then by introducing post-colonial literature (and to some extent theory) with its inevitable emphasis on power relations, the literature by women would raise the issue of feminism with equal inevitability and constancy and persuasiveness. Indeed, one of the most enjoyable aspects of the course as a whole for those teaching it was to see it take on shapes of interest and configurations of conflict that had not been predicted. It is probably too soon to know how successful the introduction to theory has been. How, for example, could the student questionnaire ask overtly about theory when it had only been introduced covertly? It did, however, ask a necessarily vague question, not well phrased I think, about 'the emphasis on critical evaluation'. The response was as follows: 55% answered 'about right'; 31% 'too weak'; 8% 'too strong'. In response to another question, concerning how well the course had succeeded in achieving its aim 'to develop skills in the critical appreciation of a wide range of literary texts', students replied: 11.5% 'very well'; 36.5% 'quite well'; 43% 'moderately'. And on the question of how well the further aim of the course had been achieved – 'that students should develop a questioning awareness of the bases of literary/critical judgement and evaluation, and be encouraged to investigate their social and political implications': 10.5% 'very well'; 40% 'quite well'; 33% 'moderately'. So the mode (or most frequent answer) in every case is in the range of positives.

The objection that the course is deficient in its 'classic' offerings and assumes too much knowledge of a traditional English Literature canon is a thorny one, for it cuts to the heart of one of the course's stated aims: to replace the notion of a central canon of essential English texts with one of an intertextual, cross-cultural dialogue between literatures, and to reveal the literary, historical and political dimensions of such dialogue. If they knew nothing of the canon beforehand, was our aim misconceived? Should the 'key' canonical texts on the syllabus have been sufficient, along with a number of lectures directly and indirectly focused on canon formation and interrogation, to open a door into that area of theoretical and ideological debate? If one wants to know about fire does one have to know about ice? Is recognition of evil by its traces sufficient to convince of the real power of good? But, then, we did not want to convince, only to question, and to stimulate genuinely 'original' thought – so perhaps the aim of 'replacement' was not well conceived, since there will always be attempts made, however tentatively or even unaware, to reform canons, as in fact many of the national literatures (or their critics) have done and continue to do.

I do not know the answer to this, and can only go by the survey results: 25.5% of students considered the 'dialogic' aim of the course in relation to the canon 'very well' achieved; 44% 'quite well' (the mode response); 23.5% 'moderately'. As to the proportion of 'canonical' texts: 62% 'about right' (mode); 25.5% 'too low'; 4% 'too high'.

The historicist objection – that the course did not take into account students' scant historical knowledge of other countries and cultures – is equally difficult to judge. Certainly, those students who were enrolled simultaneously in the first-year History course entitled 'Old Societies and New States: Rich and Poor Nations in the Modern World' seemed to benefit enormously in English I as a result – though this 'benefit' was not necessarily reflected in their final assessment results. (The focus of that History I course was, to quote from its Student Handbook, 'the transformation of Old Societies into New States which has taken place in Africa, Asia, and the Pacific region – including Australia – during the last two or three hundred years. Through an examination of key issues in social, political, and economic change, it aims at furthering our understanding of the historical processes which have shaped the modern world'.) In the first year of the course, a number of lecturers had doubts about the ability of students to handle the course:

> They commented on the students' lack of background and the difficulty they have in 'placing' a text, historically or in relation to other texts. They can get dizzy in a course that leaps from genre to genre, from country to country, from century to century, and makes such leaps deliberately as essential to the business of engaging in 'a conversation between related but differing literatures' while at the same time seeking to pay attention to the historical/political dimensions of these texts. This may be particularly difficult for those students who came to the university straight from the kind of Matriculation English ... where literature was used as a springboard for personal growth and texts were presented as somehow universal, decon-textualised. Few first-year students have a sense of history, or even much curiosity about other times and other places.[6]

On the other hand, the 'historical' focus of English I was intentionally double, if anything weighted in the direction of a synchronic rather than a diachronic perspective. That is, in some cases, the course implied a re-definition of 'history' in terms of structural relations and so sought not to privilege History as a form of narrative. Nonetheless, if I were still coordinating the course (which I am not), I would want to think through more clearly the pedagogical means of getting this de-privileged sense of history-as-narrative across to students, while still accounting for the political urgency of post-colonial literature in historical terms (as I suspect this has not been sufficiently to the foreground).

It is interesting to note that an 'average' response, calculated separately for male and female, differed marginally for some questions, and particularly in relation to the success of the course in dealing with the issues of race and gender in literary consideration. Age was not generally found to be a significant factor in the spread of responses, although students over twenty-one were marginally more positive in their answers. With regard to the degree of 'emphasis' on race, to quote from the survey-analyst's Report: '11% of all females but 20% of all males said the emphasis was strong/too strong' – and the 4% who checked 'too weak' were all female. Considering the degree of 'emphasis' on gender: 'Overall 58% thought the emphasis was reasonable, although there was a marked male/female difference, which shows up in the fact that 55% of males compared with 30% of females indicated the emphasis was strong/too strong' (Report).

Having quoted a number of students' specific objections, I should also provide a (random) sample of majority opinion:

Brilliant. *Don't drop the imperialist/colonial theme!*

I had expected a far more traditional approach and was pleasantly surprised with the structure of this year's course.

I did English I last year and withdrew because I was dissatisfied with the course – the sections on poetry, prose and drama were far too long. This year, they have been intermingled, which is a great improvement ...

This course is a great improvement on the previous English I, which I failed to complete because it was so very dull. The present English I is far more intelligent and modern in its approach.
I found the choice of texts enthralling. To study English was not a taste but a joy. There was great insight into human nature, and the world in which we live ...

I liked it – and I liked the feminist slant. There should be more of it. I found the political side of the course really interesting because it's not something you get in high school English.

Thank you for providing a stimulating and enjoyable environmental context for the study of English. Thank you for the opportunities and vistas opened out before me to provide insights into languages and thought development in English.

187

This year's course has been thoroughly enjoyable and appropriate.... The gods be praised – it was great fun – it actually fitted into and was relevant to the modern world.

Your department is to be congratulated on its courage in presenting a course that, I imagine, completely breaks with tradition. It certainly is ... a vast improvement on your competitor's product.

Thank you so much for a fabulous and entertaining year. From an auditor student (with a B.A.) who wanted a little 'no tears' learning and literary experience, the whole exercise was most worthwhile.

Student evaluation, however, is only one component of gauging the success or otherwise of a course. Peggy Mares, the person who, at the end of 1988, was commissioned to analyse independently the student response to the course, has a special research interest in the construction of English as a subject taught in schools, colleges and universities. At the time of her Report on the course, she had been looking, simultaneously and for her own purposes, at 'the interface between Year 12 [i.e. final-year high school], particularly the publicly-examined subject English, and what students are offered when they enrol for some form of English in their first year of tertiary studies' (Literacy, 19). The present English I course at the University of Adelaide became one of a number of case studies in her comparative research into the teaching of English in South Australia, the results of which were published at the end of the first year of the course (1988) in Deakin University's Journal of the Centre for Studies in Literary Education, *Typereader*. To establish some kind of framework for discussion, she begins with a series of distinctions relating to different kinds of literacy:

1. Functional Literacy – defined (from Janet Batsleer *et al.*, *Rewriting English*) as '"reading and writing for the labor market," because it includes cognitive skills and understanding'.[7]
2. Cognitive Literacy – defined (from the Gilding Report on immediate post-compulsory education in South Australia) as 'communication and cognitive skills ... such as elaboration of thought, sequencing of points, clarity of expression, understanding the language-system and functions ...'.[8]
3. Literary Literacy, or 'Literacy with a capital "L"' – defined (from the South Australian College of Advance Education's Salisbury campus 'Literary Studies' course syllabus) as 'skills, knowledge and confidence in dealing with literature' – that is, the ability 'to be literate about literature' (Literacy, 29 and 22).
4. Powerful Literacy – defined (again, from *Rewriting English*) as 'the acquisition of those relevant forms of writing and reading and speaking that confer genuine understanding and control ... "Powerful literacy" will open up the awareness and criticism of ideologies'.[9]

Mares' conclusion is: 'the Adelaide course takes Literacy with a capital "L" for granted and proceeds straight to a sophisticated study of literature. As the study confronts traditional notions of Eng. Lit., encouraging a more political reading, it is possible to see it as aiming towards powerful literacy' (Literacy, 33). Such literacy, Andrew Taylor and I claim in *(Un)Common Ground*, is 'not the ability simply to construe sentences and read texts, but rather to read what texts *do* – i.e. to understand their subtle and often not so apparent, but none the less real, social and political consequences' (3). Post-colonialism, as a teaching subject *in* English *in* Australia (or for that matter any other post-colonial culture) is a perfect vehicle for achieving the aim of powerful literacy.

There is, however, one possible problem: not everyone teaching the course agrees with that aim. Having interviewed each of the people teaching the course in 1988, Mares writes:

> Some lecturers would prefer to teach only the essential core of literature, seeing some of this year's texts as lightweight, as without 'literary value'. Others, staff and students, have commented that the course is now too political (other words they used were 'polemical', 'socialist' and 'subversive'). (Literacy, 30)

However, as I have indicated, lecturers who feel that way do not in my view undermine the aims of the course. Rather they contribute to its multivocal evocation of difference and so assist the students' developing awareness of discourse and counter-discourse and how ideology encodes itself differentially in these. Mares' comments on critical theory seem to the point in this regard:

> Several pointed out that in this course theoretical differences are implicitly conveyed by having a range of different lecturers, some of who make it clear that they are approaching the text from an identifiable critical position....
>
> ... [Another] group of comments centres on the fact that the possibilities of this course are becoming more apparent as the year progresses. Unanticipated richness is generated by the juxtapositions, and this is cumulative and recursive. For example, putting together The Tempest and Brathwaite raises the theme of colonialism, but put Frankenstein alongside and the connection becomes the recurrent myth of the outsider/monster.... For those interested in literary theory, having ten people of different persuasions giving the lectures is providing something of a critical feast this year, particularly as staff are, for the first time, attending one another's lectures. (Literacy, 31)

As to that question which had bothered a number of lecturers in relation to the previous English I course – that it seemed to rely upon false assumptions about the kind of literacy already achieved at school – my own view with the new course was more deliberately to exploit the gap, to shock students into thinking differently about literature and about the cultural debates that take place in and around it. Certainly they floundered for some time, more than the usual time, but not, thankfully, forever. I imagine that this is what the questionnaire had in mind when it asked students to what extent the course had altered their conception of what

'Literature' is: 6.5% answered 'greatly'; 28.5% 'quite a lot'; 36% 'a little'; 17.5% 'not much'; 10% 'not at all'. However, as the Report on student evaluation notes, it is 'difficult to interpret the answers to this question: it all depends on what their prior conception was, and on whether this change is for "better" or not. (And who is to say?)'

To return, as one so often does in discussion of pedagogical practice and principle, to my first paragraph, the most emphatic point about 'teaching' Post-Colonial Literature is not that it presents particular problems, but that it affords startling opportunities. 'We' do not read books in order to be comforted in our insufficiencies, but to be wrenched from them. Nor do we examine texts in a spirit of obedience to our preceptors. The study of literature, if it is to have any value, is not to induce a due reverence for great minds and nimble pens. It is not even to raise interesting questions. Literatures worth scrutiny rehearse the possibilities of being *out of control*. By its structure and procedure, and every aspect of its teaching, a 'course' in post-colonial literature rehearses these same infinite possibilities, one of which embodies the irony of course-work itself: that is, the contradiction between a course of time, fixed and finite, and a course of action, or direction – a train of thought.

How this course influences students' involvement in subsequent, often more conventional, courses in 'English' I cannot say. That is part of a dialogue yet unspoken.

[1991]

Epilogue

The course designed by Russell McDougall is still taught as 'English I' at the University of Adelaide. Although we have had to work a lot harder in recent years to earn favourable reports from our students (we can no longer rely on the initial flush of excitement that accompanies a new course to carry us through), staff generally feel that the current course is still successful and assessment by students, administered by the Advisory Centre for University Education towards the end of 1993, confirmed this. Nevertheless, some discontent has been expressed in the last few years and we have had to think seriously about this. The word has spread among students (and their former high school teachers) that we are 'politically correct'. Personally, I don't feel the need to apologise for this, but I do feel the need to defend and justify the politics of the course, and on occasions to employ more subtle strategies than I was once accustomed to use. This is not, in itself, a bad thing. Scrutiny of our motives surely is more productive than counter-productive. After all, some significantly challenging theorising encroaching on post-colonialism has been undertaken and published since 1988. (I am thinking, for example, of Anne McClintock's 'The Angel of Progress: pitfalls of the term "post-colonialism"', *Social Text*, Spring 1992, 1-15 and Aijaz Ahmad's *In Theory*, Verso, 1992.) We need to be on the ball if we are to continue promoting post-colonialism with confidence.

It is easy to bore students who think they know what is coming, and the problem will not be remedied simply by tinkering with the texts on the course. The life of a syllabus, it seems, is directly proportional to the attention span of students. Increasingly, the attention span of an English I student is proportional to the perceived productivity of the course. (For example, high marks are required for acceptance into Law. Numbers of bright students elect to do English I at the University of Adelaide primarily because they scored high marks in it in Matriculation and intend using it as a means to enter a vocational course after their first year.) With such an emphasis on productivity, we have been faced in the last few years with a strong element of conservatism among our students, such that some of the fears that Russell has already alluded to in relation to the institutions where English is taught are now more evident among the students than the teaching staff. Some students are afraid that they will leave the course without the necessary clothing (without the necessary marks – without the 'coverage' that their respected and comfortably employed elders have told them is essential). Others are afraid that they will be subjected to an arbitrary selection of texts reflecting the idiosyncratic interests of a range of staff rather than an ordered (chronological) sequence of tried and tested literary 'greats', representing better value for money. Such fears and prejudices have only served to confirm in my mind the need for teaching literatures in English with a post-colonial emphasis in Australian Universities. But we have had to improve our strategies.

One of the most worrying complaints that students have made of our course is that they have failed to find 'significant' links between set texts. Some have been clearly frustrated by a syllabus that appears fragmented and they are inclined to resist intertextual links made in lectures as 'forced'. (Ben Jonson's *Volpone* and Wole Soyinka's *The Lion and the Jewel,* for example, have been mentioned in student assessments of the course as 'having nothing in common apart from animal imagery'.) In setting canonical texts against post-colonial texts, something that we did not sufficiently take into account was the experience students had had in their Matriculation year of 'pairing' texts. In practice, such 'pairings' were generally thematic and emphasised similarities. To expect the majority of students automatically to appreciate the political dimensions of canonical/post-colonial pairings or groupings, and to expect them to understand that fragmentation and difference could be celebrated in a post-colonial context, was probably unrealistic at first-year level.

Where it was hoped, initially, that some understanding of the theoretical underpinnings of the course would enter students' minds gently, 'without pain or through the back door', it was soon apparent that we needed to be more explicit about what we were doing and we needed to demonstrate our critical positions. Feminist readings in lectures (which we now introduce with a relatively un-threatening but nevertheless *still* controversial lecture on Gender Studies) rudely awakened us to the need to demonstrate that we *were* in fact adopting critical positions and not merely spouting mad ideas off the top of our heads. ('Is that woman married?' 'What's she got against men?' were typical responses from male and female students after lectures on *Jane Eyre* and *Crusoe's Daughter.* When a male lecturer gave a feminist reading of *Frankenstein* the response was less personal, but nevertheless there was still some hostility.) This has been a major concern in the last few years and, given the rapid expansion of the teaching of and debate about literary theory in tertiary institutions, we have felt justified in making the theoretical component of the course overt rather than covert.

It is important to demonstrate that post-colonial writing intersects with literary theories that we might want to apply to writing in general. In our course, our most pressing need, it seems to me, is to reinforce the link between post-colonialism and feminism. This task will be less daunting since the publication of Laura Donaldson's *Decolonizing Feminisms Race, Gender and Empire-Building* (London: Routledge, 1994). If we can successfully address these kinds of intersections, the course should make even more sense to those students whose ears automatically close when they hear the key words of (in particular) feminist discourse. ('Easier on the feminism, honestly' and 'focus less on the oppression of women and more of what is in the text' were two typical comments volunteered on the 1993 assessment sheets.) The challenge remains, however, to justify theoretical approaches to school-leavers many of whose teachers are still actively opposed to 'all that bullshit'. Part of the problem lies in the conviction that so many students still bring with them that there *is* a 'correct' way to read each text. After all, that is how most of them have been taught to pass examinations. Lecturers are therefore perceived as deliberately withholding *the* key to meaning in any given text. We have to be patient while we wait for students to realise that different critical approaches are different kinds of keys to unlocking different kinds of meanings, and that our intention is to expand, rather than obstruct, their thinking. We have to reinforce our intentions at every opportunity and make conscious efforts to de-mystify current critical practices. ('The object of any class is to help students learn, not for Professors to boast their grasp of the English language' and 'language is for communication, not class separation' wrote students – too often to be ignored.) Theory lectures are only palatable to our first-year students when they are directly tied to texts. The lecture on Post-colonialism is currently tied to V.S. Naipaul's *Miguel Street* and Olive Senior's *Summer Lightning* and juxtaposed against a lecture on *Miguel Street* in which the lecturer identifies his position as 'liberal humanist'. This seems to work particularly well. In the 1993 student assessment of the course the overt post-colonial explanations of texts were highly praised. One of the most successful strategies employed so far in the course has been overt disagreement between lecturers on given texts. We have not exploited this fully, although we now agree that the course would be improved if we were to reduce the number of texts studied and enable different lecturers to demonstrate different approaches (including, most consistently, post-colonial readings) to the same text.

From the inception of the course we have talked a lot about 'dialogue' and 'conversations between texts'. Perhaps we should have concentrated more on 'conversations between lecturers'. We seem to have denied ourselves possibilities for demonstrating that in setting a number of canonical texts against a number of post-colonial texts, we are actually engaging in a vital critical debate. Perhaps we should have taken more notice of the effects of a particular lecture – ostensibly on *Robinson Crusoe* – in the first year that the course was offered. The lecturer concerned took the opportunity to criticise the brand new course we were offering as English I, objecting particularly to the way in which he perceived the 'great' works of English literature were being downgraded and suggesting that some of the texts students had been asked to read were not worthy of study. My students, coming straight from this lecture to their tutorial, were agog. For most, this was the first time they became aware that they were actively participating in a critical and theoretical debate in which they had to work out a position for themselves. The tutorials that followed that potentially disastrous (I would have thought at the time) episode were so exciting for me and for my students that I, for one, changed my thinking about including in the course 'traditional' readings of canonical texts. I am now convinced that the best way to enliven the course is to engage in debate *in* the lecture theatre. Last year five separate students advised us voluntarily in writing on their assessment sheets that 'where there are two lectures on the same text, get two different lecturers'.

Judging by my own experience, the life-span of a first year English course that is not a traditional survey course seems to be about five years. Last year, then, it was most important that we formally assess the current course and address criticisms that had been made unofficially in the Counter Calendar (notorious as an avenue of expression for disaffected students). Formal assessment, implemented through the Advisory Centre for University Education, indicated that the majority of students *were* content with the course. Of the 128 students who returned assessment sheets, many volunteered positive comments that were encouraging. (Most consistently recurring comments included: 'I liked new ways of viewing texts', 'I liked the awareness and insight into other cultures', 'liked reading books I wouldn't otherwise have read' and 'interesting mix of texts'). This, in itself, is a recommendation for teaching from a post-colonial position – for although we have 'tinkered' with the course as Russell originally designed it, post-colonialism is unquestionably still the dominant thread weaving through the syllabus and the theory/criticism which most students find most accessible. Last year's students were required to respond to seventeen questions about the course using a scale of 1 to 7, from 'strongly disagree' to 'strongly agree'. Bar graphs indicated that students regarded the degree of difficulty of the subject and the amount of theory content as reasonable to heavy. They agreed to strongly agreed that the subject was challenging and that they understood the subject matter presented. Responses to three of the questions, however, indicated the need for further action. There was a wide range of responses when students were asked whether (1) alternative points of view were presented where appropriate (2) the aims of the subject were implemented and (3) the connection between the various topics in the subject was made clear. General comments at the end of the survey sheet confirmed these problems, and as a result a proposal to reorganise the course, without substantially altering its nature, was drawn up and approved by the department.

The proposal introduces two six-week blocks of options, occupying the last six weeks of the first semester and the third to eighth weeks of the second semester. First years will spend fourteen weeks following the kind of teaching programme we already have, in core lectures, at the beginning, in the middle, and at the end of the course. Twelve weeks will be spent studying two out of four (or more, depending upon availability of staff) options. Options will draw upon components which have always existed within the course, but which have not been perceived by students as clearly sign-posted. By labelling options ('Canonical study' [something students have consistently asked for: 'more Shakespeare', 'more traditional texts', 'Mr Dickens where are you?'] or 'The Gothic', for example), the already existing possibilities for grouping texts will become much more obvious to students. It has also been agreed in principle that during their optional studies, students will spend more time in tutorials/seminars and less time in lectures. Comments in the ACUE assessment indicated a strong preference for interactive learning, generally favouring tutorials over lectures. Regrettably, given the (still) current crisis in funding and staffing, we may not be able to implement more tutorials immediately.

One of the most significant criticisms made of the course last year was that the lecture programme introduced texts too quickly for students to absorb ideas that were central to the course. It is our hope that by cutting down on the number of texts studied and inviting students to exercise some choice in opting to study certain texts in more detail, or to 'side with' certain ways of reading, they will respond with even greater enthusiasm and commitment to English I. A further advantage of introducing options is that it makes the course more flexible. Options can be changed from year to year, depending upon availability of staff. Furthermore, particular enthusiasms among lecturers can be demonstrated and used to the advantage of the course. It has been something of a problem in teaching the course that by no means all of the lecturers involved in English I are passionately committed to post-colonialism; students have been quick to pick this up. Last year several students commented on their course assessment sheets that some lecturers gave the impression of being uninterested in their subject matter. My feeling is that fear of a 'take-over' by voices representing the canon (which resulted in the suppression of those voices) has been counter-productive in the course, and that open debate is much closer to the spirit of post-colonial studies. This may be a dangerous game to play, given that the dissenting voices may speak rather loudly. However, if we are to regard our course as 'decolonising', we must have the confidence to be seen to be entering into dialogue with our critics, rather than just 'answering back'. Our students, after all, are rather vague (if not ignorant) about the notion of the canon when they come to us. It is hoped that the structure of the core parts of the revised course – the mixture of canonical and post-colonial texts and the clearly designated post-colonial revisions of 'great' works of British literature – will ensure that the course retains its original flavour, while the options will enable students to become more engaged in some of the issues the course asks students to consider.

My own experience, in introducing an Aboriginal text into the syllabus, is salutary. I was horrified when one of our early students complained that he was sick of all our 'bleating about slaves'. (There was originally a more substantial component of Caribbean fiction and poetry on the course than is now the case.) I had already decided that the absence of an Aboriginal text on the course, which had a strong (but still not strong enough) Australian component, was a problem that needed to be rectified, particularly when one of the set texts, Katharine Susannah Prichard's *Brumby Innes,* contained a representation of Aboriginal culture. Jack Davis's *No Sugar* was the obvious counterpart to Prichard's text, given that they are both set in the same period. This pairing was particularly useful in that it demonstrated that literary 'canons' can exist within post-colonial societies, so that notions of centre and margins cannot be fixed. My assumption had been that students would respond better to black writing that was closer to home, however I was quite unprepared for the strong reaction to my lectures from several students who indicated that they were, in effect, sick of 'bleating' about Aborigines. One student insisted on the course assessment sheet that we should remove the 'trashy low class Australian' texts, naming *Brumby Innes* and *No Sugar* specifically. Another wrote that s/he 'resented the sense of guilt felt as a result of lectures on colonialism'. Such criticisms have diminished since lectures have been rewritten to 'tone down' the (largely unconscious) element of 'preaching' or 'bleating'. *No Sugar* has, in fact, proved to be a very useful text in demonstrating that audiences in general won't be receptive to messages that are pushed too hard. Students respond well to and appreciate the 'hybridity' of *No Sugar.* Indeed, Davis's practice, of writing for two audiences, and making available different kinds of participation, has, to some extent, provided a model for improving the course. As a lecturer concerned to promote post-colonialism as a way of reading texts, the last thing I want to do is turn my students away by making them feel steam-rollered. The options that have been introduced into the course enable different kinds of reading. 'Sympathisers' can identify with post-colonialism to the nth degree, while those who are more concerned about 'coverage' or 'tradition' can exercise some degree of choice about the nature of their involvement, although they certainly cannot avoid the literary issues of post-colonialism. The course, then, is now more obviously a hybrid, which can be 'read' differently, depending upon preferences and predispositions that students bring with them when they enrol in English I. It is to be hoped, though, that the structure of the course, with its compulsory core, will continue to nudge our students into some awareness of their post-colonial context in an Australian university, and that the course will continue as an example of 'decolonised' first-year English.

Notes

1. Helen Tiffin, 'Recuperative strategies in the post-colonial novel', in William McGaw (ed.), *Inventing Countries: Essays in Post-Colonial Literatures, Span* 24 (April 1987), 29.
2. Andrew Taylor and Russell McDougall, (eds.), Introduction to *(Un)Common Ground: Essays in Literatures in English* (Adelaide: Centre for Research in the New Literatures in English, Flinders University of South Australia, 1990), 2. Further references are given in the text.
3. Wilson Harris, 'Comedy and modern allegory: A personal view', in Hena Maes-Jelinek, Kirsten Holst Petersen and Anna Rutherford (eds.), *A Shaping of Connections: Commonwealth Literature Studies – Then and Now* (Aarhus: Dangaroo Press, 1989), 128-29.
4. Harris, *The Infinite Rehearsal* (London: Faber, 1987), 1.
5. Peggy Mares, 'Report on the student evaluation of English I, 1988', unpublished. Further references are given in the text, abbreviated as 'Report'.
6. Mares, 'Literacy, Literature and First Year Studies', in *Typereader*, 1 (November 1988), 31-32. Further references are given in the text, abbreviated as 'Literacy'.
7. Literacy, 22; Janet Batsleer, Tony Davies, Rebecca O'Rourke and Chris Weedon, *Rewriting English: Cultural Politics of Gender and Class* (London: Methuen, 1985), 165.
8. Literacy, 22; *Gilding Report: Inquiry Into Post-Compulsory Secondary Education in South Australia* (1988).
9. Literacy, 22; Batsleer *et al*, *Rewriting English*, 165-66.

Postscript:
A Student's Perspective

Betty Thøgersen

I have always valued the variety of course options we had as students at the English Department of Aarhus University. When I enrolled in 1989, I thought it was rather marvellous to be given a chance to lose myself in a particular time, place and situation through subjects like 'Drama in the Elizabethan and Jacobean Period', 'America in the Great Depression' or 'Introduction to Caribbean Literature'. Later, of course, those of us who stayed long enough at the Department began to recognize a certain predictability and re-use of subjects and texts. But as post-graduate students most of us had come to specialize in one direction or the other and my interests had clearly developed within the field of post-colonial literature.

Afterwards, thinking about what spurs you on in a particular direction, it can be hard to pinpoint any concrete influences; either it touches you or it does not, just as a teacher can bring life into a subject for one student and not for another. Hence, the discussions I had with one of my fellow students concerning our academic preferences were rather fruitless, really. She blankly refused to take any interest in post-colonial studies whatsoever, asserting her disinclination to 'feel sorry for all these oppressed and marginalized victims' (she specialized in Renaissance works, which I happened to find utterly remote and stagnant). Should my interest in post-colonial literature then merely be the result of an innate or socially conditioned aptitude for sympathizing with 'victims' and 'losers'? A less simplistic study of post-colonial issues than identifying or even reversing the traditional dichotomy of 'light – darkness', 'superior – inferior' becomes related to an immensely fascinating questioning of old certainties which inevitably calls for the (re)construction of more complex truths and identities.

The gradual realization of how the colonial powers have monopolized history and culture in most parts of the world is indeed an unsettling experience – also to one who grew up outside the Commonwealth orbit – because in the process of understanding, one's notion of universality tends to become reduced to ethnocentrism, or a power issue. My own cultural certainty as a blue-eyed European with deep roots in an homogenous, independent nation has never suffered any fractures or caused me any psychic unease comparable to what is typically expressed in post-colonial texts. Yet my national heritage is by no means unquestionable or unproblematic. On the contrary, ought I not to question a cultural tradition which has relied as much on the Manichean world view as any other imperialist power? The colonial discourse that taught my parents' generation about Denmark's proud history as a colonial power is hardly unproblematic: 'Now our only colony is *Greenland*, and in this country we have carried out a great piece of work. The indigenous population has been protected from ruin and also lifted culturally' (Danish primary school geography textbook, 1933; my translation).

The days of old-time imperialism have long since been left behind us, and even since the early days of decolonization much has been achieved to correct the wrongs of the past. Marginalized voices are speaking back alongside established discourses of power, and the theorists are speaking of pluralism from various schools of thought prefixed with *post-*. As the traditional polarities of 'oppressor – oppressed' have become less marked immediately, it is tempting to complacently ignore the pain, rootlessness and injustice that still exist as a leftover from a colonial past. This applies in particular to those of us who live at a 'safe' distance from third world poverty and economic oppression, but looking at our own cultural doorstep it appears that the power of social forces and history also works in more subtle ways here.

In Australia, for example, a settler society which has witnessed a double colonization, I have experienced the white population's difficulties in coming to terms with a painful past. Over the years the cultural sentiment has changed insecurely from deep shame of colonial/convict roots to excessive pride in and exultant celebration of the same roots (particularly in connection with the Bicentenary in 1988); from politically correct goodwill towards amending the 'problems' with the Aboriginal population to indignant frustration when this goodwill fails to create the desired result of silence. I remember overhearing a conversation between two women in a theatre audience in Perth during the performance of Sally Morgan's first stage-play: 'Well, surely, it's terrible what the whites did to the Aborigines, like taking their children away, but what can *I* do about it? Done is done'.

The comment by that Australian woman reminded me of the fellow-student that I mentioned above, and it suggested to me that one can never put a lid on the issues of marginalization and colonial discourses. The wounds from the past may never heal, but the insecurity they lead to in terms of identity, I am sure, can be eased as each individual learns to deal with his memory bank of place and history in a way that denies a monopolized construction of reality.

Post-colonial studies to me became more than simply an exotic subject to become absorbed in or a cause to 'sympathize' with. An inspiring teacher and opportunities to travel helped to broaden my horizon by challenging the traditional notions of 'self' and 'other'. I have come to appreciate the culturally multidimensional experience, and now, as I am about to leave my native country to become a migrant, I shall myself have to learn to live at once with that which has been left behind and that which is here and now. *'The self that is found in exile, deepened by displacement, takes a long time to reach'* (Drusilla Modjeska).

The Contributors

Editors

Anne Collett studied and taught in England for a number of years before taking up a post as foreign lecturer at Aarhus University teaching post-colonial studies. She has now returned to her native Australia and is teaching in the English Department at Wollongong University.

Lars Jensen graduated from Aarhus University with a Master's degree. He now teaches post-colonialism at Roskilde University in Denmark, and is a Ph.D. student at Leeds University.

Anna Rutherford initiated post-colonial studies at Aarhus University, where she taught for almost thirty years until her recent retirement. She is a former chairperson of ACLALS, the Association for Commonwealth Literature and Language Studies, and is the editor of the post-colonial journal *Kunapipi*.

Other contributors

Gary Boire teaches at the Department of English, Wilfrid Laurier University, Ontario, Canada.

Margaret Daymond is a professor and Head of the Department of English at the University of Natal, South Africa.

Sam A. Dseagu teaches at the University of the North, Sovenga, South Africa.

Susan Gingell is a professor of English at the University of Saskatchewan.

Heidi Ganner is an assistant professor at the Institut für Anglistik, Innsbruck, Austria.

Alamgir Hashmi is a professor of English Literature at the University of Islamabad, Pakistan.

Sue Hosking is Head of the Department of English at the University of Adelaide, Australia.

Coral Ann Howells is Professor of English and Canadian Literature at the University of Reading, U.K.

Norman Jeffares is Honorary Life President of IASIL and Honorary Life Fellow of ACLALS, and was founding chairman of both organisations.

Russell McDougall is Senior Lecturer at the University of New England in Armidale, Australia.

Bill W. New is professor at the University of British Columbia, Vancouver, Canada.

Kirsten Holst Petersen teaches at Roskilde University Centre, Denmark.

Prem Poddar is foreign lecturer in post-colonial studies at Aarhus University.

Velma Pollard teaches at the University of the West Indies, Mona, Kingston, Jamaica.

Paul Sharrad lectures at the University of Wollongong, Australia.

Norman Simms teaches at Ben Gurion University of the Negev, Be'er Sheva, Israel.

Betty Thøgersen is currently living in Australia and has been working as a researcher for CARITAS Australia.

Kathy Trees teaches at Murdoch University, Perth, Western Australia.

Rajiva Wijesinha is the Coordinator of the English Unit at the University Grants Commission, Sri Lanka.

Abstracts

Perspectives on Home Ground, Foreign Territory
Anne Collett

Based upon an introductory lecture given to Danish students at the University of Aarhus, this essay emphasizes the importance of constructing post-coloniality within a personal, particular and culturally specific context – a process which necessarily involves the situation of 'foreign territory' on 'home ground' in order that unquestioned assumptions about identity might be questioned, analysed, re-negotiated and constantly re-defined.

An Interview with Anna Rutherford
Anne Collett

This piece takes the form of an interview which documents over thirty years' involvement in commonwealth/post-colonial literatures, and focuses upon what Rutherford feels to be the important creation and maintenance of an integral relationship between the teacher, the student and the writer – a relationship that places emphasis upon the notion of writing/reading as a living and lived experience – personal, social and political.

Teaching African Literature in Denmark
Kirsten Holst Petersen

Petersen's article traces the development of the teaching of African literature in Denmark. She argues that African studies developed out of enthusiasm rather than knowledge, but that pursuit of knowledge soon followed as a new world unfolded before the students. It was a unique situation in society that enabled the establishing of the new field; African studies was one of many pursuits for which the permissive 1960s and '70s opened the way, but it remained as a permanently established discipline with many followers.

The Definition of African Literature Revisited
S.A. Dseagu

Dseagu traces the way in which African literature has been configured since its emergence in metropolitan European languages. He argues that African literature occupies a controversial space because, unlike literatures from other continents, African literature has been represented as a single entity, 'a single continent-wide basket'. The way out of the complexities created by this representation lies in the recognition that 'many of the original political and ideological assumptions underlying the concept of African literature are no longer current and valid', and Dseagu calls instead for 'a more objective and formal definition of the literature'.

Teaching Literature under the Rubric of 'Decolonisation' in South Africa
Margaret Daymond

Daymond explores what she terms 'dissatisfaction with aspects of post-colonial literary theorising amongst some South African critics'. This becomes the point of departure for her positioning of herself as a post-colonial critic and teacher. She argues that the tensions created by the debate over post-colonialism are an intrinsic part of the ways in which South African history is understood and as such the different approaches 'reflect debates within local literary studies as well as between international and national approaches'.

'Buttered scones at 4 p.m. on Sundays': Configuring English in Colonial India
Prem Poddar

Poddar argues that the issue of 'English' in the postcolonial 'nation', especially in India, is not just a simple question of legacy. The binarism of the colonizer and the colonized was never sutured to the extent that 'local' epistemologies, whether in the form of religious traditions or schools, had no space to exist or even to resist modes of domination. After tracing the history of English in India, and discussing the reasons for the promotion of English language and literature, Poddar claims that a proper study of post-colonial literatures in English cannot be made without an understanding of the history of the status of the language in the countries concerned.

Teaching Post-Colonial Literature in Sri Lanka
Rajiva Wijesinha

Wijesinha discusses the continuation of the colonial legacy in Sri Lankan society, emphasising in particular the desire until quite recently among the establishment to be more British than the British. He then traces the development of post-colonial studies in Sri Lankan universities, and shows how after many trials and tribulations post-colonial literatures (and in particular current Sri Lankan writing) have become accepted in some curricula. The article contains a suggestion for a course on Sri Lankan literature as well as an accompanying bibliography.

English Studies in Pakistan
Alamgir Hashmi

In a personal survey of the development of post-colonial studies in Pakistan since the 1970s, Hashmi shows how the change from the traditional teaching of British canonical texts to a broader consideration of literatures in English was motivated both by changes elsewhere in the Commonwealth and by changes within Pakistan itself. The consequence was an awakening recognition and inclusion of Pakistani literature in English Departments at Pakistani University. At first the integration took shape under the umbrella of Commonwealth literature, but later the emphasis shifted towards a recognition of the post-colonial status of Pakistani literature.

The How and the Wherefore
A. Norman Jeffares

This survey article traces the various stages post-colonialism has passed through since it first emerged in the form of an interest in Commonwealth literature. Jeffares, who has been one of the prime movers of the incorporation of Commonwealth literature into university curricula, explains how the field developed from its modest beginnings in the 1950s, how Leeds University became a centre for the study of Commonwealth literature, and how he later introduced the field to Stirling University in Scotland.

The Role of Literature from the English-speaking World in the EFL Classroom: Short Prose Fiction from the New English Literatures
Heidi Ganner

Ganner contextualises post-colonial writing in relation to English language teaching in Europe. While post-colonial writing is now well established on the European book market, including the market for ELT readers, the teaching of post-colonial texts still represents a challenge. Ganner uses selected short texts by post-colonial writers to illustrate how their writing can be used in work on language while at the same time broadening school students' socio-cultural horizons.

Teaching Canadian Literature outside Canada
Coral Ann Howells

Howells defines the texts and contexts of teaching a course on Canadian Women's Writing in England. She remarks that the emphasis in a course on contemporary literature must necessarily lie in the charting of change – 'the mapping of new territory' – both in terms of writers and readers; and she particularly notes 'the difficulty of "translation" from the conceptual and narrative frameworks of one culture to another' – a difficulty that is encountered by all those who teach in the area of comparative literature.

'Avowels': Notes on Ambivalence and a Post-colonial Pedagogy
Gary Boire

Gary Boire examines the difficulties of gaining recognition for post-colonial literature and criticism within traditionally configured English Departments. He states: 'I want to consider the nature of the inseminating canonized pedagogical beast, as well as some possible ways to "fix" it (in the veterinarian sense of course). My discussion deals in varying ways with the interrelated triad of "theory", "pedagogy", and "politics".'

Strategies for not Teaching Post-Colonial Literature: The Better Part of Valor
Norman Simms

Simms's article is a testimony to the controversy of teaching post-colonial literature. It is an argument that questions the losses incurred when teaching literature from the overtly politicised position of a post-colonial stance. Simms argues against the dangers of reproducing victim and oppressor roles, because such futile gestures are equally unproductive for both. He uses his present position in Israel to illustrate the continuity of oppression and the complexities of colonisation, and to argue against the perpetuation of the fatal impact of colonisation.

Poetic Language and the Construction of Post-coloniality: A New Zealand Example
W.H. New

New discusses the ways in which language in literary practice – he uses the terms *word choice*, *structural form*, and sometimes *subject* – constructs the political positions of colonial and post-colonial writers. He uses New Zealand poems as text examples to show what particular forms post-coloniality takes in the context of a white settler society, and how texts operate in the space between white settlers and indigenous cultures.

Teaching Pacific Literature
Paul Sharrad

Sharrad begins his article with a discussion of the contexts in which Pacific literatures have traditionally been placed, and the merits and drawbacks such approaches have. He then presents a history of the development of Pacific literatures, and includes references to some of the landmark publications in the area. He contextualises Pacific literatures in relation to both the overall umbrella of post-colonial criticism and more traditional canonical representations of literary traditions. The article contains a bibliography of source material and criticism.

Firing the can(n)on: Teaching Post-colonialism in a Pacific Context
Lars Jensen

In this article on teaching Australian, New Zealand and Pacific literatures, Jensen explores the possibility of approaching Australian and New Zealand literatures from outside their traditional confines of a nationalistic paradigm. The article also discusses ways of contextualising Pacific literatures in an effort to incorporate interdisciplinary texts, thus challenging traditional representations of the Pacific cultures.

The politics of post-colonial reading practices as they relate to the work of Aboriginal writers
Kathryn Trees

Trees writes from two viewpoints. She is an academic scholar teaching and researching on Aboriginal writing, and she works with the Australian Judiciary, where she designs cross-cultural awareness programmes 'so that magistrates and judges are better informed about Aboriginal people and their cultures before making decisions about them'. The article demonstrates the links between the political and the literary, and also shows how the teaching of Aboriginal literature is particularly necessary, although fraught with pitfalls, in a society where the majority of the population know little about the country's indigenous peoples.

Pedagogy and Resistance in the Context of Commonwealth/Post-Colonial Literatures
Susan Gingell

Susan Gingell's contribution is a practical example of how post-colonial encodings and decodings of texts may be exercised in a classroom. Through a comparative reading of the Australian poet A.D. Hope's poem 'Imperial Adam' and the Caribbean writer Dionne Brand's poem 'October 25th, 1983', Gingell shows how the very different positions from which post-colonial writers speak open up a variety of ways to contextualise their texts, and that the politics of gender, race, resistance and nationalism are intrinsic to the relationship between literary texts and cultural contexts.

From Periphery to Centre – Teaching Caribbean Literature within a Post-colonial/Commonwealth Context
Velma Pollard

Pollard begins her article by making a distinction between 'literature whose content is culturally remote from the reader ... and literature which is culturally accessible'. She argues the distinction has a particular applicability in a Caribbean context, where schools until fairly recently taught only European literature; this told Caribbean children little about themselves. Pollard traces the development of a distinctly Caribbean tradition and shows how that has changed the ways in which people in the Caribbean see themselves and in which they relate to issues of colonialism and post-colonialism.

The Trials, Tribulations and Ironies of Teaching Post-Colonialism as 'English I' in an Australian University
Russell McDougall, with an Epilogue by Sue Hosking

The article describes an effort to introduce post-colonialism in a form which would integrate post-colonial literatures into the overall framework of the curricula in university English departments. It presents the results of a survey of student opinions relating to a course with a structure that incorporates the work of teachers outside post-colonial studies and which juxtaposes post-colonial texts with traditional canonical texts. Sample student responses – positive and negative – are included.

Postscript: A Student's Perspective
Betty Thøgersen

As a former student of the University of Aarhus, Thøgersen describes the impact which a course on post-colonial studies had on her – though not all her fellow-students responded in the same way. The course forced her to see herself and her society in a new light, and gave her a fresh perspective on the world.

The Dolphin

The following back issues are still available:

1. *Pride and Prejudice*
6. Culture and Narcissism
8. Joyce Centenary Offshoots
9. Coyote Was Here
10. George Orwell and 1984
11. Inventing the Future
13. Communicative Competence in Foreign Language Learning and Teaching
14. British Drama in the Eighties
15. Displaced Persons
16. Something to Believe in
18. Translation: A Means to an End
19. The Impact of the French Revolution on English Literature
20. Where? Place in Modern Americn Fiction
21. New Thinking in TEFL
22. Literary Pedagogics after Deconstruction
23. Cracking the Ike Age: Aspects of Fifties America
24. Screen Shakespeare
25. O Canada. Essays on Canadian Literature and Culture
26. The Lost Decade: America in the Seventies

The Literary Man:
Essays presented to
Donald W. Hannah

Edited by Karl-Heinz Westarp with contributions by
Michael Böss, Jørn Carlsen, Inger H. Dalsgaard, Niels Bugge Hansen, Hans Hauge, Seamus
Heaney, Earle Labor, Lee Morgan, Per Serritslev Petersen, Lars-Ole Sauerberg, Michael
Skovmand, Knud Sørensen and Claus B. Østergaard.

Professor Donald W. Hannah taught English literature at the University of Aarhus for nearly
forty years, and retired in August 1996. Friends, colleagues and former students pay tribute
to Donald Hannah with this collection of essays, which spans the breadth of his own life
work, from literary history to aesthetics and criticism, from Shakespeare and Samuel
Johnson to D.H. Lawrence, Graham Greene, Jack London, Colm Toibin and Flannery
O'Connor.

240 pages, 17 x 24 cm. 1996. ISBN 87 7288 540 8